lonely planet

D0172693

BERLIN
ENCOUNTER

ANDREA SCHULTE-PEEVERS

Berlin Encounter

Published by Lonely Planet Publications Pty Ltd
ABN 36 005 607 983

Australia   Locked Bag 1, Footscray,
(Head Office)   Vic 3011
                     ☎ 03 8379 8000 fax 03 8379 8111
                     talk2us@lonelyplanet.com.au
USA   150 Linden St, Oakland, CA 94607
                     ☎ 510 250 6400
                     toll free 800 275 8555
                     fax 510 893 8572
                     info@lonelyplanet.com
UK   2nd fl, 186 City Rd
                     London EC1V 2NT
                     ☎ 020 7106 2100 fax 020 7106 2101
                     go@lonelyplanet.co.uk

This title was commissioned in Lonely Planet's London
office and produced by: **Commissioning Editors**
Suzannah Shwer, Caroline Sieg, Clifton Wilkinson
Coordinating Editors Michelle Bennett, Charlotte Orr
Coordinating Cartographer Peter Shields **Layout
Designer** Jessica Rose **Assisting Cartographer**
Khanh Luu **Senior Editor** Helen Christinis **Managing
Cartographer** David Connolly, Herman So **Cover
Designer** Naomi Parker **Cover** Image research provided
by lonelyplanetimages.com **Project Managers** Craig
Kilburn, Michelle Lewis **Series Designer** Michael Ruff
Managing Layout Designer Sally Darmody **Thanks
to** Lucy Birchley, David Carroll, Ryan Evans, Annelies
Mertens, Wayne Murphy, Naomi Parker, Trent Paton,
Lyahna Spencer

ISBN 978 1 74179 289 8

Printed through Colorcraft Ltd, Hong Kong.
Printed in China.

Acknowledgement Berlin S+U-Bahn Map © 2009
Berliner Verkehrbetriebe (BVG).

HOW TO USE THIS BOOK
Colour-Coding & Maps
Colour-coding is used for symbols on maps and in
the text that they relate to (eg all eating venues on
the maps and in the text are given a green knife and
fork symbol). Each neighbourhood also gets its own
colour, and this is used down the edge of the page
and throughout that neighbourhood section.

   Shaded yellow areas on the maps denote areas
of interest — for their historical significance, their
attractive architecture or their great bars and restaurants. We encourage you to head to these areas
and just start exploring!

Send us your feedback We love to hear from
readers — your comments help make our books better. We read every word you send us, and we always
guarantee that your feedback goes straight to the
appropriate authors. The most useful submissions are
rewarded with a free book. To send us your updates
and find out about Lonely Planet events, newsletters
and travel news visit our award-winning website:
lonelyplanet.com/contact

Note: We may edit, reproduce and incorporate
your comments in Lonely Planet products such as
guidebooks, websites and digital products, so let us
know if you don't want your comments reproduced or
your name acknowledged. For a copy of our privacy
policy visit **lonelyplanet.com/privacy**.

ANDREA SCHULTE-PEEVERS

Andrea has travelled the distance to the moon and back in her visits to over 60 countries and carries her dog-eared passport like a badge of honour. Her fascination with Berlin's mystique goes back to her first stay in the summer of 1989, a few months shy of the Wall's collapse. During many return trips she has watched Berlin shed its Cold War–era brooding and blossom into a vibrant, creative, seductive and confident metropolis. Born and raised in Germany and educated in London and at UCLA, Andrea has built a career on writing about her native country for two decades. She's authored or contributed to more than 40 Lonely Planet titles, including the first edition of this guide, and all six editions of the *Berlin* city guide and the *Germany* country guide. For this trip she again traded her house in Los Angeles for a teensy rooftop apartment in Berlin – and loved every minute of it.

ANDREA'S THANKS

Vielen Dank to Alex, Anna, Anne, Annika, Ariela, Christina, Erez, Gabriella, Henrik, Holm, Kerstin, Katja and everyone else who's pounded Berlin's turf with me. Heartfelt thanks to Caroline Sieg and the LP folks responsible for producing this kick-ass book. The biggest thanks, though, go to David, my loyal companion in love and life.

Our readers Many thanks to the travellers who wrote into us with helpful hints, useful advice and interesting anecdotes. Irene Siekman, Wim Vandenbussche.

Cover photograph Altes Museum, Berlin; S Tauqueur/Photolibrary. **Internal photographs** p169 Juergen Henkelmann Photography/Alamy. All other photographs by Lonely Planet Images, and by David Peevers except p45 Jon Davison; p36, p51, p115 Krzysztof Dydynski; p166 Lou Jones; p32 (top right and bottom), p34, p161 Jean-Pierre Lescourret; p6, p152 Guy Moberly; p24, p26, p31, p38, p65, p128, p156 Martin Moos; p6 (bottom), p21, p49, p75, p87, p142, p146, p162, p163 Richard Nebesky; p135 Jonathan Smith; p16 Thomas Winz.

All images are copyright of the photographers unless otherwise indicated. Many of the images in this guide are available for licensing from **Lonely Planet Images:** lonelyplanetimages.com

Kaiser-Wilhelm-Gedächtniskirche (p135), perfectly framed by Matschinsky-Denninghoff's striking *Berlin* sculpture

CONTENTS

THE AUTHOR	**03**
THIS IS BERLIN	**07**
HIGHLIGHTS	**08**
BERLIN DIARY	**25**
ITINERARIES	**31**
NEIGHBOURHOODS	**38**
>MITTE – UNTER DEN LINDEN & MUSEUMSINSEL	42
>MITTE – ALEXANDERPLATZ AREA	56
>MITTE – SCHEUNENVIERTEL	62
>REICHSTAG & GOVERNMENT QUARTER	76
>POTSDAMER PLATZ & TIERGARTEN	80
>PRENZLAUER BERG	88
>EASTERN KREUZBERG & KREUZKÖLLN	100
>WESTERN KREUZBERG	112
>FRIEDRICHSHAIN	122
>CHARLOTTENBURG	132
>SCHÖNEBERG	144
SNAPSHOTS	**148**
>ACCOMMODATION	150
>FOOD	152
>GAY & LESBIAN	154
>GALLERIES	156
>JEWISH BERLIN	158
>THE BERLIN WALL	160
>BACK TO THE GDR	162
>CLUBBING	163
>DRINKING	164
>FASHION	165
>KIDS	166
>MUSEUMS	167
>MUSIC	168
>SEX & FETISH	169
>SHOPPING	170
BACKGROUND	**171**
DIRECTORY	**181**
INDEX	**192**

THIS IS BERLIN

Twenty years after its post-Wall rebirth, Berlin is a scene-stealing combo of glamour and grit, teeming with top museums and galleries, grand opera and guerrilla clubs, gourmet temples and ethnic snack shacks. Whether your tastes run to posh or punk, you can sate them in Berlin.

Chronic fiscal woes aside, when it comes to fashion, art, design and music, the German capital is the city to watch. A global influx of creatives has turned it into a cauldron of cultural cool reminiscent of New York in the '80s. What draws them is Berlin's legendary climate of tolerance, openness and experimentation infused with an edgy undercurrent that gives this 'eternally unfinished' city its street cred. Cheap rents don't hurt either.

All this trendiness is a triumph for a town that's long been in the cross-hairs of history: Berlin staged a revolution, was headquartered by fascists, bombed to bits, ripped in half and finally reunited – and that was just in the 20th century! Famous landmarks such as the Reichstag, the Branden-burg Gate, Checkpoint Charlie and what's left of the Berlin Wall are like a virtual 3-D textbook in a city where you'll find history staring you in the face every time you turn a corner.

Perhaps it's because of its heavy historical burden that Berlin is throw-ing itself into tomorrow with such contagious energy. At times the entire city seems to be bubbling over into one huge party. Cafes are jammed at all hours, drinking is a religious rite and clubs host their scenes of frenzy and hedonism until the wee hours. Sleep? Fuhgeddaboutit!

Yet despite its often hectic pace, Berlin functions on an exquisitely human scale. Traffic flows freely, public transportation is brilliant, you can walk without fear at night, clubs have no velvet ropes and your restaurant bill would only buy you a starter back home. Come and join the party and be swept away by the riches, quirks and vibrancy of this fascinating city.

Top left Popular and pleasant-on-the-purse Monsieur Vuong (p70) **Top right** Contemporary art at the multifaceted Berlinische Galerie (p114) **Bottom** Berlin and booze go hand-in-hand (p164). Drink too much *grün* Berliner Weisse and you'll be green too

>1 Going ape for antiquities at the Pergamonmuseum 10

>2 Getting palace envy at Schloss Charlottenburg 12

>3 Losing your weekend on Berlin's sizzling dance floors 13

>4 Shopping for kitsch and couture in the Scheunenviertel 14

>5 Confronting the ghosts of the Cold War at the East Side Gallery 15

>6 Standing in awe of history at the Reichstag 16

>7 Gaining insight into Jewish life at the Jewish Museum 17

>8 Mingling with Old Masters at the Gemäldegalerie 18

>9 Roaming, picnicking and carousing in the Tiergarten 19

>10 Hobnobbing with high society on Kurfürstendamm 20

>11 Posing for pictures with the Brandenburg Gate 21

>12 Exploring Prenzlauer Berg on a DIY saunter 22

>13 Experiencing 'Roaring Twenties' glam at a cabaret 23

>14 Touring the highlights on two wheels 24

Graffiti, bourgeois-bohemian style, in ubertrendy Prenzlauer Berg (p22)

>1 PERGAMONMUSEUM

GOING APE FOR ANTIQUITIES AT THE PERGAMONMUSEUM

An Aladdin's cave of treasures from ancient realms, the Pergamon-museum is an essential entry on any list of must-see sights. Inside the vast complex, custom built on Museumsinsel (Museum Island) in 1930, awaits a feast of classical sculpture and monumental architecture from Greece, Rome, Babylon and the Middle East that will amaze and enlighten. Most of it was excavated and spirited to Berlin by German archaeologists at the turn of the 20th century. Note that in coming years some sections may be closed while the museum is renovated.

The Pergamonmuseum unites three major collections, each with their own signature sights, which are described on the excellent free audioguide. The undisputed highlight of the Antikensammlung (Collection of Classical Antiquities) is the museum's namesake, the Pergamon Altar (165 BC), which cuts a commanding presence in the first hall. This gargantuan raised marble shrine hails from the ancient Greek metropolis of Pergamon (now Bergama in Turkey) and centres on a steep, 20m-wide staircase. Climbing up the stairs you arrive at a colonnaded courtyard adorned with a vivid frieze featuring episodes from the life of Telephos, the mythical founder of Pergamon.

But it's another frieze, reconstructed along the walls of the hall, that deservedly hogs most visitors' attention. About 113m long, it shows the gods locked in an epic battle with the giants; it was origi-nally a painted and gilded band wrapped around the entire altar. The anatomical detail, the emotional intensity and the dramatic composi-tion of the figures show Hellenic art at its finest.

The next room opens onto another key exhibit: the giant Market Gate of Miletus (2nd century AD), a masterpiece of Roman architec-ture. Merchants and customers once flooded through here into the market square of this trading town (also in today's Turkey), which functioned as a link between Asia and Europe.

Pass through it and enter another culture and civilisation: Babylon during the reign of King Nebuchadnezzar II (604–562 BC). You're now in the Vorderasiatisches Museum (Museum of Near Eastern An-tiquities), where it's impossible not to be awed by the reconstructed Ishtar Gate, the Processional Way (pictured) leading up to it and the

facade of the king's throne hall. All are sheathed in glazed bricks glistening in radiant blue and ochre. The strutting lions, horses and dragons, which represent major Babylonian gods, are so striking that you can almost hear the roaring and the fanfare.

A staircase delivers you to the third collection, the Museum für Islamische Kunst (Museum of Islamic Art). Standouts here include the fortresslike 8th-century caliph's palace from Mshatta in today's Jordan and the 17th-century Aleppo Room from the house of a Christian merchant in Syria, featuring richly painted, wood-panelled walls. If you look closely, you can make out *The Last Supper* and *Mary and Child* amid all the ornamentation (straight ahead, to the right of the door). Also see p50.

HIGHLIGHTS

>2 SCHLOSS CHARLOTTENBURG

GETTING PALACE ENVY AT SCHLOSS CHARLOTTENBURG

An exquisite baroque palace, Schloss Charlottenburg evokes the one-time grandeur of the Prussian royals. It's a wonderful place to visit, especially in summer when you can fold a stroll, sunbathing session or picnic in the lush palace park into a day of peeking at royal treasures.

The palace started out rather modestly as the summer retreat of Sophie Charlotte, whose husband later became King Friedrich I. Subsequent rulers dabbled with the compound, updating and enlarging it into today's lavish 505m-long edifice.

The central – and oldest – section is the Altes Schloss (Old Palace), fronted by Andreas Schlüter's epic equestrian statue of the Great Elector (see p172). Inside are the private chambers of Friedrich I and Friedrich Wilhelm IV, while Frederick the Great set himself up in the Neuer Flügel (New Wing), added in 1746.

Additional sightseeing gems hidden among the groomed paths, mature trees and pretty lake of the palace park are the Neuer Pavillon (New Pavilion), the charming Belvedere with its porcelain collection, and the sombre Mausoleum. For more about the Schloss, see p136.

>3 CLUB CULTURE

LOSING YOUR WEEKEND ON BERLIN'S SIZZLING DANCE FLOORS

Berlin's reputation for intense and unbridled nightlife is rooted in the libertine 1920s when everyone from Marlene Dietrich to Christopher Isherwood partied like it was 1999. After reunification the club scene exploded, with the most vital venues taking over all sorts of dark, disused and derelict locations, from postal offices to power stations, bunkers to factories. From here, hard-edged techno conquered the world, using the impetus of reunification to tap into the simultaneous explosion of the UK rave scene and the popularity of ecstasy.

Musicwise, techno is still tops, but all sorts of splinter genres of electronic music have percolated into the club scene, which is as diverse as ever. Venues range from designer dens such as Cookies (p55) to hedonistic pleasure pits like Berghain/Panoramabar (p130) and trash dives like Rosi's (p131). Illegal and underground parties, meanwhile, continue to thrive, often taking over S-Bahn stations and trains, abandoned buildings, ATM foyers and other unlikely locales – at least until the police show up.

>4 SCHEUNENVIERTEL

SHOPPING FOR KITSCH AND COUTURE IN THE SCHEUNENVIERTEL

Retail therapy gets a unique Berlin twist in the Scheunenviertel, the ultimate shopping mecca for individualists. Boutiques here are edgy, stylish and definitely light years from high-street conformity. From couture to streetwear, home decorations to gourmet foods, accessories to art, you'll find a diverse and mostly home-grown selection in this villagelike labyrinth of lanes. Despite the recent landing of a small flock of corporate flagship eagles such as Hugo Boss and Tommy Hilfiger, most stores here still reflect the vision, philosophy and taste of the shopkeepers and resident fashionistas.

Spending euros in the Scheunenviertel is not a chore but a journey of discovery. What makes the area so special is simply the great variety of outlets. On an aimless wander you're bound to bump into stylish concept stores such as 14OZ (p67), quirky speciality places like 1. Absinth Depot Berlin (p67; pictured), local designer showrooms like Berlinerklamotten (p67), artisanal outlets including the old-fashioned candy maker Bonbonmacherei (p68) and tourist-oriented havens such as Ampelmann Galerie (p67). Auguststrasse is the haunt of progressive galleries like Kunst-Werke Berlin (p64), while brand-name boutiques are concentrated around Hackescher Markt, and along Münzstrasse and Neue Schönhauser Strasse.

>5 EAST SIDE GALLERY
CONFRONTING THE GHOSTS OF THE COLD WAR AT THE EAST SIDE GALLERY

The year was 1989. After 28 years the Berlin Wall, that grim and grey divider of humanity, had finally met its maker. East Germany was free, reunification imminent. Most of the Wall was quickly dismantled, but along Mühlenstrasse a 1.3km stretch was spared. It became the East Side Gallery, drenched in over 100 colourful murals that collectively make up the world's largest open-air gallery. Dozens of international artists translated the era's global euphoria and optimism into a mix of political statements, drug-induced musings and truly artistic visions.

Birgit Kinder's *Test the Best,* showing a Trabant car (Trabi, for short) bursting through the Wall, is a shutterbug favourite. Alas, time, taggers and tourists insisting on signing their favourite picture took their toll over the years. In 2009, though, the entire thing got a total makeover and is looking better than ever, even though a short section was removed so that the O2 World arena could have its own boat landing docks. Encroaching development is also threatening the survival of the beach bars set up on the Spree side of the gallery. Also see p124.

>6 REICHSTAG

STANDING IN AWE OF HISTORY AT THE REICHSTAG

Likely to give you more flashbacks to high-school history than any other Berlin landmark, this grand old building by Paul Wallot (1894) is where the German parliament, the Bundestag, has been hammering out its policies since 1999. This followed a total makeover by Lord Norman Foster, who preserved only the building's historical shell while adding the striking glass dome (pictured), which is accessible by lift.

The Reichstag has witnessed many milestones in German history. After WWI Philipp Scheidemann proclaimed the German Republic from one of its windows. The Reichstag fire in February 1933 allowed Hitler to blame the communists and helped catapult him to power. A dozen years later, victorious Red Army troops raised the Soviet flag on the bombed-out building.

In the '80s, megastars including David Bowie, Pink Floyd and Michael Jackson performed concerts on the lawn of the Reichstag, which rubbed up against the western side of the Berlin Wall. When word got out that East German fans were trying to eavesdrop from the other side, the stars turned some of the loudspeakers around, thus almost provoking an international incident!

Fortunately, the Wall collapsed soon afterwards, paving the way to German reunification, which was enacted in the Reichstag in 1990. Five years later, the building made worldwide headlines once again when the artist couple Christo and Jeanne-Claude wrapped it in fabric. Foster set to work shortly thereafter. See p78 for more information.

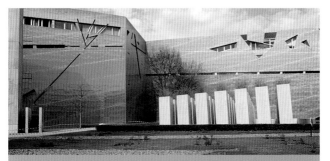

>7 JEWISH MUSEUM

GAINING INSIGHT INTO JEWISH LIFE AT THE JEWISH MUSEUM

Berlin's Jewish Museum (Jüdisches Museum) is an eye-opening, emotional and interactive journey through 2000 years of Jewish history in Germany. Yup, 2000 and not just the 12 Nazi horror years that such presentations often focus on, although those are of course addressed as well. This exhibit deftly navigates through all major historic periods, from the Roman era to the community's current renaissance, with stops in the Middle Ages and the Enlightenment. You'll learn about Jewish cultural contributions, holiday traditions, the difficult road to Emancipation (see p158) and outstanding individuals such as the philosopher Moses Mendelssohn and jeans inventor Levi Strauss.

Just as poignant as the exhibit itself is Daniel Libeskind's stunning museum building that's essentially a 3-D allegory for Jewish suffering. Its zigzag outline symbolises a broken Star of David; its silvery zinc walls are sharply angled; and instead of windows there are only small gashes piercing the building's gleaming skin. Inside, a steep staircase leads to three intersecting walkways. Called 'axes', they represent the fates of Jews during the Nazi years: death, exile and continuity. Only the latter leads to the actual exhibit, but it too is a cumbersome journey up several steep flights of stairs. Libeskind's architecture is a powerful language indeed.

See p115 for additional details.

>8 GEMÄLDEGALERIE

MINGLING WITH OLD MASTERS AT THE GEMÄLDEGALERIE

When the Gemäldegalerie (Picture Gallery) opened in its custom-built space at the Kulturforum in 1998, it marked the happy reunion of an outstanding collection of European paintings separated by the Cold War for half a century. Some had remained at the Bodemuseum in East Berlin, the rest went on display in the West Berlin suburb of Dahlem. Today about 1500 works span the arc of artistic vision between the 13th and 18th centuries, with key canvasses by Rembrandt, Titian, Goya, Botticelli, Holbein, Gainsborough, Canaletto, Hals, Rubens, Vermeer and other heavy hitters.

Standouts include the *Portrait of Hieronymus Holzschuher* (1529; Room 2), painted by his friend Albrecht Dürer with utmost precision down to the furrows and wrinkles. In the moralistic yet humorous *Dutch Proverbs* (1559; Room 7), Pieter Bruegel magically managed to illustrate 119 proverbs in a single seaside village scene. Lucas Cranach the Elder's hilarious *Fountain of Youth* (1546; Room III) shows old crones leaping into a pool and emerging as dashing hotties – this fountain would surely put plastic surgeons out of business. Other highlights include Correggio's naughty *Leda with the Swan* (1532; Room XV), Petrus Christus' chilling *Last Judgement* (1452; Room IV) and Frans Hals' fantastically witchy *Malle Babbe* (1633; Room 13). For more details, see p82.

>9 TIERGARTEN

ROAMING, PICNICKING AND CAROUSING IN THE TIERGARTEN

Berlin's rulers used the grounds to hunt boar and pheasants before having them shaped into a public park by master landscape architect Peter Lenné in the 18th century. With its huge shady trees, groomed paths, woodsy groves, lakes, creeks and meadows, the Tiergarten is one of the world's largest city parks and a wonderful retreat from the city bustle. It's popular for strolling, jogging, Frisbee tossing, picnicking, grill parties, sunbathing and, yes, gay cruising (especially around the Löwenbrücke).

Walking across the entire park takes about an hour, but even a shorter stroll has its rewards. The most idyllic spots include the Rousseauinsel (Rousseau Island), a memorial to the 18th-century French philosopher, and the flowery Luiseninsel (Louise Island). The largest lake is the Neuer See (New Lake), where you can rent boats or quaff a cold one at the Café am Neuen See (p86) beer garden. Kids love the critters in the famous Berlin Zoo (p134) just beyond the Landwehr-kanal (Landwehr canal).

Tiergarten is bisected east–west by Strasse des 17 Juni, home to a Soviet WWII memorial and a traditional flea market. Big festivals, including the annual Christopher Street Day celebration (p28), are staged along here and around the Siegessäule (Victory Column; p85).

>10 KURFÜRSTENDAMM

HOBNOBBING WITH HIGH SOCIETY ON KURFÜRSTENDAMM

No trip to Berlin would be complete without a saunter along Kurfürstendamm (Ku'damm for short) in Charlottenburg. Along with its continuation, the Tauentzienstrasse, it's the city's longest and busiest shopping strip, lined with everything from big department stores to high-street chains and designer boutiques for size zero fembots. Amid all this, the Gedächtniskirche (Memorial Church; p135) stands quietly, if incongruously, as a poignant reminder of the absurdity of war.

This 3.5km-long ribbon of style began as a bridle path to the royal hunting lodge in the Grunewald forest. In the early 1870s, Otto von Bismarck, the Iron Chancellor, decided that the capital of the new German Reich needed its own representative boulevard, bigger and better even than the Champs Élysées. Kurfürstendamm quickly became *the* top address in town, lined with fashionable town houses and extrawide pavements for promenading in style.

The 1920s added luxury hotels and shops, art galleries and restaurants, plus enough theatres and movie palaces to give Berlin its own version of Broadway. More recently built architectural gems include Helmut Jahn's Neues Kranzler Eck (Map p133, E2).

>11 BRANDENBURG GATE

POSING FOR PICTURES WITH THE BRANDENBURG GATE

So where were you when the Berlin Wall fell? For tens of thousands the answer is 'at the Brandenburg Gate'. Who can forget the images of the crowds of euphoric revellers perched atop the Wall, hugging complete strangers and shaking hands with border guards? Amid cheers and champagne, the Cold War was over and a new era of hope and freedom began.

Carl Gotthard Langhans looked to the Acropolis in Athens for inspiration for this elegant triumphal arch, which came into existence in 1791 as the royal entrance gate to the city. If you look closely, you'll see that the columns are not evenly spaced. Only the royal family was allowed to enter through the extrawide middle arch. Its entourage used the adjacent walkways, while common folk had to squeeze through the narrow outer ones.

The gate is topped by the *Quadriga,* Johann Gottfried Schadow's sculpture of the winged goddess of victory piloting a chariot drawn by four horses. After trouncing Prussia in 1806, Napoleon kidnapped the lady and held her hostage in Paris until she was freed by a gallant Prussian general in 1815.

The neatly restored gate is now the backdrop for raucous New Year's Eve parties and mega-events. See p46 for more.

>12 PRENZLAUER BERG

EXPLORING PRENZLAUER BERG ON A DIY SAUNTER

Once a neglected backwater, Prenzlauer Berg went from rags to riches after reunification and is now one of Berlin's most appealing neighbourhoods. There are no major sights, which is just fine because its true charms reveal themselves in subtler, often unexpected ways. Look up at gorgeously ornamented facades that not long ago bore the scars of war. Push open a sturdy door to stumble upon quiet courtyards such as the artsy Hirschhof (Map p89, B3; enter between Oderberger Strasse 18 and 19) or the radical Tuntenhaus (Map p89, B4; Kastanienallee 86), a gay punk co-op. Browse for unique clothes and accessories in indie designer boutiques on boho-trendy Kastanienallee and Oderberger Strasse, or carve out a spot in a cafe to observe the parade of students, yuppies, mummies and kool kids.

Kastanienallee culminates at Eberswalder Strasse U-Bahn station, where Konnopke's Imbiss (p95) is a cult sausage purveyor. West of here, the Mauerpark (Wall Park; p90; pictured) has been reclaimed from the 'death' strip and is home to a Sunday flea market (p92) and a short stretch of Berlin Wall that's an official practice ground for budding street artists. East of Schönhauser Allee, the Kulturbrauerei (p99) is a former brewery turned bustling cultural centre and gateway to the beautiful, if heavily yuppified, Kollwitzplatz area (p90). North of Danziger Strasse, around Helmholtzplatz and along Stargarder Strasse, the vibe is still less polished, the crowd edgier, the bars busier and the shops more eccentric. For the full low-down, see p88.

>13 CABARET & VARIETÉ

EXPERIENCING 'ROARING TWENTIES' GLAM AT A CABARET

Cabaret may have been born in 1880s Paris, but it became a wild and libidinous grown-up in 1920s Berlin. In those giddy Weimar years, creativity and decadence blossomed despite – or perhaps because of – raging inflation and political instability. Cabarets provided a titillating fantasy of play and display where transvestites, singers, magicians, dancers and other entertainers made audiences forget about the harsh realities of daily life. It's a world vividly portrayed in the 1930 movie *The Blue Angel,* starring Marlene Dietrich, and of course in Bob Fosse's acclaimed film musical *Cabaret* (1972), with Liza Minnelli.

Over the last decade, cabaret has made a big comeback, thanks in large part to post-reunification euphoria and a renewed unleashing of creativity. More mainstream and less lurid than in the Roaring Twenties, today's shows are mostly a series of snazzily choreographed variety acts. The edgiest venue is the Bar jeder Vernunft (p143), whose reprise of *Cabaret* plays to sell-out audiences. Across town, the Friedrichstadtpalast (p74) is Europe's largest revue theatre, where leggy, feather-clad dancers strut their stuff. If you'd like a smaller, more intimate venue, try Chamäleon Varieté (p74), while Admiralspalast (p54; pictured) offers musicals and comedies. Note that cabarets should not be confused with *Kabarett,* which is essentially stand-up political satire.

>14 CYCLING

TOURING THE HIGHLIGHTS ON TWO WHEELS

Strap on your helmet! Flat as a pancake, Berlin is tailor-made for two-wheeling. From students to lawyers, nannies to nuns, locals of all ages and walks of life love getting from A to B by bicycle. In fact, the number of bicyclists has more than doubled in the last decade to 400,000 riders daily, accounting for 12% of total traffic in the city. Bicycles are chained to posts and racks in the streets. They crowd apartment-building lobbies and courtyards. Cars yield to them at crossroads. And it doesn't hurt that the biking infrastructure is fantastic. After pumping €2.5 million into expanding the bike-lane system, the city now has 130km of dedicated paths in the streets or on the pavements.

For visitors, too, a bicycle is an ideal way to get around. Riding one is nonpolluting, keeps you fit and lets you cover a lot of ground more quickly and comfortably than on foot. If you want to get away from road traffic, take your human-powered vehicle on the U-Bahn and S-Bahn trains and head out to a lake, river or forest. Or, if you're feeling ambitious, follow the 160km-long Berliner Mauerweg (p161), a signposted path along the former border fortifications with 40 multilingual information stations posted along the way.

See p183 for information on bike hire and p187 for guided bike tours.

>BERLIN DIARY

Berlin is very much a party town with a busy year-round calendar of concert series, street parties, sports events, trade shows and festivals celebrating everything from film to fetish, music to fashion, porn to travel. Major events such as Christopher Street Day or New Year's Eve bring hundreds of thousands of revellers to town, filling hotels, restaurants and venues to capacity. Berlin's tourist office (www.visit berlin.de) has a searchable events calendar and can also help you book tickets and hotels. The listings magazines *Tip* (www.tip-berlin.de, in German) and *Zitty* (www .zitty.de, in German) are the best sources for up-to-the-minute events listings.

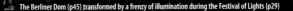

The Berliner Dom (p45) transformed by a frenzy of illumination during the Festival of Lights (p29)

When sand in your camera is no big deal: sensational sculpture at Sandsation (p28)

JANUARY

Internationale Grüne Woche
www.gruenewoche.de
The week-long International Green Week, a consumer fair for food, agriculture and gardening, is a great excuse for gorging on exotic morsels from around the world.

Lange Nacht der Museen
www.lange-nacht-der-museen.de
Culture meets entertainment on the last Saturday of January (and August) when up to 100 museums keep their doors open until at least midnight.

Transmediale
www.transmediale.de
Digital media art gets full bandwidth at this progressive festival that also investigates how digital technologies shape today's society and artistic endeavours.

FEBRUARY

Berlinale
www.berlinale.de
Berlin International Film Festival draws stars, starlets, directors, critics and the world's A-to-Z-list celebrities for two weeks of screenings and glamour parties. The lucky ones go home with a Golden or Silver Bear. Screenings often sell out, so book early.

MARCH

Internationale Tourismus Börse
www.itb-berlin.de
Take a virtual trip around the globe at the world's largest international travel expo. It opens to the public at the weekend.

MaerzMusik
www.maerzmusik.de
This contemporary music festival presents a boundary-pushing palette of sounds, from full orchestral symphonies to experimental tonescapes, many of them new or commissioned.

APRIL

Achtung Berlin
www.achtungberlin.de
Flicks about Berlin produced by Berlin companies get the nod at this festival held at the Kino Babylon (p72) with many authors, directors and producers in attendance.

Festtage
www.staatsoper-berlin.org
Founded by state opera boss Daniel Barenboim in 1996, this is a star-studded 10-day festival of high-profile gala concerts and operas with an emphasis on works by Richard Wagner.

MAY

Karneval der Kulturen
www.karneval-berlin.de
Berlin's answer to London's Notting Hill Carnival celebrates the city's multicultural spirit with parties, exotic nosh and a fun parade of flamboyantly costumed dancers, singers, DJs, artists and musicians shimmying through the streets of Kreuzberg.

Theatertreffen Berlin
www.theatertreffen-berlin.de
The Berlin Theatre Gathering is a three-week showcase of new productions by emerging and established German-language ensembles from Germany, Austria and Switzerland.

MAY DAY MADNESS
Not for those of a nervous disposition, May Day (1 May) sees Berlin's central districts (Kreuzberg especially) become the venue of large-scale anticapitalist, antiglobalisation, antiwhatever demonstrations. Traditionally, right-wing groups schedule their marches for the same day, the police turn out in force and within a couple of hours there's chaos. That means violence, vandalism and burning vehicles – we only mention this at all so you can stay out of the way.

JUNE

Christopher Street Day
www.csd-berlin.de
No matter your sexual persuasion, everybody's welcome to paint the town pink at this huge pride parade with naked torsos, strutting trannies and more queens than you'd find at a royal wedding.

Fête de la Musique
www.lafetedelamusique.com, in German
Summer (21 June) starts with good vibrations thanks to hundreds of free concerts during this global music festival that first came online in Paris in 1982.

Sandsation
www.sandsation.de
A fantasy world built from sand takes shape from early June through to the end of August next to the Hauptbahnhof (main train station). At more than 6m high, these ain't your little brother's sandcastles.

JULY

Classic Open Air Gendarmenmarkt
www.classicopenair.de
Five days and five alfresco concerts delight an adoring crowd hunkered on bleachers before the Konzerthaus. No ticket? No problem. Just eavesdrop with the penniless masses from outside the fence.

Museumsinsel Festival
www.museumsinselfestival.info
Listen to Mongolian shaman drumming, be transported by Argentine electrotango or take a Bollywood dance workshop at this summerlong international festival in the Lustgarten.

AUGUST

Berliner Bierfestival
www.bierfestival-berlin.de, in German
Who needs Oktoberfest when you can have the 'world's longest beer garden'? Pick your poison from around 250 breweries from dozens of countries along 2km of Karl-Marx-Allee.

Fuckparade
www.fuckparade.org, in German
Relax, it's not what you think but simply your average antifascist demonstration. Wear black and dark mascara or risk not fitting in.

Internationale Funkausstellung
www.ifa-berlin.de
Find out what gadgets everyone will want for Christmas at this huge international consumer electronics fair.

SEPTEMBER

Berlin Marathon
www.berlin-marathon.com
Sweat it out with the other 50,000 runners or just cheer 'em on during Germany's biggest street race – which has seen nine world records set since 1977.

Giving Santa a helping hand at one of Berlin's many Christmas markets (p30)

Internationales Literaturfestival
www.literaturfestival.com
Dozens of authors from all corners of the world celebrate the power of the pen with the literary public through readings, workshops and events.

Musikfest Berlin
www.berlinerfestspiele.de
World-renowned orchestras, conductors and soloists come together for two weeks of concerts at the Philharmonie (p87) and adjacent Kammermusiksaal (Map p81, E2).

OCTOBER

Art Forum Berlin
www.art-forum-berlin.com
Find out what's hot in art at this well-established international contemporary art fair that brings together leading galleries, artists, collectors and the merely curious.

Festival of Lights
www.city-stiftung-berlin.eu
For two weeks Berlin's all about 'light-seeing' as historical landmarks such as

the TV Tower, the Berliner Dom and the Brandenburg Gate sparkle with illuminations, projections and fireworks.

Porn Film Festival

www.pornfilmfestivalberlin.de

Vintage porn, Japanese porn, indie porn, sci-fi porn – the 'Berlinale' of sex brings alternative skin flicks out of the smut corner and onto the big screen.

You Berlin

www.you.de, in German

Stay ahead of the fashion, sports, beauty and lifestyle curve at Europe's largest youth fair, complete with concerts, live TV tapings and roving casting agents.

NOVEMBER

Berlin Biennale

www.berlinbiennale.de

Presenting new art in unusual sites around town, this biennial exhibition of contemporary art was launched in 1997 by the nonprofit Kunst-Werke Berlin (p64).

Jazzfest Berlin

www.jazzfest-berlin.de

This top-rated jazz festival has 'doo-wopped' in Berlin since 1964 and presents fresh and big-time talent in dozens of performances all over town.

DECEMBER

Christmas Markets

www.berlin.de/orte/weihnachtsmaerkte, in German

Pick up shimmering ornaments or get smashed on mulled wine at dozens of Yuletide markets held throughout December in such locales as Breitscheidplatz (Map p133, F2) and Alexanderplatz (Map p57, C1).

New Year's Eve

www.silvester-in-berlin.de

Ring in the New Year hugging strangers, cooing at fireworks, guzzling *Sekt* (sparkling wine) straight from the bottle and generally misbehaving. The main action is at the Brandenburg Gate (p46), but pros and purists prefer the Kreuzberg hill in Viktoriapark (Map p113, A5).

>ITINERARIES

Imagine the grandeur of Prussian royalty at Schloss Charlottenburg (p12)

ITINERARIES

Don't let Berlin's great size intimidate you: most of its trophy sites are squished into the compact city centre and the rest is just a quick U-Bahn or bus ride away. Here are some ideas on how you might plan your stay.

DAY ONE

Get up early to beat the crowds to the dome of the Reichstag (p78), then head south to snap a picture of the Brandenburg Gate (p46) before exploring the maze of the Holocaust Denkmal (Holocaust Memorial; p48), followed by a stroll around Potsdamer Platz (p80). From here take the U2 to Stadtmitte station, hook south to Checkpoint Charlie (p114) to ponder Cold War history, then double back for a dose of retail therapy in the Friedrichstadtpassagen (p52). Grab a quick bite, then saunter over to the beautiful Gendarmenmarkt (p47) and north to Unter den Linden (p42). Follow the historic boulevard east to the Berliner Dom (p45) but leave Museumsinsel (Museum Island) for another day, saving your energy for a leisurely meander through the winding lanes of the Scheunenviertel (p62). After foraging for mostly home-grown art, fashions and accessories, wind down the day with dinner, perhaps at Schwarzwaldstuben (p70). If you're not ready to go home, hit the wooden dance floor amid hilarious retro decor at Clärchens Ballhaus (p74).

DAY TWO

Follow the one-day itinerary, then devote day two's morning to ancient treasure at the Pergamonmuseum (p50) and Queen Nefertiti at the Neues Museum (p49). Outside the museums, hop on tram M1 and head north to the Eberswalder Strasse stop to saunter leisurely around boho-chic and beautifully restored Prenzlauer Berg. Swing by the Kulturbrauerei (p99), then stroll over to leafy Kollwitzplatz (p90) before resting over coffee and cake at Anna Blume (p96). Next, check out the indie boutiques along Kastanienallee and Oderberger Strasse on your way to the Mauerpark and Bernauer Strasse (p90), which were at the epicentre of Berlin Wall history. Dinner options abound in this area; try Fellas (p93), Oderquelle (p95) or Si An (p96), then cap off the day with a drink at Klub der Republik (p98).

Top left Bergmannstrasse (p112), western Kreuzberg's shopping and eating darling **Top right** It's all light and form at the Museumsinsel's bodacious Bodemuseum (p46) **Bottom** Aquadom's awe-inspiring aquatic denizens, Sea Life Berlin (p59)

DAY THREE

After breakfast on day three, head to Schloss Charlottenburg where you should miss neither the Neuer Flügel (New Wing; p136) nor a spin around the lovely palace gardens. In nice weather you could follow up your visit with a leisurely boat ride (p188) back to Mitte from the landing docks just east of the palace. Alternatively (and assuming it's not Sunday), take the U2 from Sophie-Charlotte-Platz to Wittenbergplatz to satisfy your shopping cravings at the KaDeWe (p146) department store with its mind-boggling food hall. For extended retail therapy, head west on Tauentzienstrasse to the famous Kurfürstendamm, which has all the international chains. Or, if your tastes run more in the boho vein, take the M19 bus from Wittenbergplatz to Mehringdamm in Kreuzberg. Refuel with *Currywurst* (curried sausage) at Curry 36 (p118), then poke around the little

Feeling free by the Spree

stores along lovely Bergmannstrasse. For dinner, you could go haute at Hartmanns (p103) or local at Henne (p104) or Hasir (p104). Finish up with drinks at Freischwimmer (p107) or Club der Visionäre (p110).

FOR FREE

It's no secret that you can get more bang for your euro in Berlin than in any other Western capital, and there are ways to stretch your budget even further. And we're not talking second-rate stuff here! The lift ride to the Reichstag dome (p78) – free. The Berlin Wall at East Side Gallery (p124) – free. And the Holocaust Denkmal (p48) – you guessed it, free as well. Simply walking down city streets costs nothing either, of course, and Berlin has some great strips, including historic Unter den Linden and flashy Friedrichstrasse (p42), bohemian Bergmannstrasse (p112) and monumental Karl-Marx-Allee (p124). The Spree promenade, meanwhile, opens up exciting views of the new government quarter. Check the listings magazines *Tip* (www.tip-berlin.de, in German) and *Zitty* (www.zitty .de, in German) for gallery openings, festivals, readings and other events that don't charge a cover. Examples include jazz at A-Trane (p142), lunchtime concerts at the Berliner Philharmonie (p87), and the occasional rock concert at Magnet (p99).

FORWARD PLANNING

Two or three months before you go Check the website of Berlin's tourist office (www.visit berlin.de), which comes with a searchable database of major upcoming special events and also gives you the option of buying tickets using a credit card. Performing-arts venues usually have their own online calendars and booking facilities. Tickets to the Berliner Philharmonie (p87) and the Staatsoper Unter den Linden (p55) often sell out and should be booked as early as possible. The same is true for key football (soccer) games such as the German football league final in late May or classic Bundesliga (Germany's premier league) derbies, such as between local club Hertha BSC and arch rival FC Bayern. Tickets to regular Saturday matches, though, are usually available on game day.

One month before you go Sign up for the weekly newsletter of Berlin Unlike (http://berlin .unlike.net) to keep tabs on the latest trends and openings around the town, and also check the online versions of the listings magazines *Tip* (www.tip-berlin.de, in German) and *Zitty* (www.zitty.de, in German).

One week before you go Make weekend dinner reservations at hot or upmarket restaurants such as Uma (p53) or Spindler & Klatt (p105). For other restaurants, calling one day ahead is usually sufficient.

RAINY DAY

With more museums than rainy days, there's no shortage of quality things to do in Berlin when the weather gods are in a foul mood. The classic way to start the day is with a leisurely breakfast, served until well into the afternoon at such places as Anna Blume (p96), Brel (p140) and Tomasa (p118). Afterwards, lug your full belly to one of the 175 museums, which range from mega hits such as the Pergamonmuseum (p50) to such speciality gems as the Käthe-Kollwitz-Museum (p135). Shopaholics won't have a problem giving their credit cards a workout during a couple of dry hours spent at KaDeWe (p146) or the Friedrichstadtpassagen (p52). Or head to the Liquidrom (p119), an ethereal pool, sauna and bar, where a dreary winter afternoon is quickly forgotten. Celebrity watchers can scan the crowd over coffee or cocktails in the lobby lounge of the legendary Hotel Adlon (p48). Also check *Tip* (www.tip-berlin.de, in German) and *Zitty* (www.zitty.de, in German) for what's playing at the all-English cinema Cinestar Original (p87) or the Arsenal (p87) art-house cinema, both at the Sony Center.

Not your average shopping mall: stylish, yesteryear Quartier 206 at Friedrichstadtpassagen (p52)

ON A SUNDAY

Unlike other metropolises, Berlin doesn't sink into a pious stupor on Sundays and – except for the shops – is pretty much open for business. This goes for all the museums, sights, boat cruises, cinemas, theatre and concert stages, cabarets and other entertainment venues. Cafes are in full swing all day long, serving big brunch buffets until the last bleary-eyed night owls have had their fill, ie about 3pm or 4pm. In the afternoon, the time-honoured German tradition of coffee and cake brings out people of all generations and walks of life. If you're suffering from shopping withdrawal, get your fix at a flea market. Flohmarkt am Mauerpark (p92) and Flohmarkt am Arkonaplatz (p91) are among the city's best and conveniently close to each other. For diehard dancers, there are plenty of afterparties; the waterfront Club der Visionäre (p110) has one of the best vibes in town. Weekly Sunday-night parties include Café Fatal at SO36 (p110) with dance lessons, a show and disco dancing; and GMF at Weekend (p61) for our queer friends.

>1 Mitte – Unter den Linden & Museumsinsel   42
>2 Mitte – Alexanderplatz Area   56
>3 Mitte – Scheunenviertel   62
>4 Reichstag & Government Quarter   76
>5 Potsdamer Platz & Tiergarten   80
>6 Prenzlauer Berg   88
>7 Eastern Kreuzberg & Kreuzkölln   100
>8 Western Kreuzberg   112
>9 Friedrichshain   122
>10 Charlottenburg   132
>11 Schöneberg   144

An enchanted evening in tucked-away, art-nouveau-style Hackesche Höfe (p64)

NEIGHBOURHOODS

Built upon the ashes of WWII, Berlin is a modern, sprawling and well-structured mosaic of distinctive neighbourhoods or, as locals affectionately say, *Kieze*.

The areas of greatest visitor interest are fairly well defined and the flat terrain and superb public transport make it easy to get around quickly. The central district is historic Mitte, a fantastic cocktail of culture, architecture, commerce and such blockbuster sights as the Brandenburg Gate, the Holocaust Denkmal (Holocaust Memorial), Museumsinsel (Museum Island) and the TV Tower. The federal government quarter with the historic Reichstag is northwest of the Brandenburg Gate, while east of it the grand boulevard Unter den Linden recalls the glory days of royal Prussia and Friedrichstrasse is a swanky shopping and entertainment artery. North of bustling Alexanderplatz, the Scheunenviertel is the historic Jewish quarter, jammed with bars, restaurants, galleries and urban designer boutiques.

North of Mitte, residential Prenzlauer Berg has a vibrant cafe culture, leafy avenues and a bevy of owner-run boutiques. South of Mitte, Kreuzberg is one of Berlin's most diverse and vibrant neighbourhoods. The eastern section is the local Turkish population's hub and there's rocking nightlife along the Spree River, Oranienstrasse and around Kottbusser Tor. Western Kreuzberg around Bergmannstrasse has more of a boho-chic vibe. Checkpoint Charlie and the Jewish Museum are the district's key sights.

Across the river, Friedrichshain blends a working-class, socialist past with a youthful, future-oriented outlook. Its assets include a lively party scene, the longest surviving stretch of the Berlin Wall and Karl-Marx-Allee, East Berlin's grand socialist boulevard.

West of the Brandenburg Gate, Mitte segues into Tiergarten park, a fantastic urban playground that rubs up against Potsdamer Platz, Berlin's biggest post-reunification construction project. On the park's western edge is Charlottenburg, the heart of the western city centre, with great shopping along Kurfürstendamm and the royal splendour of Schloss Charlottenburg. Much of Charlottenburg is upmarket residential, as is adjoining Schöneberg, despite its throbbing gay and lesbian quarter around Nollendorfplatz.

PRENZLAUER BERG
p89

MITTE –
SCHEUNENVIERTEL
p63

MITTE –
ALEXANDERPLATZ
AREA
p57

FRIEDRICHSHAIN
p123

EASTERN
KREUZBERG
& KREUZKÖLLN
p101

Treptow

Nikolaiviertel

Kreuzberg

REICHSTAG
& GOVERNMENT
QUARTER
p77

MITTE – UNTER
DEN LINDEN &
MUSEUMSINSEL
p43

Panke

WESTERN
KREUZBERG
p113

Kreuzberg

Kulturforum

POTSDAMER
PLATZ & TIERGARTEN
p81

Tiergarten

Spree River

SCHÖNEBERG
p145

CHARLOTTENBURG
p133

Wilmersdorf

1 km
0.5 miles

0
0

>MITTE – UNTER DEN LINDEN & MUSEUMSINSEL

Even cynics can't deny it: historic Mitte has magnetism. Once trapped behind the Berlin Wall, it's now the glamorous heart of the city, where famous landmarks line up like Prussian soldiers for inspection along elegant Unter den Linden boulevard. This 1.5km-long ribbon of baroque beauties and haughty neoclassical edifices stretches from the Brandenburg Gate to the giant treasure chest of the Museumsinsel (Museum Island), a cluster of five museums, including the newly reopened Neues Museum.

MITTE – UNTER DEN LINDEN & MUSEUMSINSEL

◉ SEE

Alte Nationalgalerie	1	E1
Altes Museum	2	E2
Bebelplatz	3	D3
Berliner Dom	4	F2
Berliner Schloss Infocenter	5	E3
Bodemuseum	6	E1
Brandenburg Gate	7	A3
Deutsche Guggenheim Berlin	8	D2
Deutscher Dom	9	D4
Deutsches Historisches Museum	10	E2
DZ Bank	11	B3
Emil Nolde Museum	12	D3
Französischer Dom	13	D3
Friedrichswerdersche Kirche	14	E3
Gendarmenmarkt	15	D3
Hitler's Bunker	16	B4
Holocaust Denkmal	17	A3
Holocaust Denkmal Ort der Information	18	B3
Hotel Adlon Kempinski	19	B3
IM Pei Bau	20	E2

Kennedy Museum	21	B2
Madame Tussauds	22	B2
Neue Wache	23	E2
Neues Museum	24	E2
Pariser Platz	25	B3
Pergamonmuseum	26	E1
Reiterdenkmal Friedrich des Grossen	27	D2
Site of Former Palast der Republik/Future Humboldt Forum	28	F2
Temporäre Kunsthalle	29	F2

◉ SHOP

Berlin Story	30	C2
Contemporary Fine Arts	31	E2
Dussmann – Das Kulturkaufhaus	32	C2
Fassbender & Rausch	33	D4
Friedrichstadt-passagen	34	D4
Galeries Lafayette	35	D3
Quartier 205	36	D4
Quartier 206	37	D3

🍴 EAT

Cookies Cream	38	C3
Grill Royal	39	C1
Ishin	40	C2
Sagrantino	41	D3
Uma	42	B3
Zwölf Apostel	43	D1

🍷 DRINK

Bebel Bar	44	D3
Tadschikische Teestube	45	E2
Tausend	46	C1
Windhorst	47	C2

★ PLAY

Admiralspalast	48	C1
Berliner Ensemble	49	C1
Cookies	50	C2
Felix Clubrestaurant	51	B3
Konzerthaus Berlin	52	D3
Staatsoper Unter den Linden	53	E3

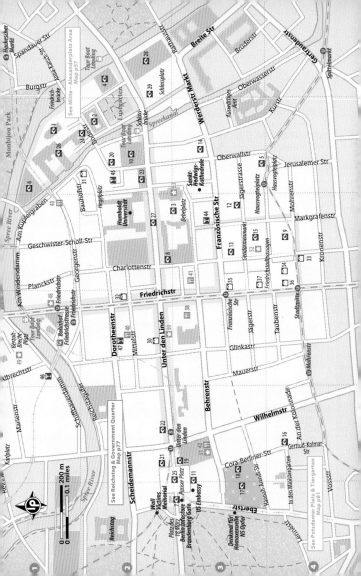

Across the street, on Schlossplatz, a big lawn and an art-exhibit hall fill the temporary void created by the demolition of the German Democratic Republic–era Palast der Republik building. If all goes to plan, the reconstruction of the royal city palace it replaced will begin in 2011.

Unter den Linden itself is pretty dead after dark, but Friedrichstrasse, which bisects it, has reclaimed its historic role as a luxury hub with shopping, dining, party and imbibing stations fit for the Prada brigade. The poshness spills over into nearby Gendarmenmarkt, Berlin's most beautiful square. North of Unter den Linden, Friedrichstrasse leads into the city's vibrant theatre district.

◉ SEE

◎ ALTE NATIONALGALERIE

Old National Gallery; ☎ 2090 5577; www .smb.spk-berlin.de/ang; Bodestrasse 1-3; adult/under 16/concession €8/free/4, last 4hr Thu free; ☺ 10am-6pm Tue, Wed & Fri-Sun, to 10pm Thu; ⊟ 100, 200 or TXL; ⌖

This Greek-temple building on Museumsinsel is an elegant backdrop for an exquisite collection of 19th-century European art. Drawcards include Caspar David Friedrich's mystical landscapes, sensitive portraits by Max Liebermann and Adolph Menzel's epic glorifications of Prussian military might.

◎ ALTES MUSEUM

Old Museum; ☎ 2090 5577; www.smb .spk-berlin.de; Am Lustgarten; adult/ under 16/concession €8/free/4, last 4hr Thu free; ☺ 10am-6pm Tue, Wed & Fri-Sun, to 10pm Thu; ⊟ 100, 200 or TXL; ⌖ Karl Friedrich Schinkel pulled out all the stops for this grand, column-fronted museum with its Pantheon-inspired rotunda. It houses a prized collection of Greek and Roman art and sculpture but is scheduled for restoration as part of the Museumsinsel update, so may be fully or partly closed in coming years.

◎ BEBELPLATZ

Bebel Square; ⊟ 100, 200 or TXL On this stark square books by Brecht, Mann, Marx and other 'subversives' went up in flames during the first big official Nazi

BARGAIN BOX

If you're visiting more than one museum on Museumsinsel, a day pass for €12 (concession €6) is your ticket to savings. It's valid for one-time, same-day admission to the Altes Museum, Bodemuseum, Alte Nationalgalerie and Pergamonmuseum. Note that it is not valid at the Neues Museum. Admission at any is free if you're under 16 and for everyone during the last four opening hours on Thursday. Special exhibits cost extra.

book burning in 1933. Michael Ul-
lmann's underground installation,
Empty Library, beneath a glass
pane at the square's centre, commemorates the event. The stately
buildings framing Bebelplatz date
back to the reign of Frederick the
Great, who surveys his domain
from horseback in Christian
Rauch's epic sculpture, **Reiterdenk-
mal Friedrich des Grossen,** nearby on
Unter den Linden.

🎧 BERLINER DOM
**Berlin Cathedral; ☎ 2026 9136; www
.berliner-dom.de; Am Lustgarten;**
**adult/under 14/concession €5/free/3,
with audioguide €8/free/6; ⏰ 9am-8pm
Mon-Sat, noon-8pm Sun Apr-Sep, to 7pm
Oct-Mar; 🚌 100, 200 or TXL; ♿**
Pompous yet majestic, the former
royal court church (1905) does
triple duty as house of worship,
museum and concert hall. Climb
up to the gallery for glorious city
views and close-ups of the glass
mosaics decorating the inner
dome. The 7269-pipe Sauer organ
and the elaborate sarcophagi
made for the Great Elector, King
Friedrich I and their wives are
other top draws.

Soaring towards heaven for very different reasons: the grand Berliner Dom and the TV Tower (p59)

'LOUVRE ON THE SPREE'

The Museumsinsel repositories collectively became a Unesco World Heritage site in 1999. The distinction was at least partly achieved because of an ambitious master plan that will unite four of the five buildings into a self-contained complex representing 6000 years of human history, art and culture. By 2015 all but the Alte Nationalgalerie will be linked by a subterranean walkway dubbed the Archaeological Promenade. The complex will be entered through a colonnaded modern structure called the James-Simon-Galerie. To learn more, go to www.museumsinsel-berlin.de.

☉ BODEMUSEUM

☎ 2090 5577; www.smb.spk-berlin .de/bode; Monbijoubrücke; adult/under 16/concession €8/free/4, last 4hr Thu free; ☽ 10am-6pm Fri-Wed, to 10pm Thu; ⊠ Hackescher Markt or Oranienburger Strasse; ♿

On the northern tip of Museumsinsel, this mighty museum houses Byzantine art, a coin collection, old paintings and, most importantly, European sculpture from the Middle Ages to the 18th century. Look out for masterpieces by Tilmann Riemenschneider, Donatello, Giovanni Pisano and Ignaz Günther.

☉ BRANDENBURG GATE

Brandenburger Tor; Pariser Platz; admission free; ☽ 24hr; ⊠ Unter den Linden; ♿

A symbol of division during the Cold War, this landmark now epitomises German reunification. The 1791 structure by Carl Gotthard Langhans is the only surviving one of 18 city gates

and is crowned by the *Quadriga* sculpture, a horse-drawn chariot piloted by the winged goddess of victory. See p21 for more.

☉ DEUTSCHE GUGGENHEIM BERLIN

☎ 202 0930; www.deutsche-guggen heim.de; Unter den Linden 13-15; adult/concession/family €4/3/8, Mon free; ☽ 10am-8pm Fri-Wed, to 10pm Thu; ⊠ 100, 200 or TXL; ♿

This small, minimalist gallery may not compare to the other Guggenheims in New York or Bilbao but the changing exhibits here still spotlight big-name talent such as Eduardo Chillida, Georg Baselitz and Gerhard Richter.

☉ DEUTSCHES HISTORISCHES MUSEUM

German Historical Museum; ☎ 203 040; www.dhm.de; Unter den Linden 2; adult/under 18 €5/free; ☽ 10am-6pm; ⊠ 100, 200 or TXL; ♿

If you're wondering what the Germans have been up to for the past 2000 years, take a spin around this engaging museum. A startling highlight is the big globe that originally stood in the Nazi Foreign Office with bullet holes where Germany should be. In the courtyard, Andreas Schlüter's baroque mask sculptures of dying soldiers make a strong case against war. High-calibre temporary exhibits take up a strikingly geometrical annexe designed by IM Pei and hence called the **IM Pei Bau**.

◪ EMIL NOLDE MUSEUM
☎ 4000 4690; www.nolde-stiftung.de; Jägerstrasse 55; adult/concession incl audioguide €10/5; ⌚ 10am-7pm; ⦿ Französische Strasse or Hausvogteiplatz; ⛊
Bright flowers, stormy seas and red-lipped women with jaunty hats – the paintings and watercolours of Emil Nolde (1867–1956) are intense, sometimes melancholic and always captivating. Admire a rotating selection of works by this key German expressionist in a brightly converted 19th-century bank building.

◪ FRIEDRICHSWERDERSCHE KIRCHE
☎ 2090 5577; www.smb.spk-berlin.de; Werderscher Markt; admission free; ⌚ 10am-6pm; ⦿ Hausvogteiplatz; ⛊
This perkily turreted ex-church by Karl Friedrich Schinkel now

shelters 19th-century sculpture. Schinkel groupies should report to the upstairs gallery for background on the architect's life and times.

◪ GENDARMENMARKT
⦿ Französische Strasse
Berlin's most graceful square gets its name from the Gens d'Armes, a Prussian regiment consisting of French Huguenot immigrants. Local Huguenots worshipped at the **Französischer Dom** (French Dome), where a small museum now chronicles their story. The cathedral closely mirrors the **Deutscher Dom** (German Dome) opposite, home to a hopelessly academic exhibit on German democracy. Completing the trio is Schinkel's beautiful Konzerthaus Berlin (p55).

◪ HITLER'S BUNKER
In den Ministergärten & Gertrud-Kolmar-Strasse; ⧇ Unter den Linden
Berlin was burning and Soviet tanks advancing relentlessly when Adolf Hitler put a gun to his head in his bunker. Today there's just a parking lot and an information panel with a diagram of the vast bunker network, technical data on how it was constructed and information on what happened to it after WWII.

☉ HOLOCAUST DENKMAL

Holocaust Memorial; ☎ 2639 4336; www.holocaust-mahnmal.de; Cora-Berliner-Strasse 1; admission free; ⏰ memorial 24hr, Ort der Information 10am-8pm Tue-Sun Apr-Sep, to 7pm Oct-Mar, last admission 45min before closing; 🚉 Unter den Linden; ♿

This poignant memorial to the Jewish victims of the Nazi-planned genocide was designed by Peter Eisenmann and consists of 2711 sarcophagi-like columns rising up in sombre silence from undulating ground. For context, visit the subterranean **Ort der Information** (Information Centre), whose exhibits will leave no one untouched.

☉ HOTEL ADLON KEMPINSKI

☎ 226 10; www.hotel-adlon.de; Unter den Linden 77; 🚉 Unter den Linden; ♿

Overlooking the Brandenburg Gate, Berlin's poshest caravanserai was the original *Grand Hotel*, where the 1932 movie starring Greta Garbo was filmed. A celeb magnet since its 1907 opening, it has sheltered Charlie Chaplin, Albert Einstein and even Michael Jackson. Remember him dangling his baby out the window? It happened at the Adlon.

☉ KENNEDY MUSEUM

☎ 2065 3570; www.thekennedys.de; Pariser Platz 4a; adult/concession €7/3.50; ⏰ 10am-6pm; 🚉 Unter den Linden; ♿

US president John F Kennedy of '*Ich bin ein Berliner!*' fame is the focus of this intimate, nonpolitical exhibit set up like a walk-through family photo album. Besides pictures there are scribbled notes, JFK's crocodile-leather briefcase, Jackie's Persian lamb pillbox hat and a hilarious *Superman* comic book edition starring the president.

☉ MADAME TUSSAUDS

☎ 4000 4600; www.madametussauds.com/berlin; Unter den Linden 74; adult/child/concession €19/14/18; ⏰ 10am-7pm, last admission 6pm; 🚉 Unter den Linden; 🚌 100; ♿

No celebrity in town to snare your stare? Don't fret: at this legendary wax museum Brangelina, Leo and Obama stand still – very still – for you to snap their picture. Sure, it's an expensive haven of kitsch and camp but where else can you cuddle with Robbie Williams or hug the Pope?

☉ NEUE WACHE

New Guardhouse; Unter den Linden 4; admission free; ⏰ 10am-6pm; 🚌 100, 200 or TXL; ♿

Karl Friedrich Schinkel's columned, templelike structure was originally a Prussian royal guardhouse and is now an antiwar memorial centred on Käthe Kollwitz' heart-wrenching sculpture of a mother cradling her dead soldier son.

NEUES MUSEUM

New Museum; ☎ 2090 5555; www.smb
.spk-berlin.de; Bodestrasse 1-3; adult/
under 16/concession €8/free/4; 10am-
6pm Fri-Wed, to 10pm Thu; 100, 200
or TXL;

After 10 years and €200 million,
the reconstructed Neues Museum
finally reopened to an adoring
public in October 2009. Architect
David Chipperfield harmoniously
incorporated remnants of the war-
damaged structure into the new
building, which houses the Egyptian Museum (including the famous bust of Queen Nefertiti), the
Papyrus Collection, the Museum of
Pre- and Early History and the Collection of Classical Antiquities.

PARISER PLATZ

Unter den Linden; 100, 200 or TXL

The Brandenburg Gate stands
sentinel over this elegant square,
which spent the Cold War trapped
just east of the Berlin Wall but
now is again framed by embassies, banks and the fancy Hotel
Adlon, just as it was during its
19th-century heyday. Pop into the
Frank Gehry–designed **DZ Bank** for
a peek at the atrium's outlandish

Suite at Hotel Adlon Kempinski with one helluva sweet view of the Brandenburg Gate

PRUSSIAN POMP, 21ST-CENTURY STYLE

Nothing of today's Schlossplatz evokes memory of the grand palace where the Prussian rulers made their home for 500 years. Despite international protests, the GDR government razed the barely war-damaged structure in 1951 and replaced it with a multipurpose hall called **Palast der Republik** (Palace of the Republic). This was where the GDR parliament hammered out policy and common folk came to hear Harry Belafonte or party on New Year's Eve.

After the fall of the Wall, the Palast closed instantly because of asbestos contamination. Years of debate resulted in the demolition of the behemoth and the plan to build an exact replica of the Prussian palace shell but with a modern interior. To be called **Humboldt Forum**, it will shelter art and artefacts from Africa, Asia, Oceania and the Americas currently on display in the far-flung suburb of Dahlem, as well as a library and a research facility. It's slated to be completed in time for the 25th anniversary of reunification in 2015. For a preview of what's to come, drop by the **Berliner Schloss Infocenter** (☎ 2067 3093; www.berliner -schloss.de; Hausvogteiplatz 3; admission free; 🕙 9.30am-6pm; 🚇 Hausvogteiplatz).

In the meantime, part of the empty lot is occupied by the **Temporäre Kunsthalle** (☎ 2045 3650; www.kunsthalle-berlin.com; Schlossplatz; admission varies; 🕙 11am-6pm Sun-Fri, to 9pm Sat; 🚌 100, 200 or TXL), an exhibition hall showcasing statement-making pieces by international artists living in Berlin.

conference room. Next door, the new **US Embassy** opened in 2008.

🄲 PERGAMONMUSEUM

☎ 2090 5555; www.smb.spk-berlin.de; Am Kupfergraben 5; adult/under 16/ concession €8/free/4, last 4hr Thu free; 🕙 10am-6pm Fri-Wed, to 10pm Thu; 🚌 100, 200 or TXL; ♿

On Museumsinsel, this Aladdin's cave of treasures from ancient worlds pulls in more people than any other museum in town. Admission includes an excellent audio-guide describing all the must-see exhibits, including the massive Pergamon Altar, the radiantly blue Ishtar Gate and a caliph's palace. For the full low-down, see p10.

🄲 SHOP

🄱 BERLIN STORY
Books

☎ 2045 3842; www.berlinstory.de; Unter den Linden 26; 🕙 10am-8pm; 🚇 🚆 Friedrichstrasse

Berlin in a nutshell. This is the ultimate one-stop shop for Berlin-related books, maps, DVDs, CDs and magazines, in English and 11 other languages, some even published in-house. Also check out the free historical movie about Berlin and the basement exhibit with its GDR-era Trabant car (Trabi, for short) and 1930 Berlin city model.

🖼 CONTEMPORARY FINE ARTS *Gallery*

☎ 288 7870; www.cfa-berlin.com; Am Kupfergraben 10; 🕙 10am-1pm & 2-6pm Tue-Fri, 11am-4pm Sat; Ⓓ Ⓡ Friedrichstrasse

In an elegantly minimalist new building by David Chipperfield, this top gallery is a must for art buffs wanting to take the city's aesthetic pulse. Artists represented include Georg Baselitz, Sarah Lucas, Jonathan Meese and Daniel Richter.

🖼 DUSSMANN – DAS KULTURKAUFHAUS *Books & Music*

☎ 2025 1111; www.kulturkaufhaus .de, in German; Friedrichstrasse 90; 🕙 10am-midnight Mon-Sat; Ⓓ Ⓡ Friedrichstrasse

It's easy to lose track of time in this huge book, film and music

Stopping off on a Berlin bicycle tour at Friedrichswerdersche Kirche (p47)

emporium with reading nooks, a cafe and a performance space used for concerts, political discussions and book readings, often featuring high-profile authors.

🏛 FASSBENDER & RAUSCH
Food

☎ 2045 8443; www.fassbender-rausch.de; Charlottenstrasse 60; ⌚ 10am-8pm Mon-Sat, 11am-8pm Sun; Ⓜ Französische Strasse

If the Aztecs thought of chocolate as the elixir of the gods, then this depot of truffles and pralines must be heaven. Bonus: the chocolate volcano and the giant replicas of Berlin landmarks.

🏛 FRIEDRICHSTADTPASSAGEN
Shopping Mall

☎ 209 480; www.lafayette-berlin.de, in German; Friedrichstrasse 76; ⌚ 10am-8pm Mon-Sat; Ⓜ Französische Strasse

Get your mitts on international couture, edgy Berlin fashions, gourmet treats and other goodies in this strikingly designed and interlinked trio of ritzy shopping complexes (called *Quartiere*). Don't miss Jean Nouvel's shimmering glass funnel inside the **Galeries Lafayette**, the dazzlingly patterned art-deco-style **Quartier 206** and John Chamberlain's tower made from crushed automobile parts in **Quartier 205**.

🍴 EAT

🍴 COOKIES CREAM
Vegetarian €€€

☎ 2749 2940; www.cookiescream.com; Friedrichstrasse 158; ⌚ from 7pm Tue-Sat; Ⓜ Französische Strasse; ✗ Ⓥ

Combining coolness with substance, Cookies is one of Berlin's favourite hidden eateries, reached via the smelly service alley of the Westin Grand Hotel. Upstairs awaits an elegantly industrial space where flesh-free but flavour-packed dishes are brought to linen-draped tables. It's all so good and gorgeous, even diehard meatheads should have no complaints.

🍴 GRILL ROYAL
International €€€

☎ 2887 9288; www.grillroyal.com; Friedrichstrasse 105b; ⌚ from 6pm; Ⓜ 🚋 Friedrichstrasse

A platinum card is a handy accessory at this 'look-at-me' temple where power politicians, A-listers, Russian oligarchs, pouty models and 'trust-afarians' can be seen slurping oysters and tucking into their *wagyu* steak. The entrance is on the canalside below the hotel.

🍴 ISHIN *Asian* €

☎ 2067 4829; www.ishin.de, in German; Mittelstrasse 24; ⌚ 11am-10pm Mon-Sat; Ⓜ 🚋 Friedrichstrasse; ✗

This cafeteria-style sushi parlour scores two for looks and 10 for freshness and value. The combination platters are ample and the sushi-meisters often sneak in an extra piece or two. Prices drop even lower during Happy Hour (all day Wednesday and Saturday and 11am to 4pm on other days). Nice touch: the unlimited free green tea.

▯ SAGRANTINO
Italian €€

☎ 2064 6895; www.sagrantino-winebar.de; Behrenstrasse 47; ⏱ 7.30am-midnight Mon-Fri, 9am-noon & 5pm-midnight Sat; ▣ Französische Strasse; ✗

The ambience here is so classically Italian, you'd half expect to see a sprawling vineyard out the window. That would be a vineyard in Umbria, for that's the region showcased at this fantastic little spot that usually gets mobbed at lunchtime for its good-value pasta-salad combos (€5.90).

▯ UMA *Japanese* €€€

☎ 301 117 333; www.ma-restaurants.de; Behrenstrasse 72; ⏱ 6pm-midnight Mon-Sat; ▣ Unter den Linden; ▯ 100, 200 or TXL; ✗

Japanese for horse, Uma is the 'casual' sister of Michelin-starred Tim Raue's stunning MA restau-

rant complex. Flavours are woven together like fine tapestries in such dishes as pork cheeks with papaya and sorrel or 'pizza' with yellow-fin tuna. Alas, you'll need three or four plates (each costing between €10 and €30) to fill your tummy.

▯ ZWÖLF APOSTEL
Italian €€

☎ 201 0222; www.12-apostel.de, in German; Georgenstrasse 2; ⏱ 11am-midnight; ▣ Friedrichstrasse; ✗

A pleasant pit stop between museums, this place beneath the railway arches has over-the-top religious decor and tasty thin-crust pizzas named after the 12 apostles. All cost a mere €6.90 from 11.30am to 4pm Monday to Friday.

▾ DRINK

▾ BEBEL BAR *Bar*

☎ 460 6090; www.hotelderome.com; Behrenstrasse 37; ⏱ from 9am; ▣ Französische Strasse; ✗

Channel your inner Cary Grant and belly up to the bar at this smooth, mood-lit thirst parlour at the Hotel de Rome. Blending fresh fruit, exotic herbs and spices with quality booze, cocktails here have a progressive, sexy edge that goes over well with the global Armani crowd.

☕ TADSCHIKISCHE TEESTUBE
Cafe

☎ 204 1112; Am Festungsgraben 1; ⏱ 5pm-midnight Mon-Fri, from 3pm Sat & Sun; 🚌 100, 200 or TXL; ✗

This authentic Tajik tearoom inside an 18th-century town palace feels like a fairy-tale retreat. Students, old hippies and curious tourists loll on thick oriental carpets drinking steaming teas poured from silvery samovars. The exotic room was a gift to the East German leadership by the Soviets in the 1970s. Skip the food.

🍸 TAUSEND *Bar*

☎ 460 6090; www.tausendberlin.com; Schiffbauerdamm 11; ⏱ from 9pm Tue-Sat; Ⓜ 🚇 Friedrichstrasse; ✗

The living room of the see-and-be-seen scene. No sign, no light, no bell, just a heavy steel gate beneath a railway bridge with a small window through which you shall be assessed. Once inside the black-and-metal tunnel, though, there's expert cocktails and easy-on-the-eyes fellow sippers.

🍸 WINDHORST *Bar*

☎ 2045 0070; Dorotheenstrasse 65; ⏱ from 6pm Mon-Fri, from 9pm Sat; Ⓜ 🚇 Friedrichstrasse

Discerning drinkers wishing to unwind in a sophisticated setting will find a thoroughly five-star ambience at this postage-stamp-sized bar where your host, the eponymous Günter Windhorst, 'shakes' things up with a passion.

⭐ PLAY

🎭 ADMIRALSPALAST
Theatre

☎ 4799 7499; www.admiralspalast.de, in German; Friedrichstrasse 101-102; Ⓜ 🚇 Friedrichstrasse

This beautifully restored 1920s party palace stages plays, concerts and musicals to pleased crowds in its elegant historic hall, and more intimate shows, including comedy, readings, dance, concerts and theatre, on two smaller stages.

🎭 BERLINER ENSEMBLE
Theatre

☎ 2840 8155; www.berliner-ensemble.de, in German; Bertolt-Brecht-Platz 1; tickets €5-30; Ⓜ 🚇 Friedrichstrasse

The company founded by Bertolt Brecht in 1949 is based at the neobaroque theatre where his *Threepenny Opera* premiered in 1928. Current artistic director Claus Peymann keeps the master's legacy alive while also peppering the repertory with works by Schiller, Beckett and other European playwrights. Quality is high, tickets are cheap.

⭐ COOKIES *Club*
www.cookies-berlin.de; Friedrichstrasse
158-164; ☽ 9pm-5am Tue, Thu & Sat;
cover €10; ⊕ Französische Strasse
This legendary party palace used
to be midweek only but now also
runs a Saturday party called Crush.
It's in a glamorous former East
Berlin cinema tucked behind the
Westin Hotel. There's no sign, a
tough door, great cocktails and a
grown-up ambience. Celeb sightings possible. The entrance is next
to the KPM store.

⭐ FELIX CLUBRESTAURANT
Club
☎ 206 2860; www.felixrestaurant.de;
Behrenstrasse 72; cover €10; ☽ Thu-Sat;
🚇 Unter den Linden; 🚌 100, 200 or TXL
Once past the rope of this exclusive
supper club at the Hotel Adlon,
you too can shake your booty to
'international club sounds', sip
champagne cocktails and – who
knows? – maybe even meet your
very own Carrie or 'Mr Big'. The flirt
factor is through the roof at Thursday's after-work party (from 9pm).

⭐ KONZERTHAUS BERLIN
Classical Music
☎ 203 090; www.konzerthaus.de;
Gendarmenmarkt 2; tickets €10-100;
⊕ Französische Strasse
This Schinkel-designed top-
ranked classical-music venue
counts the Konzerthausorchester
as its 'house band' but others,
such as the Rundfunk-Sinfonie-
orchester Berlin, perform here
as well.

⭐ STAATSOPER UNTER DEN
LINDEN *Opera*
☎ 2035 4555; www.staatsoper-berlin.de;
Unter den Linden 5-7, until 2013 performances at Bismarckstrasse 110; tickets
€5-160; ⊕ Französische Strasse
While the grand dame of Berlin's
opera houses is getting a facelift
(probably until 2013), you'll have
to travel to the **Schiller Theater** in
Charlottenburg (Map p133) to at-
tend the high-calibre productions
staged under Daniel Barenboim.
All operas are sung in their original
language.

>MITTE – ALEXANDERPLATZ AREA

Noisy, hectic and chaotic, Alexanderplatz (Alex for short) is not the kind of square that invites lingering, but at least it's easy to locate thanks to the TV Tower. Simply look up and chances are pretty good that you will see this famous landmark sticking out from the city skyline like Yao Ming surrounded by pygmies.

The tower was the crowning glory in the square's 1960s conversion into a poster child of socialist architecture. Despite post-reunification attempts to temper the austere look, Alexanderplatz remains an oddly cluttered, soulless spot that's all concrete, no trees. The main plaza is anchored by the German Democratic Republic–era Fountain of Friendship Among the Peoples, where pierced punks and their pit bulls linger next to field-tripping school kids and foot-weary tourists hunched over their city maps. The rest of Alex is confusingly bifurcated by roads, train and tram tracks and littered with a hotchpotch of architectural styles.

To find some open space, wander west of the TV Tower. This was where East German city planners tore down whatever was left of Old Berlin, leaving only the Marienkirche and the Berliner Rathaus (town hall). After the deed was done, they built the mock-medieval Nikolaiviertel quarter nearby. Go figure.

MITTE – ALEXANDERPLATZ AREA

🅞 SEE
DDR Museum	1	A2
Marienkirche	2	B2
Neptunbrunnen	3	B2
Nikolaiviertel	4	B3
Rotes Rathaus	5	B3
Sea Life Berlin	6	A2
TV Tower	7	C2

🅐 SHOP
Alexa	8	D2
Ausberlin	9	C1
Galeria Kaufhof	10	C1

🍴 EAT
Atame	11	B1
Dolores	12	C1
Zur Letzten Instanz	13	D3

⭐ PLAY
Bohannon	(see 11)	
Casino Berlin	14	D1
Kino International	15	F2
Weekend	16	D1

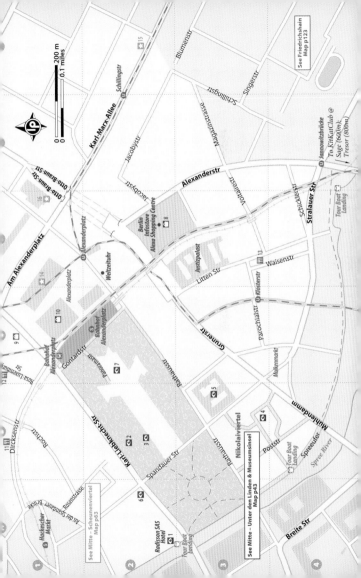

200 m
0.1 miles

See Friedrichshain
Map p123

Schillingstr

Blumenstr

Singerstr

Karl-Marx-Allee

Jacobystr

Schillingstr

Magazinstr

Janowitzbrücke
To KitKatClub @
Sage (600m);
Tresor (800m)

Otto-Braun-Str

Alexanderstr

Voltairestr

Schicklerstr

Stralauer Str

Am Alexanderplatz

Alexanderplatz

Berlin
InfoStore
Alexa Shopping Centre

Tour Boat
Landing

Alexanderplatz

Weltzeituhr

Justizpalast

Litten Str

Waisenstr

Klosterstr

Parochialstr

Grunerstr

Bahnhof
Alexanderplatz

Kaufhof
Alexanderplatz

Gontardstr

Panoramastr

Rathausstr

Molkenmarkt

Rosa-Luxemburg-Str

Dircksenstr

Rochstr

Karl-Liebknecht-Str

Spandauer Str

Rathausstr

Nikolaiviertel

Mühlendamm

Poststr

Tour Boat
Landing

Spreeufer

Spree River

Breite Str

Hackescher
Markt

An der Spandauer Brücke

An der Rosenstraße

Radisson SAS
Hotel

Tour Boat
Landing

See Mitte – Scheunenviertel
Map p63

See Mitte – Unter den Linden & Museumsinsel
Map p43

SEE

DDR MUSEUM

GDR Museum; ☎ 847 123 731; www
.ddr-museum.de; Karl-Liebknecht-
Strasse 1; adult/concession €5.50/3.50;
⏱ 10am-8pm Sun-Fri, to 10pm Sat;
🚌 100, 200 or TXL; ♿
East German kids were put through
collective potty training, engineers
earned little more than farmers and
everyone, it seems, went on nudist
holidays. Such are the fascinating nuggets you'll learn at this
hands-on museum dedicated to
teaching the rest of us about daily
life beyond the Iron Curtain. A must
for *Good Bye, Lenin!* fans.

Neptunbrunnen beauty outside Marienkirche

MARIENKIRCHE

Church of St Mary's; ☎ 242 4467; www
.marienkirche-berlin.de; Karl-Liebknecht
-Strasse 8; ⏱ 10am-9pm Apr-Oct, to 6pm
Nov-Mar; 🚌 100, 200 or TXL; ♿
This 13th-century brick gem is entered via a vestibule gruesomely
decorated with a (badly faded)
Dance of Death fresco created after
the plague of 1486. Outside the
church is the epic 1891 **Neptunbrunnen** (Neptune Fountain) by Rein-
hold Begas, with buxom beauties
representing major rivers.

NIKOLAIVIERTEL

Nicholas Quarter; 🚇 Klosterstrasse
Bounded by Rathausstrasse,
Spandauer Strasse, Mühlendamm
and the Spree River, the twee
Nicholas Quarter is a Disney-esque
attempt at re-creating Berlin's
medieval birthplace around the
1230 Nikolaikirche, the city's oldest building. The maze of cobbled
lanes is worth a quick stroll, but
you won't find too many Berliners patronising the pricey cafes,
restaurants and cutesy shops.

ROTES RATHAUS

Red Town Hall; ☎ 902 60;
Rathausstrasse 15; ⏱ closed to the
public; 🚇 🚊 Alexanderplatz
The hulking 1860 town hall is
where Berlin's governing mayor
and senators have their offices. It
sits smack dab in the city's geo-

graphical centre and is called Rotes Rathaus in reference to the colour of its bricks – not (necessarily) the political leanings of its occupants.

👁 SEA LIFE BERLIN

☎ 992 800; www.sealifeeurope.com; Spandauer Strasse 3; adult/concession €17/12; ⏲ 10am-7pm, last admission 6pm; 🚌 100, 200 or TXL; ♿

Pricey but entertaining, this aquarium follows the Spree River into the North Atlantic, introducing you to local aquatic denizens along the way. Visits conclude with a glacial lift ride through the Aquadom, a 16m-tall cylindrical tropical fish tank. Catch a free preview from the lobby of the Radisson SAS Hotel.

👁 TV TOWER

Fernsehturm; ☎ 242 3333; www.berlin erfernsehturm.de; Panoramastrasse 1a; adult/under 16 €10/5.50, VIP €19.50; ⏲ 9am-midnight Mar-Oct, from 10am Nov-Feb; 🚇 🚊 Alexanderplatz; ♿

The TV Tower is the tallest structure in Germany, soaring 368m above Berlin since 1969. Come early to beat the queue for the lift ride to the panorama level at 203m, where views are unbeatable on clear days. Pinpoint city landmarks from here or the upstairs cafe, which makes one revolution every 30 minutes. If you want to skip the line, buy a VIP ticket.

🛍 SHOP

🛍 ALEXA Shopping Mall

☎ 269 3400; www.alexacentre.de, in German; Grunerstrasse 20; ⏲ 10am-9pm; 🚇 🚊 Alexanderplatz

Power shoppers love this XXL-sized megamall near Alexanderplatz. Besides the usual mainstream retailers, there's a store by German rapper Bushido, the Kindercity interactive indoor playground and Loxx, the world's largest model railway.

🛍 AUSBERLIN Gifts & Souvenirs

☎ 4199 7896; www.ausberlin.de, in German; Karl-Liebknecht-Strasse 17; ⏲ 10am-8pm Mon-Sat, noon-8pm Sun; 🚇 🚊 Alexanderplatz

This unpretentious store has made it its mission to discover, promote and sell only articles made in Berlin. We're not talking trashy souvenirs but wallet-friendly stuff you might actually want or need, including T-shirts, accessories, toys, chocolates, music, lingerie and jewellery by dozens of local designers.

🛍 GALERIA KAUFHOF
Department Store

☎ 247 430; www.galeria-kaufhof.de, in German; Alexanderplatz 9; ⏲ 9.30am-8pm Mon-Wed, to 10pm Thu-Sat; 🚇 🚊 Alexanderplatz

A total renovation has turned the GDR-era Centrum Warenhaus into a 21st-century retail cube with a glass-domed court and a travertine skin that glows green at night.

🍴 EAT

🍴 ATAME Spanish €€

☎ 2804 2560; www.atame-tapasbar.de; Dircksenstrasse 40; 🕑 from 10am Mon-Fri, from 11am Sat & Sun; 🚇 🚈 Alexanderplatz; 🚈 Hackescher Markt; ✖

The Spanish tapas tradition translates well to the easygoing Berlin lifestyle but oddly there aren't many good bars around. Atame is the genuine item with a colourfully tiled bar, smiling Spanish staff and delicious nibbles served in satisfying portions.

🍴 DOLORES Mexican €

☎ 2809 9597; www.dolores-berlin.de, in German; Rosa-Luxemburg-Strasse 7; 🕑 11.30am-10pm Mon-Fri, 1-10pm Sat & Sun; 🚇 🚈 Alexanderplatz; ✖ Ⓥ

A lunchtime favourite, Dolores wins hearts and tummies with the best burritos this side of San Francisco's Mission district. Select your preferred combo of marinated meats or tofu, rice, beans, veggies, cheese

and salsa and the cheerful staff will build it for you on the spot. Great homemade lemonade, too.

🍴 ZUR LETZTEN INSTANZ German €€

☎ 242 5528; www.zurletzteninstanz.de; Waisenstrasse 14-16; 🕑 noon-1am Mon-Sat, to 11pm Sun; 🚇 Klosterstrasse; ✖

Oozing folksy Old Berlin charm, this rustic eatery has been an enduring hit since 1621 and has fed everyone from Napoleon to Beethoven to Angela Merkel. Quality remains high when it comes to such local rib-stickers as Eisbein (pork knuckle) and Bouletten (meat patties).

⭐ PLAY

⭐ BOHANNON Club

☎ 6950 5287; www.bohannon.de, in German; Dircksenstrasse 40; cover €7-10; 🕑 from 11pm Mon, Fri & Sat; 🚈 Hackescher Markt

Seventies disco legend Hamilton Bohannon inspired the name of this basement club where groovemeisters such as Barney Millah, B.Side and visiting DJ royalty spin a wicked mix of funk, hip hop,

GRILLWALKERS: MOBILE WURST

On Alexanderplatz, emerging from the northern U2 station exit or the eastern S-Bahn exit, you have to run a veritable gauntlet of Grillwalkers or what we've come to call 'Self-Contained Underpaid Bratwurst Apparatus', aka SCUBA. Picture this: young guys with a mobile gas grill strapped around their bellies where an array of sizzling bratwursts waits for customers. And at just €1.20 a pop, squished into a roll and slathered with mustard or ketchup, they're going fast.

reggae and dancehall with as much emphasis on tunes as beats.

⭐ CASINO BERLIN *Casino*
☎ 2389 4144; www.casino-berlin.de, in German; Park Inn Hotel, Alexanderplatz 8; admission €5; ⏱ 3pm-3am; ♿ 🚇 Alexanderplatz

Craps with a view. Berlin's highest den of vice is on the 37th floor of the Park Inn Hotel, offering all the usual card and random-chance games. Minimum age 18, tie and jacket required (may be borrowed).

⭐ KINO INTERNATIONAL
Cinema & Gay Club
☎ 2475 6011; www.yorck.de, in German; Karl-Marx-Allee 33; tickets €5.50-8; 🚇 Schillingstrasse

With its camp cavalcade of glass chandeliers, glitter curtain and undulating ceiling, this socialist-era cinema is a show in itself. Monday is 'MonGay' with homo-themed classics and imports. The first Saturday of the month it's 'raining men' at Klub International, the largest gay party in town (midnight start).

⭐ KITKATCLUB @ SAGE
Club
☎ 278 9830; www.kitkatclub.de; Köpenicker Strasse 76, enter Brückenstrasse 3; cover €6-12; ⏱ Fri-Sun; 🚇 Heinrich-Heine-Strasse

This kitty is naughty, sexy and decadent, listens to techno and house, and fancies leather and lace, vinyl and whips. It hides out at Sage with its four dance floors, fire-breathing dragon and shimmering pools. Check the website for dress-code instructions at Berlin's most (in)famous erotic nightclub.

⭐ TRESOR *Club*
☎ 6953 7713; www.tresorberlin.de; Köpenicker Strasse 70; cover €10; ⏱ from midnight Wed, Fri & Sat; 🚇 Heinrich-Heine-Strasse

After a few years' hiatus, this techno pioneer is back on the scene in a former East Berlin power station. The ace booking policy brings in big-time DJs who make the beats pound on three floors: the battery room, the +4 Bar with balcony overlooking the cavernous power station's belly, and a dank cellar reached via a long, dark tunnel. Still an essential player.

⭐ WEEKEND *Club*
www.week-end-berlin.de; Am Alexanderplatz 5; cover €10-12; ⏱ Thu-Sat; ♿ 🚇 Alexanderplatz

This hot 'n' heavy club in the GDR-era 'House of Travel' high-rise delivers awesome views, sleek design and high-profile spinners such as Tiefschwarz, Phonique and Dixon. When in full swing, there are three floors of action: the 12th with its panoramic windows, the inky black 15th and the rooftop lounge.

V

NEIGHBOURHOODS

MITTE – ALEXANDERPLATZ AREA

>MITTE – SCHEUNENVIERTEL

It's hard to imagine that, until reunification, the dapper Scheunenviertel was a neglected barrio with tumbledown buildings and dirty streets. Fanning out northwest of Alexanderplatz, it's since catapulted from drab to fab and teems with restaurants, bars, clubs, cabarets, concept stores and owner-run boutiques.

The Scheunenviertel's name (Barn Quarter) hearkens back to the 17th century, an age of wooden houses and poor fire-fighting techniques, which is why all flammable crops had to be stored outside the city walls. Later it evolved into Berlin's main Jewish quarter, a role it has been gradually reprising since reunification.

The area's most charismatic side reveals itself in the villagelike labyrinth of lanes off Oranienburger Strasse, its main drag. On an aimless wander you'll find surprises lurking around every corner: here an intriguing public sculpture, there a bleeding-edge gallery, a cosy watering

MITTE – SCHEUNENVIERTEL

◎ SEE

Alter Jüdischer Friedhof	**1**	D3
Hackesche Höfe	**2**	D3
Heckmannhöfe	**3**	C3
Kunsthaus Tacheles	**4**	B3
Kunst-Werke Berlin	**5**	C3
Museum für Naturkunde	**6**	A2
Neue Synagoge & Centrum Judaicum	**7**	C3
Ramones Museum	**8**	C3
Rosenhöfe	**9**	D3
Sammlung Boros	**10**	B3
Sophie-Gips-Höfe & Sammlung Hoffmann	**11**	D3

⬚ SHOP

1. Absinth Depot Berlin	**12**	E3
140z	**13**	D3
Ampelmann Galerie	**14**	D3
Berlinerklamotten	**15**	D3
Blush Dessous	**16**	E3
Bonbonmacherei	**17**	C3
IC! Berlin	**18**	E3
Lala Berlin	**19**	E3

⬚ EAT

Bandol sur Mer	**20**	C2
Barcomi's Deli	**21**	D3
Café Nord-Sud	**22**	C3
Dada Falafel	**23**	B3
Kasbah	**24**	D3
Kuchi	**25**	E3
Monsieur Vuong	**26**	E3
Schwarzwaldstuben	**27**	C2
Susuru	**28**	E3
Tartane	**29**	B2
Weinbar Rutz	**30**	B2
Zagreus Projekt	**31**	D2

⬚ DRINK

Bar 3	**32**	F3
Café Bravo	(see 4)	
Eschschloraque	**33**	D3
Greenwich	**34**	D3

⬚ PLAY

Ackerkeller	**35**	C2
Babylon Mitte	**36**	F3
B-Flat	**37**	D3
Box + Bar	(see 41)	
Chamäleon Varieté	**38**	D3
Clärchens Ballhaus	**39**	C3
Delicious Doughnuts	**40**	C3
Deutsches Theater	**41**	A3
Friedrichstadtpalast	**42**	B3
Kaffee Burger	**43**	E2
Volksbühne am Rosa-Luxemburg-Platz	**44**	F3

hole or 19th-century ballroom. A particularly enchanting feature are the quarter's *Höfe,* interlinked hidden courtyards filled with cafes, stores and party venues. The Hackesche Höfe is the best known but the Heckmann-höfe (Oranienburger Strasse 32) and Sophie-Gips-Höfe (Sophienstrasse 21) are also lovely.

SEE

⬤ ALTER JÜDISCHER FRIEDHOF

Old Jewish Cemetery; Grosse Hamburger Strasse; 🚇 **Hackescher Markt;** ♿
What looks like a small park was in fact Berlin's first Jewish cemetery, destroyed by the Nazis in 1943. Some 12,000 people were buried here between 1672 and 1827, including the philosopher Moses Mendelssohn. His tombstone (not the original) stands representative for all the six-feet-under residents.

⬤ HACKESCHE HÖFE

Hackesche Courtyards; ☎ **2809 8010; www.hackesche-hoefe.com, in German;** 🕐 **24hr; enter from Rosenthaler Strasse or Sophienstrasse;** 🚇 **Hackescher Markt;** ♿
Thanks to its congenial mix of cafes, galleries, boutiques and entertainment venues, this attractively restored complex of eight interlinked courtyards is a major tourist magnet. Court 1, festooned with patterned art nouveau tiles, is the liveliest, while Court VII leads off to the whimsical **Rosenhöfe** with a sunken rose garden and tendril-like balustrades.

⬤ KUNSTHAUS TACHELES

Art House Tacheles; ☎ **282 6185; www .tacheles.de; Oranienburger Strasse 54-56;** Ⓜ **Oranienburger Tor**
The 'Sistine Chapel of Graffiti', the Tacheles may look scary-ass but it is actually a beloved-as-a-puppy-dog collective art and culture space born during the heady post-reunification days. Inside you'll find a warren of studios, galleries, a cinema and a cafe-bar. In summer quaff a cold one among the surreal installations in the backyard beer garden. Alas, its future is uncertain and it may soon fall victim to development. Stay tuned.

⬤ KUNST-WERKE BERLIN

☎ **243 4590; www.kw-berlin.de; Auguststrasse 69; adult/concession €6/4;** 🕐 **noon-7pm Tue, Wed & Fri-Sun, to 9pm Thu;** 🚇 **Oranienburger Strasse;** ♿
In an old margarine factory, non-profit KW helped chart the fate of the Scheunenviertel as Berlin's original post-Wall art district. Today it still enjoys an international reputation as a laboratory for new trends in contemporary art.

◉ MUSEUM FÜR NATURKUNDE

Museum of Natural History; ☎ 2093 8591; www.naturkundemuseum -berlin.de, in German; Invalidenstrasse 43; adult/concession/family €3.50/2/7; ⏱ 9.30am-5pm Tue-Fri, 10am-6pm Sat & Sun; ⓜ Zinnowitzer Strasse; ♿
Take the opportunity to meet dinosaurs and travel back to the beginning of time at this beautiful university-affiliated museum. The star of the show is the world's largest mounted lizard, a 23m-long and 12m-high Brachiosaurus,

who's joined by a dozen other Jurassic buddies and an ultrarare archaeopteryx. Other halls demystify the Big Bang, why zebras are striped and other cool stuff.

◉ NEUE SYNAGOGE & CENTRUM JUDAICUM

New Synagogue; ☎ 8802 8300; www .cjudaicum.de; Oranienburger Strasse 28-30; adult/concession €3/2; ⏱ 10am-8pm Sun & Mon, to 6pm Tue-Thu, to 5pm Fri (to 2pm Mar & Oct) Apr-Sep, 10am-6pm Sun-Thu, to 2pm Fri Nov-Feb; ⓡ Oranienburger Strasse; ♿

No bones about it, the Museum für Naturkunde is dino-mite

STUMBLING UPON HISTORY

Look down and you'll see them everywhere, but especially in the Scheunenviertel: small brass paving stones engraved with names and placed in front of house entrances. Part of a nationwide project initiated by Berlin-born artist Gunter Demnig, these so-called *Stolpersteine* (stumbling blocks) are essentially mini-memorials to the people (usually Jews) who lived in that building before being killed by the Nazis. Berlin's Jewish community suffered tremendously during the regime of the Third Reich. In 1933 there were 160,000 Jews living in Berlin; by 1945, 55,000 had been murdered, 100,000 had emigrated and only 5000 survived. Today about 13,000 Jews live in town, most of them recent arrivals from Russian republics (see p158 for more information about Berlin's Jewish community).

The gleaming gold dome of the New Synagogue is the most visible symbol of Berlin's revitalised Jewish community. The 1866 original seated 3200 people and was Germany's largest synagogue. Partly reconstructed, it is not so much a house of worship but a museum and cultural centre. Inside are displays on its history and architecture as well as on the lives of the people who worshipped here. The dome can be climbed.

RAMONES MUSEUM

☎ 7552 8890; www.ramonesmuseum .com; Krausnickstrasse 23; admission incl button & badge €3.50; ☼ 8.30am-6pm Tue-Thu, to 8pm Fri, 10am-8pm Sat, noon-6pm Sun; ⓡ Oranienburger Strasse

They sang 'Born to Die in Berlin' but the legacy of the Ramones punk pioneers is kept very much alive in the German capital thanks to superfan Florian Hayler. His two-room shrine is crammed with vintage T-shirts, signed album covers, Marky Ramone's drumsticks, Johnny Ramone's jeans and other flotsam and jetsam, and there's an on-site cafe (free wi-fi) to swap stories with other fans.

SAMMLUNG BOROS

Boros Collection; ☎ 2759 4065; www .sammlung-boros.de; Reinhardtstrasse 20; tours €10; ☼ tours Sat & Sun, must be booked online; ⓞ Oranienburger Tor; ⓞ ⓡ Friedrichstrasse

Book early to join art aficionados and the merely curious on a trippy tour of a Nazi-era bunker where ad guru Christian Boros shares his exalted collection of contemporary works with the public. The concrete maze is the perfect backdrop for such artworld darlings as Olafur Eliasson, Damien Hirst, Sarah Lucas and Wolfgang Tillmans.

🛍 SHOP

For more scoop on retail therapy in the Scheunenviertel, see p14.

🛍 1. ABSINTH DEPOT BERLIN
Food & Drink

☎ 281 6789; www.erstesabsinth depotberlin.de, in German; Weinmeister-strasse 4; ⏲ 2pm-midnight Mon-Sat; Ⓜ Weinmeisterstrasse

Van Gogh, Toulouse-Lautrec and Oscar Wilde were among the fin-de-siècle artists who drew inspiration from the 'green fairy', as absinthe is also known. This quaint little shop has over 60 varieties and an expert owner who'll happily help you pick out the perfect bottle for your own mind-altering rendezvous.

🛍 14OZ *Fashion*

☎ 2804 0514; www.14oz-berlin.de; Neue Schönhauser Strasse 13; ⏲ 10am-6pm Mon-Sat; Ⓜ Weinmeisterstrasse

Stylistas worship at the altar of 14oz, a sleek concept store brought to you by the organisers of the Bread & Butter fashion fair. Join them in circling for premier denim by Citizens of Humanity and PRPS, far-out fashions by Velvet and Lot 78, and bold necklaces by King Baby, all under one impossibly chic but slightly snooty roof.

🛍 AMPELMANN GALERIE
Souvenirs

☎ 4472 6438; www.ampelmann.de; Court V, Hackesche Höfe; ⏲ 9.30am-10pm Mon-Sat, 10am-7pm Sun; 🚊 Hackescher Markt

It took a vociferous grassroots campaign to save the little Ampelmann, the endearing fellow on the pedestrian traffic lights who helped generations of East Germans safely cross the street. Now a beloved cult figure, his likeness fills an entire store's worth of T-shirts, towels, onesies, key rings, cookie cutters and other knick-knacks.

🛍 BERLINERKLAMOTTEN
Fashion

www.berlinerklamotten.de; Court III, Hackesche Höfe; ⏲ 11am-8pm Mon-Sat; 🚊 Hackescher Markt

Keen on keeping tabs on what's humming on the sewing machines of Berlin's indie designers? Flip through the racks of this arbiter of fashion cool to dig up outfits – casual to couture – with that urban, cheeky and fresh capital twist. On weekends a DJ pumps out high-energy sounds to get you into party mood.

🛍 BLUSH DESSOUS *Lingerie*

☎ 2809 3580; www.blush-berlin.de, in German; Rosa-Luxemburg-Strasse 22; ⏲ noon-8pm Mon-Fri, to 7pm Sat; Ⓜ Rosa-Luxemburg-Platz

NEIGHBOURHOODS

MITTE – SCHEUNENVIERTEL

It's all five-star sex appeal at this little boudoir (right down to its giant 1960s bed and casually arranged vibrators). Stocking a supreme selection of women's scanties, here you can dress up (or down) in ensembles by Princess Tam Tam and Cosabella and accessorise with sweet little silk-satin eye covers.

BONBONMACHEREI Food
☎ 4405 5243; www.bonbonmacherei .de, in German; Oranienburger Strasse 32, Heckmannhöfe; ☷ noon-8pm Wed-Sat; 🚊 Oranienburger Strasse
The old-fashioned art of handmade sweets has been lovingly revived in this basement-store-cum-show-kitchen. Watch candy masters Katja and Hjalmar using their antique equipment to churn out tasty treats right before your eyes.

IC! BERLIN Eyewear
☎ 2472 7200; www.ic-berlin.de; Max-Beer-Strasse 17; ☷ 11am-8pm Mon-Sat; 🚇 Rosa-Luxemburg-Platz
What looks like a bachelor pad, with worn sofas, wacky art and turntables, is the flagship store of this internationally famous eyewear maker. The feather-light frames with their klutzproof screwless hinges have added 'spec appeal' to celebs from Madonna to the king of Morocco.

LALA BERLIN Fashion
☎ 6579 5466; www.lalaberlin.de; Mulackstrasse 7; ☷ noon-8pm Mon-Sat; 🚇 Rosa-Luxemburg-Platz
Former MTV editor Leyla Piedayesh makes top-flight women's fashion that flatters both the twig-thin and the well-upholstered. Check out the elegant knitwear in jewel-like hues or her witty takes on logo-obsession via a collection of soft, sensuous scarves. Her fan base includes Claudia Schiffer.

Sleek Susuru (p70): slurp your way to happiness

🍴 EAT

🍴 BANDOL SUR MER

French   €€€

☎ 6730 2051; Torstrasse 167; ⏰ from 6pm; ⊖ Rosenthaler Platz

OK, so Brad Pitt ate here. But even without a Hollywood endorsement, this teensy bistro in a former *döneria* (doner kebab shop) on Torstrasse's evolving restaurant row is worthy of a culinary Oscar. The blackboard menu mixes reliable classics such as entrecôte steak with out-there combos, eg pink lamb with rhubarb. Dining is done in two seatings (6pm and 9pm). Reservations essential.

🍴 BARCOMI'S DELI

American   €

☎ 2859 8363; www.barcomis.de, in German; 2nd courtyard, Sophie-Gips-Höfe, Sophienstrasse 21; ⏰ 9am-9pm Mon-Sat, 10am-9pm Sun; ⊖ Weinmeisterstrasse; ✕ Ⓥ

Train your java radar onto this New York–meets–Berlin deli where latte-rati, families and expats meet for coffee, bagels with lox, deli-style sandwiches and possibly the best brownies and cheesecake this side of the Hudson River.

🍴 CAFÉ NORD-SUD *French*   €

☎ 9700 5928; Auguststrasse 87; ⏰ noon-3pm & 5-11pm Mon-Sat; 🚇 Oranienburger Strasse; ✕

Truth be told, we'd rather keep this place secret. It's just one of those little gems; you know, always packed to the rafters thanks to Jean-Claude's Gallic charm, the kitchen's formidable skills and, let's face it, the rock-bottom prices. A mere €7.50 for three courses – how do they do it? Don't ask: score a table and find out.

🍴 DADA FALAFEL

Middle Eastern   €

☎ 2759 6927; Linienstrasse 132; ⏰ 10am-2am; ⊖ Oranienburger Tor; ✕

Famished tourists join local loyalists at this teensy pit stop with jazzy decor for freshly prepared falafel doused with a tangy home-made sauce.

🍴 KASBAH *Moroccan*   €€

☎ 2759 4361; www.kasbah-berlin.de; Gipsstrasse 2; ⏰ 6pm-midnight Tue-Sun; ⊖ Weinmeisterstrasse or Rosenthaler Platz; ✕

Take your tastebuds on a magic carpet ride at this exotic salon where owner Driss welcomes each guest with a big smile. Eating here is a sensory immersion that starts with rinsing your hands in rose water before digging into such tasty treats as flaky *b'stilla* (chicken-stuffed filo) or tangy *tagine* (stew). Dishes pair well with a palate-cleansing mint tea or superb Moroccan wine.

🍴 KUCHI *Asian* €€

☎ 2838 6622; www.kuchi.de;
Gipsstrasse 3; 🕐 noon-midnight;
🚇 **Weinmeisterstrasse;** 🔀

Sushi purists might shudder at Kuchi's 'extreme' creations, but scenesters gobble 'em up like M&Ms. Fried eel, tempura or crispy chicken skin add a quirky twist to maki rolls, while yakitori, stir-fries, *donburi* (rice bowl) and noodle soups take you back to more familiar culinary territory.

🍴 MONSIEUR VUONG
Asian €

☎ 9929 6924; www.monsieurvuong.de;
Alte Schönhauser Strasse 46; 🕐 noon-midnight; 🚇 **Weinmeisterstrasse;** 🔀

This upbeat Indochina nosh stop hasn't lost a step despite becoming a fixture on the tourist circuit. Pick from a small menu of flavour-packed soups and three or four healthy mains, then sit back and enjoy your leftover money. Alas, the never-ending queue does not make for leisurely meals. Afternoons are slowest.

🍴 SCHWARZWALDSTUBEN
German €€

☎ 2809 8084; **Tucholskystrasse 48;**
🕐 9am-midnight; 🚇 **Oranienburger Strasse;** 🔀

The tongue-in-cheek olde-worlde decor is as delicious as the authentic southern German food

served in gut-busting portions at this cosy corner joint. We can't get enough of the *'geschmelzte Maultaschen'* (sautéed ravioli-like pasta) and the giant schnitzel. Everything goes down well with a Rothaus Tannenzäpfle beer, straight from the Black Forest.

🍴 SUSURU *Asian* €€

☎ 211 1182; www.susuru.de, in German; **Rosa-Luxemburg-Strasse 17;** 🕐 11.30am-11.30pm; 🚇 **Rosa-Luxemburg-Platz;** 🔀 📶 🅅

Go ye forth and slurp! Susuru is Japanese for slurping and, quite frankly, that's really the best way to get a handle on the big bowls of steaming udon or *nabe* (hotpot dishes) at this stylishly minimalist noodle bar. It's all healthy and delicious and served in sleek designer environs.

🍴 TARTANE *American* €€

☎ 4472 7036; **Torstrasse 225;** 🕐 6pm-2am; 🚇 **Oranienburger Tor**

The banister, lamps and Meissen tile mural are scavenged from the demolished GDR-era Palast der Republik, but otherwise this stylish gastropub is very much in the here and now. Most nights tables buzz with an arty, local crowd wolfing Tartane's luscious signature burgers or downing glasses of refreshing Kölsch beer from Cologne.

☷ WEINBAR RUTZ
International   €€€

☎ 2462 8760; www.rutz-weinbar.de; Chausseestrasse 8; ☾ 5pm-midnight Mon-Sat; ⊖ Oranienburger Tor; ✗

Marco Müller's creations strike just the right balance between adventure and comfort, an approach that won him a Michelin star in 2008. The cellar, meanwhile, is stocked with 1001 bottles of the finest vintages, many available by the glass with dinner or in the downstairs wine bar, which serves a few home-style dishes (€9 to €17).

☷ ZAGREUS PROJEKT
International   €€€

☎ 2809 5640; www.zagreus.net; Brunnenstrasse 9a; ☾ call for hours, reservations required; ⊖ Rosenthaler Platz; ✗

Chef-artist-gallery-owner Ulrich Krauss takes the art and food crossover concept to new heights in his backyard basement studio. Every two months or so he invites a different artist to design a site-specific installation, then composes a multicourse dinner inspired by the work. Guests then 'rent a chair' at a long communal table and dine right in the middle of the art (three-/four-course dinners €30 to €35). Very unique, very Berlin.

☰ DRINK

There are plenty of tourist-oriented bars all along Oranienburger Strasse, but you may have to skip around waist-cinched, platform-booted street workers to get to any of them. The better places are tucked into the side streets.

☰ BAR 3 *Bar*
☎ 2804 6973; Weydinger Strasse 20; ☾ from 9pm Tue-Sat; ⊖ Rosa-Luxemburg-Strasse; ✗

With its wraparound glass windows, black decor and dim lighting, this small bar seems to be jostling for *Wallpaper* coverage but is actually a laid-back lair for local lovelies, artists and professionals. Scope out the action bellied up to the U-shaped bar and guzzling delicious Kölsch imported from the owner's hometown of Cologne.

☰ CAFÉ BRAVO *Cafe*
☎ 2345 7777; www.cafebravo.de, in German; Auguststrasse 69; ☾ 9am-7pm or 8pm; 🚇 Oranienburger Strasse; ✗

Is it art? Is it a cafe? Answer: it's both. The glass-and-chrome cube in the courtyard of the Kunst-Werke art institute was dreamed up by US artist Dan Graham and is a suitably edgy – if self-service – refuelling stop on any Scheunenviertel saunter.

Y ESCHSCHLORAQUE *Bar*

☎ 0172 311 1013; www.eschschloraque
.de, in German; Rosenthaler Strasse 39;
🕙 from 2pm; 🚇 Hackescher Markt; ✗

This trashy-chic bar is a rare bulwark against Mitte's creeping yuppification. Find it past the trash cans at the end of the courtyard of Haus Schwarzenberg, one of the few unrenovated houses left around here. We love the surreal monster decor by the Dead Chickens art collective, the comfy sofas, the strong cocktails and the eccentric live music – if only the staff laid off the snootiness.

Y GREENWICH *Bar*

☎ 2809 5566; Gipsstrasse 5; 🕙 from 8pm; 🚇 Weinmeisterstrasse; ✗

So hip it doesn't even bother with a sign, this highfalutin fixture on the cocktail circuit is another Midas-touch venture by Heinz Gindullis, the man behind Cookies (p55). You'll have plenty of time to study the mamba-green bar and sofas, illuminated aquariums and eye-candy crowd while you're waiting for your expert cocktail.

⭐ PLAY

For more on cabaret, see p23.

⭐ ACKERKELLER
Gay Pub & Club

☎ 3646 1356; www.ackerkeller.de, in German; Bergstrasse 68; cover €3-5;

🕙 pub from 8pm Tue-Fri, from 6pm Sun, parties 10pm Tue, Fri & Sat;
🚇 Rosenthaler Platz

This snug and alternative lesbigay pub, run by a nonprofit group, spins its cellar into a party venue thrice weekly with rock, pop, electro and even Balkanbeats keeping the dance floor grooving. Party themes include: Schlagernacktparty (no clothes), Clean Party (no booze, no drugs) and Morisseylicious (mope rock). Best day is Tuesday.

⭐ BABYLON MITTE *Cinema*

☎ 242 5969; www.babylonberlin.de, in German; Rosa-Luxemburg-Strasse 30; tickets €6.50; 🚇 Rosa-Luxemburg-Platz

This gorgeously restored expressionist cinema delivers a well-curated program of retrospectives, tributes, cult classics, foreign films and other stuff you'd never catch at the multiplex. For the silent movies, the original theatre organ is put through its paces.

⭐ B-FLAT *Live Music*

☎ 283 3123; www.b-flat-berlin.de, in German; Rosenthaler Strasse 13; cover €10; 🕙 from 8pm;
🚇 Weinmeisterstrasse; ✗

Cool cats of all ages come out to this intimate venue where the audience quite literally sits

Henrik Tidefjärd
Founder of Berlinagenten (p188) – lifestyle, culinary and adventure tours

You were born in Sweden and have lived in London and Barcelona. Why did you come to Berlin? Because of its quirky aspects, stunning experiences and diversity of lifestyle in each district. Berlin is not a snobbish, mainstream and conservative city but a creative, sexy and open-minded 'beast'. Everyone is individual. **What makes Mitte fascinating?** The mixture of architecture, fashion, art, history and people of all kinds. Pretty much inspiring and eye-catching. **Favourite hidden spots in Mitte?** Café Bravo (p71), tucked into the courtyard of the Kunst-Werke art space. **Any cool buys in Mitte?** The IC! Berlin shop (p68) is just what Berlin is about: off the beaten track, confusing and great fun. **Anything to avoid?** The 'EasyJetSet' on Oranienburger Strasse and the pub crawls. **Favourite restaurant?** Susuru (p70). **You've lived in Berlin for eight years. How has Mitte changed?** New shops, galleries and restaurants mushroom all the time, especially around Hackescher Markt. Maybe only 10% of all locations existed on my arrival.

within spitting distance of the performers. The emphasis is on acoustic music, mostly jazz, world beats, afro-Brazilian and other soundscapes. Wednesday's free jam session often brings down the house.

⭐ CHAMÄLEON VARIETÉ
Cabaret

☎ 400 5930; www.chamaeleonberlin.de, in German; Hackesche Höfe, Rosenthaler Strasse 40/41; tickets €31-42; 🚉 Hackescher Markt; ✂

An alchemy of art nouveau charms and high-tech theatre trappings, this intimate former ballroom presents classy variety shows – comedy, juggling acts and singing – often in sassy, sexy and unconventional fashion.

⭐ CLÄRCHENS BALLHAUS
Club-Restaurant

☎ 282 9295; www.ballhaus-mitte.de, in German; Auguststrasse 24; cover free-€3; 🕑 from 10pm Mon, 9pm Tue-Thu, 8pm Fri & Sat, 3pm Sun; 🚉 Oranienburger Strasse; ✂

Yesteryear is now at this late, great 19th-century dance hall, where groovers and grannies swing their legs to tango, swing, waltz, disco and pop, all without even an ounce of irony. In the daytime, the garden's a nice spot for pizza and German soul food (served from 12.30pm).

⭐ DELICIOUS DOUGHNUTS
Club

☎ 2809 9279; www.delicious.doughnuts.de, in German; Rosenthaler Strasse 9; cover €3-5; 🕑 from 9pm; 🚇 Weinmeisterstrasse

A sweet Mitte staple, Doughnuts is a lounge-club hybrid with a welcoming vibe, a small but lively dance floor and almost daily afterparties that go well into midmorning.

⭐ DEUTSCHES THEATER
Theatre

☎ 2844 1225; www.deutschestheater.de, in German; Schumannstrasse 13a; tickets €5-45; 🚇 🚉 Friedrichstrasse

Berlin's top stage has reeled in numerous thespian awards, including Theatre of the Year in 2008. Plays are also performed in the smaller Kammerspiele next door and at **Box + Bar**, an 80-seat space with cocktail bar that presents edgy and experimental fare (tickets €6 to €16).

⭐ FRIEDRICHSTADTPALAST
Theatre

☎ 2326 2326; www.friedrichstadtpalast.de; Friedrichstrasse 107; tickets €17-100; 🚇 🚉 Friedrichstrasse

Marlene Dietrich and Ella Fitzgerald have graced the stage of this 1920s vintage palace, but today Europe's largest revue theatre does mostly glitzy-glam Vegas-style

Kaffee Burger comes with the lot: country and western, Balkanbeats, punk, you name it

productions with leggy showgirls in skimpy costumes and feather boas. Alas, since it's hard to fill those 2000 seats night after night, its future is uncertain.

☆ KAFFEE BURGER Club
☎ 2804 6495; www.kaffeeburger.de, in German; Torstrasse 60; cover €3-5; 🕒 from 8pm Mon-Thu, 9pm Fri & Sat, 7pm Sun; ⓜ Rosa-Luxemburg-Platz
Madonna once mixed it up with wrinkle-free hipsters at this skanky, sweaty cult club with original East German decor. But even without a celebrity in sight, the home of Wladimir Kaminer's twice-monthly Russendisko is always a fun-for-all party pen

(indie, punk, rock, Balkanbeats) with dancing, concerts, readings and cheap drinks.

☆ VOLKSBÜHNE AM ROSA-LUXEMBURG-PLATZ Theatre
☎ 2406 5777; www.volksbuehne-berlin.de, in German; Rosa-Luxemburg-Platz; tickets €10-30; ⓜ Rosa-Luxemburg-Platz
Nonconformist, provocative, radical: performances at the 'People's Stage' are not for the squeamish. *Enfants terribles* Frank Castorf and Christoph Schlingensief regularly tear down the confines of the proscenium stage with *Zeitgeist*-critical productions that are somehow both populist and elitist.

>REICHSTAG & GOVERNMENT QUARTER

Berlin's government quarter snuggles neatly into the Spreebogen, a horseshoe-shaped bend in the Spree River. Its historic anchor is the Reichstag (parliament building), which once rubbed against the western side of the Berlin Wall and is now part of the Band des Bundes (Band of the Federal Buildings), a series of glass-and-concrete buildings symbolically linking the two city halves across the Spree. North of the river looms the solar-panel-clad Hauptbahnhof (central train station), which is poised to get several hotels and possibly a contemporary art hall as neighbours in the coming years.

Not a single structure had to be torn down to make room for the new power district. That job had already been done by the Nazis, who demolished an entire high-end residential quarter to make room for a massive – though thankfully never realised – domed Great Hall capable of holding 180,000 people.

Today's government buildings are considerably more modest, and fit quite smoothly into the urban tapestry. Kids fly kites and play football (soccer) on the sprawling lawns, and a leisurely stroll along the river promenade takes you past beer gardens and beach bars and allows for interesting perspectives. The quarter looks most impressive at night when buildings are illuminated from within.

REICHSTAG & GOVERNMENT QUARTER

◉ SEE
Berliner Medizinhistorisches
   Museum 1 C2
Bundeskanzleramt 2 B5
Halle am Wasser 3 C1
Hamburger Bahnhof – Museum
   für Gegenwart 4 C2
Reichstag 5 C5

ᵞ⁴ EAT
Sarah Wiener im Hamburger
   Bahnhof .... (see 4)

★ PLAY
2BE 6 B1
Haus der Kulturen der
   Welt 7 A5
Tape 8 B1

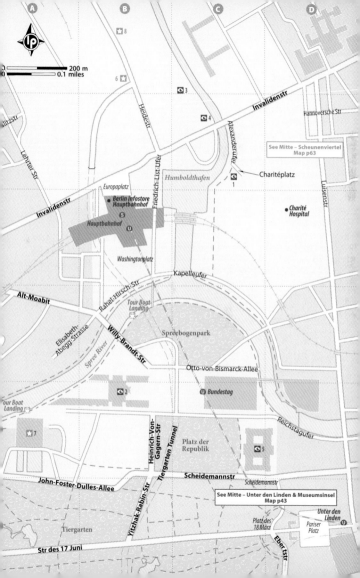

A

B

C

D

$\bigcirc$UP

0 _____ 200 m
0 _____ 0.1 miles

★ 8

Heidestr

6 ★

🕐 3

Invalidenstr

🕐 4

Hannoversche Str

Alexanderufer

See Mitte – Scheunenviertel
Map p63

🕐 1 ← Charitéplatz

Luisenstr

Europaplatz

Humboldthafen

Berlin Infostore S
Hauptbahnhof

● Charité
Hospital

Friedrich-List-Ufer

Hauptbahnhof

Ⓤ

Washingtonplatz

Kapelleufer

Alt-Moabit

Rahel-Hirsch-Str

Tour Boat
Landing

Spreebogenpark

Willy-Brandt-Str

Elisabeth-
Abegg-Strasse

Spree River

Otto-von-Bismarck-Allee

Ⓤ Bundestag

Reichstagufer

Tour Boat
Landing

★ 7

🕐 2

Heinrich-Von-
Gagern-Str

Platz der
Republik

🕐 5

John-Foster-Dulles-Allee

Tiergarten Tunnel

Scheidemannstr

Scheidemannstr

Yitzhak-Rabin-Str

See Mitte – Unter den Linden & Museumsinsel
Map p43

Tiergarten

Str des 17 Juni

Platz des
18 März

Ebertstr

Unter den
Linden

Ⓤ

Pariser
Platz

NEIGHBOURHOODS

REICHSTAG & GOVERNMENT QUARTER

◉ SEE

◉ BERLINER MEDIZINHISTORISCHES MUSEUM

Berlin Medical History Museum; ☎ 450 536 156; www.bmm.charite.de; Charité Hospital Mitte, Charitéplatz 1; adult/ concession/family €5/2.50/10; ◷ 10am-5pm Sun, Tue, Thu & Fri, to 7pm Wed & Sat; ◚ Hauptbahnhof; ◐

This grisly pathology museum is essentially a 3-D medical textbook on human disease and deformities. Monstrous tumours, Siamese twins and a colon the size of an elephant's trunk are all pickled in formalin and neatly displayed in glass jars. Definitely not for the squeamish. Anyone under 16 must be accompanied by an adult.

◉ BUNDESKANZLERAMT

Federal Chancellery; Willy-Brandt-Strasse 1; closed to the public; ◚ Hauptbahnhof; ◚ 100

Germany's chancellor keeps his or her office in this H-shaped compound designed by Axel Schultes and Charlotte Frank. From Moltkebrücke bridge or the northern river promenade you can best appreciate the circular openings that inspired the building's nickname 'washing machine'. Eduardo Chillida's rusted-steel *Berlin* sculpture graces the forecourt.

◉ HALLE AM WASSER

Hall by the Water; Invalidenstrasse 50/51; ◚ Hauptbahnhof; ◐

The Berlin art scene has a new hot spot in this row of contemporary art galleries ensconced in a canalside warehouse behind the Hamburger Bahnhof. Top-flight occupants include Arndt & Partner, Frisch and Loock.

◉ HAMBURGER BAHNHOF – MUSEUM FÜR GEGENWART

Hamburger Bahnhof – Museum of Contemporary Art; ☎ 3978 3439; www .hamburgerbahnhof.de; Invalidenstrasse 50-51; adult/under 16/concession €8/ free/4, last 4hr Thu free; ◷ 10am-6pm Tue-Fri, 11am-8pm Sat, 11am-6pm Sun; ◚ Hauptbahnhof; ◐

Berlin's premier contemporary art museum presents career-spanning bodies of work by Andy Warhol, Roy Lichtenstein, Anselm Kiefer, Joseph Beuys and other heavyweights. Occupying a cleverly converted 19th-century railway station and an adjacent 300m-long warehouse, it also has great temporary exhibits, a well-stocked art bookshop and the popular Sarah Wiener cafe (opposite).

◉ REICHSTAG

☎ 2273 2152; www.bundestag.de; Platz der Republik 1; admission free; ◷ 8am-midnight, last lift 10pm; ◚ 100; ◐

For a knockout panorama, catch the lift to the top of the German federal parliament building, then continue via a spiralling ramp wrapped around the mirror-clad funnel of the glass dome. Queues are shortest early or at night, or skip 'em altogether by going on an organised tour or by making reservations at the pricey rooftop restaurant. Also see p16.

🍽 EAT

🍽 SARAH WIENER IM HAMBURGER BAHNHOF
Austrian €€

☎ 7071 3650; www.sarahwieners.de, in German; Invalidenstrasse 50/51; 🕙 10am-6pm Tue-Fri, 11am-8pm Sat, 11am-6pm Sun; 🚇 Hauptbahnhof; ✖
Discuss the latest Hamburger Bahnhof art exhibit over coffee or schnitzel at Berlin's smartest museum cafe, the domain of culinary star Sarah Wiener. A long bar, patterned stone floor and leather banquettes add character and texture to what used to be the train station waiting hall.

⭐ PLAY

⭐ 2BE *Club*

www.2be-club.de; Heidestrasse 73; cover €8; 🕙 Fri & Sat; 🚇 Hauptbahnhof
At the 'place to be' for friends of Black Music, resident DJs B.Side,

Beathoavenz and Rybixx, and visiting royalty such as Grandmaster Flash spin a bootylicious mix of hip hop, R&B and dancehall, largely for wrinkle-free hotties.

⭐ HAUS DER KULTUREN DER WELT *Performance Space*

House of World Cultures; ☎ 397 870; www.hkw.de; John-Foster-Dulles-Allee 10; admission varies; 🕙 10am-9pm Tue-Sun; 🚌 100; 🛜 ♿
This eccentric building with its gravity-defying parabolic roof brings the world to Berlin with dance, readings, films, exhibits and theatre from Latin America, Asia and Africa. Chime concerts ring out at noon and 6pm daily from the nearby 68-bell carillon.

⭐ TAPE *Club*

www.tapeberlin.de; Heidestrasse 14; cover €10; 🕙 from midnight Sat, sometimes Fri; 🚇 Hauptbahnhof
There's a tantalising underground vibe to this dancing den, no doubt helped along by an obscure location in an industrial area north of the Hauptbahnhof. Top local and visiting DJs get clued-in clubbers going with Chicago- and Detroit-influenced house, deephouse, dubhouse and dubtechno. Watch out for the 'Tape Modern' party series, a fusion of club and art expo. Superb sound system, too.

>POTSDAMER PLATZ & TIERGARTEN

Despite the name, Potsdamer Platz is not really just a square but Berlin's newest quarter, birthed from terrain once bifurcated by the Berlin Wall. It became a showcase of urban renewal in the 1990s, drawing an international cast of 'starchitects' that included Renzo Piano and Helmut Jahn.

Potsdamer Platz 2.0 is essentially a modern reinterpretation of the historic original, which was the equivalent of New York's Times Sq until WWII sucked all life out of the area. It's divided into three slices: DaimlerCity with a large mall, public art and high-profile entertainment venues; the flashy Sony Center built around a central plaza canopied by a glass roof that shimmers in different colours at night; and the comparatively subdued Beisheim Center, which was inspired by classic American skyscraper design.

Potsdamer Platz is easily combined with a trip to the Kulturforum, a cluster of museums and concert halls, including the famous Philharmonie. Black limousines are a common sight further west in the Diplomatenviertel (Diplomatic Quarter), the streets of which are studded with some bold contemporary architecture. And if your head is spinning after all that cultural stimulus, the leafy paths of the vast Tiergarten, Berlin's response to New York's Central Park, will likely prove to be a restorative antidote.

POTSDAMER PLATZ & TIERGARTEN

○ SEE
Bauhaus Archiv/Museum
  für Gestaltung **1** B3
Daimler
  Contemporary **2** F3
Gedenkstätte Deutscher
  Widerstand **3** D3
Gemäldegalerie **4** D3
Kunstgewerbemuseum ...**5** D2
Kupferstichkabinett **6** D3
Legoland Discovery
  Centre **7** E2
Museum für Film und
  Fernsehen **8** E2

Musikinstrumenten-
  Museum **9** E2
Neue Nationalgalerie ...**10** D3
Panoramapunkt **11** F3
Siegessäule **12** B1

○ SHOP
Potsdamer Platz
  Arkaden **13** E3

⊞ EAT
Edd's **14** D4
Facil **15** E3

Joseph-Roth-Diele **16** D4
Vapiano **17** F2

⊺ DRINK
Café am Neuen See **18** A2

★ PLAY
Arsenal ....(see 8)
Berliner
  Philharmonie **19** E2
Cinestar Original &
  IMAX 3D..................**20** E2

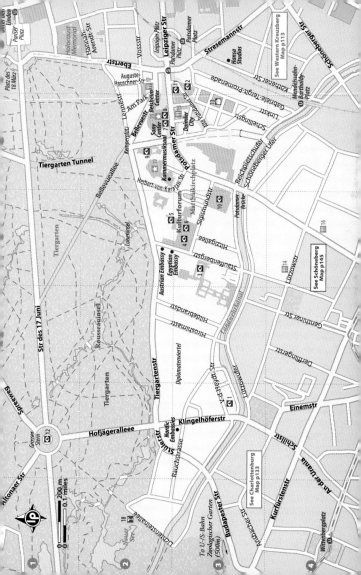

Unter den Linden
Pariser Platz

Holocaust Memorial

Platz des 18 März

Hannah-Arendt-Str
Vossstr
Leipziger Platz
Leipziger Str
Potsdamer Platz

Stresemannstr
Schöneberger Str

See Western Kreuzberg Map p113

Hansa Studios

Ebertstr
Auguste-Hauschner-Str

Potsdamer Platz

Gabriele-Tergit-Promenade
Köthener Str

Linkstr

Mendelssohn-Bartholdy-Platz

Bellevuestr
Am Park
Beisheim Center

Schellingstr

Sony Center
Daimler City

Tiergarten Tunnel

Kemperplatz
Tennisstr

Kammermusiksaal
Potsdamer Str

Reichpietschufer
Schöneberger Ufer

Herbert-von-Karajan-Str

Bellevueallee

Lützeninsel

Kulturforum

Potsdamer Brücke

Matthäikirchplatz

Sigismundstr

Str des 17 Juni

Tiergarten

Rousseauinsel

Hitzigallee

Stauffenbergstr

See Schöneberg Map p145

Lützowstr

Austrian Embassy
Egyptian Embassy

Hildebrandstr

Gentiner Str

Grosser Stern

Spreeweg

Hiroshimastr

Landwehrkanal

Derfflingerstr

Altonaer Str

Diplomatenviertel

Von-der-Heydt-Str

Einemstr

Hofjägeralleee

Klingelhöferstr

Nordic Embassies

Stülerstr
Rauchstrasse

See Charlottenburg Map p133

Kurfürstenstr

Schillstr

An der Urania

Wittenbergplatz

Ansbacher Str

To U-/S-Bahn Zoologischer Garten (500m)

Lichtensteinallee

Budapester Str

200 m
0.1 miles

◉ SEE

For the best bird's-eye views in Berlin, take what's billed as Europe's fastest lift to the observation deck of the **Panoramapunkt** (☎ 2529 4372; www.panoramapunkt.de; Potsdamer Platz 1; adult/concession €3.50/2.50; ☽ 11am-8pm). For more on the Tiergarten, see p19.

◉ BAUHAUS ARCHIV/ MUSEUM FÜR GESTALTUNG

Bauhaus Archive/Museum for Design; ☎ 254 0020; www.bauhaus.de; **Klingelhöferstrasse 14; adult/concession incl audioguide €5/3; ☽ 10am-5pm Wed-Mon; 🚌 100; ♿**

Bauhaus school (1919–33) founder Walter Gropius himself designed the avant-garde building that now houses this important design exhibit. The study notes, workshop pieces, models, blueprints and other items by Klee, Kandinsky, Schlemmer and other Bauhaus practitioners underline the movement's enormous influence on all aspects of 20th-century architecture and design.

◉ DAIMLER CONTEMPORARY

☎ 2594 1420; www.sammlung.daimler .com; Weinhaus Huth, Alte Potsdamer Strasse 5; admission free; ☽ 11am-6pm; ◉ Ⓢ Ⓡ Potsdamer Platz; ♿

Enjoy international abstract, conceptual and minimalist artworks

at this quiet loft-style gallery on the top floor of the historic Weinhaus Huth. Ring the bell to be buzzed in.

◉ GEDENKSTÄTTE DEUTSCHER WIDERSTAND

German Resistance Memorial Center; ☎ 2699 5000; www.gdw-berlin.de; **Stauffenbergstrasse 13-14; admission free; ☽ 9am-6pm Mon-Wed & Fri, to 8pm Thu, 10am-6pm Sat & Sun; 🚌 200; ♿**

This important exhibit on German Nazi resistance occupies the very rooms where high-ranking officers led by Claus Schenk Graf von Stauffenberg plotted the ill-fated assassination attempt on Hitler on 20 July 1944. There's a memorial in the courtyard where the main conspirators were shot right after the failed coup. The story was poignantly retold in the 2008 movie *Valkyrie*. An English audioguide is available.

◉ GEMÄLDEGALERIE

Picture Gallery; ☎ 266 2951; www.smb .spk-berlin.de/gg; Matthäikirchplatz 8; **adult/concession incl audioguide €8/4; ☽ 10am-6pm Tue, Wed & Fri-Sun, to 10pm Thu; ◉ Ⓢ Ⓡ Potsdamer Platz; 🚌 200 or M29; ♿**

This gallery of European art from the 13th to the 18th centuries is famous for its exceptional quality and breadth. Take advantage of the excellent audioguide to get the low-down on selected works by such heavy hitters as Rembrandt, Dürer, Hals, Vermeer and Gainsborough. A tour of all 72 rooms covers almost 2km. Also see p18.

KUNSTGEWERBEMUSEUM

Museum of Decorative Arts; ☎ 266 2951; www.smb.spk-berlin.de/kgm; Tiergartenstrasse 6; adult/concession €8/4; ⏰ 10am-6pm Tue-Fri, 11am-6pm Sat & Sun; ⓐ ⓡ Potsdamer Platz; 🚌 200 or M29; ♿

This cavernous museum brims with seven centuries' worth of fancy knick-knacks from all over Europe. From medieval gem-encrusted reliquaries to art deco ceramics and Philippe Starck furniture, it's all here. Don't miss the Guelph Treasure and the Lüneburg silver collection.

KUPFERSTICHKABINETT

Museum of Prints & Drawings; ☎ 266 2951; www.kupferstichkabinett.de; Matthäikirchplatz 8; adult/concession €8/4; ⏰ 10am-6pm Tue-Fri, 11am-6pm Sat & Sun; ⓐ ⓡ Potsdamer Platz; 🚌 200 or M29; ♿

Drawings, watercolours, pastels and oil sketches produced since the 14th century by the top dogs in the art world – including Dürer, Rembrandt and Picasso – are what's in store at this museum.

LEGOLAND DISCOVERY CENTRE

☎ 3010 4010; www.legolanddiscovery centre.com; Sony Center, Potsdamer Strasse 4; adult/child €16/13; ⏰ 10am-7pm, last admission 5pm; ⓐ ⓡ Potsdamer Platz; ♿

This cute indoor amusement park wows the elementary-school set with a 4-D cinema, a Lego 'factory', a Jungle Trail where Lego crocs lurk in the dark, and a mini-Berlin with landmarks made entirely from those little plastic bricks.

MUSEUM FÜR FILM UND FERNSEHEN

Museum of Film & TV; ☎ 300 9030; www.filmmuseum-berlin.de; Potsdamer Strasse 2; adult/concession/family €6/4.50/12; ⏰ 10am-6pm Tue, Wed & Fri-Sun, to 8pm Thu; ⓐ ⓡ Potsdamer Platz; ♿

From silent movies to sci-fi, this hi-tech museum charts the major

BARGAIN ALERT

A ticket to any one Kulturforum museum entitles you to same-day admission to the permanent collection of the other four. Participating museums are: Neue Nationalgalerie, Gemäldegalerie, Kunstgewerbemuseum, Kupferstichkabinett and Musikinstrumenten-Museum. Admission to any of them is free during the last four opening hours on Thursdays and always to anyone under 16.

NEIGHBOURHOODS

POTSDAMER PLATZ & TIERGARTEN

milestones in German film and TV history. You'll get more out of it with the excellent audioguide as you skip around galleries dedicated to pioneers such as Fritz Lang, groundbreaking movies such as *Olympia* by Leni Riefenstahl, and legendary divas like Marlene Dietrich. The TV exhibit is not nearly as engrossing, although if you ever wondered what *Star Trek* sounds like in German, this is your chance.

⊙ MUSIKINSTRUMENTEN-MUSEUM

Musical Instruments Museum; ☎ 2548 1178; www.mim-berlin.de, in German; Tiergartenstrasse 1; adult/concession incl audioguide €4/2; ⏱ 9am-5pm Tue, Wed & Fri, to 10pm Thu, 10am-5pm Sat & Sun; ⊕ ⊛ Potsdamer Platz; ♿

This niche museum is stuffed with precious and rare sound machines that are quite interesting even if

Germany on the silver and small screens: the Museum für Film und Fernsehen (p83)

you only play the triangle. Look for a glass harmonica invented by Ben Franklin, a flute played by Frederick the Great, and Johann Sebastian Bach's cembalo. The Mighty Wurlitzer organ – with more buttons and keys than a troop of Beefeater guards – is cranked up at noon on Saturday.

◎ NEUE NATIONALGALERIE

New National Gallery; ☎ 266 2951; www.neue-nationalgalerie.de; Potsdamer Strasse 50; adult/concession €8/4; ⏲ 10am-6pm Tue, Wed & Sun, to 10pm Thu, to 8pm Fri & Sat; ◉ ▣ Potsdamer Platz; ▤ 200 or M29; ♿

This edgy glass temple by Ludwig Mies van der Rohe shelters early-20th-century European paintings and sculpture. Besides the usual suspects from Picasso to Dalí, there's an outstanding collection of such German expressionists as Georg Grosz and Ernst Kirchner. Note that the permanent collection occasionally yields to visiting blockbuster shows.

◎ SIEGESSÄULE

Victory Column; ☎ 391 2961; www .monument-tales.de; Grosser Stern, Tiergarten; adult/concession €2.20/1.50; ⏲ 9.30am-6.30pm Mon-Fri, to 7pm Sat & Sun Apr-Oct, 10am-5pm Mon-Fri, to 5.30pm Sat & Sun Nov-Mar; ▤ 100

This ego-boosting triumphal column, built as a monument to

Prussian military victories, now doubles as a symbol of Berlin's gay community. The gilded lady on top represents the goddess of Victory, but locals irreverently call her Gold Else. The so-so views from below her skirt take in mostly the Tiergarten park.

🛍 SHOP

🛍 POTSDAMER PLATZ ARKADEN *Shopping Mall*

☎ 255 9270; www.potsdamer-platz -arkaden.de, in German; Alte Pots-damer Strasse; ⏲ 10am-9pm Mon-Sat; ◉ ▣ Potsdamer Platz

You'll find all your basic shopping needs met at this attractive indoor mall that also has two supermarkets, a food court and decadent ice cream upstairs at Caffé & Gelato.

🍴 EAT

🍴 EDD'S *Thai*   €€

☎ 215 5294; www.edds-thairestaurant .de; Lützowstrasse 81; ⏲ 11.30am-3pm & 6pm-midnight Tue-Fri, from 5pm Sat, from 2pm Sun; ◉ Kurfürstenstrasse or Mendelssohn-Bartholdy-Platz; ✗

Edd's grandma used to cook for Thai royals and the man himself has regaled Berlin foodies for over two decades with such palate-pleasers as twice-roasted duck, chicken steamed in banana leaves, and curries that are poetry on a plate. Reservations essential.

🍴 FACIL French €€€

☎ 590 051 234; www.facil-berlin.de;
5th fl, Mandala Hotel, Potsdamer Strasse
3; ⏱ noon-3pm & 7-11pm Mon-Fri;
🚇 🚌 Potsdamer Platz; ✗
Michael Kempf's Michelin-starred
fare is hugely innovative yet deliciously devoid of needless flights
of fancy. Enjoy it while draped into
a sleek Donghia chair in the glass
garden dining room – the setting,
at the Mandala Hotel, is every bit as
cutting-edge as the food. Budget
gourmets should come for lunch.

🍴 JOSEPH-ROTH-DIELE
German €

☎ 2636 9884; www.joseph-roth
-diele.de, in German; Potsdamer
Strasse 75; ⏱ 10am-midnight Mon-Fri;
🚇 Kurfürstenstrasse; ✗
Conversation rarely seems to
flag in this lovable 1920s retreat
named for an Austrian Jewish
writer who lived next door before
being forced into exile by the
Nazis. The menu is simple: two

hearty hot dishes at lunch and din-
nertime, otherwise German-style
sandwiches and cake. At lunchtime, staffers from the nearby
Tagesspiegel newspaper invade.

🍴 VAPIANO Italian €

☎ 2300 5005; www.vapiano.de; Potsdamer Platz 5; ⏱ 10am-1am Mon-Sat,
to midnight Sun; 🚇 🚌 Potsdamer
Platz; ✗
Matteo Thun's jazzy decor is a great
foil for this self-service joint's tasty
Italian fare. Mix-and-match pasta
dishes, creative salads and crusty
pizzas are prepared *à la minute*
before your eyes. Nice touch: a
condiment basket with fresh basil.
Your order is recorded on a chip
card and paid for upon leaving.

🍸 DRINK

🍸 CAFÉ AM NEUEN SEE
Beer Garden

☎ 254 4930; Lichtensteinallee 2;
⏱ from 10am daily Mar-Oct, Sat & Sun
Nov-Feb; 🚇 🚌 Zoologischer Garten; ✗

MAKING CLASSIC COOL

Mozart, Beethoven and Grieg instead of techno and beats – that's the concept of the **Yellow
Lounge** (www.yellowlounge.de, in German), a roving monthly club night of classical music.
It's an ingenious stunt by Universal Music to win new audiences for its Deutsche Grammophon
classical music label – and it works. The sold-out cult concerts pack some of the hottest clubs
in town, including **Berghain** (p130), **Weekend** (p61) and **Cookies** (p55). Resident DJ David
Canisius, himself a violinist with the Deutsches Kammerorchester, treats mostly youthful ears
to musical jewels from the past centuries. The evenings' highlights, though, are live performances by such top artists as the Emerson String Quartet, Anna Gourari and Sting.

This lakeside Bavarian-style beer garden in Tiergarten park feels like a microvacation from the city bustle. Cold beers go well with the Bratwurst and pretzels, and there's pizza to boot. Romantic types can even rent a boat and take their sweetie for a spin.

PLAY

ARSENAL *Cinema*
☎ 2695 5100; www.arsenal-berlin.de, in German; Sony Center, Potsdamer Strasse 2; adult/child €6.50/3; Ⓖ Ⓡ Potsdamer Platz

This artsy twin-screen cinema is the antithesis of popcorn culture, with a bold, daily changing flick schedule that hopscotches from Japanese satire to Brazilian comedy and German road movies. Many films have English subtitles.

BERLINER PHILHARMONIE
Classical Music
☎ 2548 8999; www.berliner-philharm oniker.de; Herbert-von-Karajan-Strasse 1; tickets €7-150; Ⓖ Ⓡ Potsdamer Platz

This world-famous concert hall has supreme acoustics and, thanks to Hans Scharoun's clever terraced vineyard design, not a bad seat in the house. It's the home base of the Berliner Philharmoniker, currently led by Sir Simon Rattle. Bonus: free Tuesday lunchtime concerts (1pm, September to June).

Ludwig presiding over the Berliner Philharmonie

CINESTAR ORIGINAL & IMAX 3D *Cinema*
☎ 2606 6260; www.cinestar.de, in German; Sony Center, Potsdamer Strasse 4; adult/concession €9/7; Ⓖ Ⓡ Potsdamer Platz

This state-of-the-art cinema in the Sony Center shows the latest Hollywood blockbusters, all in English, all the time, plus some cool 3-D Imax flicks.

>PRENZLAUER BERG

Ageing divas know that a facelift can quickly pump up a drooping career, and it seems the same can be done with entire neighbourhoods. It helps that Prenzlauer Berg has always had great bone structure, so to speak. Badly pummelled but not destroyed during WWII, the district was among the first to show up in the cross-hairs of developers after the Wall collapsed. Now pretty as a polished penny, its town houses sparkle in prim pastels, their sleekly renovated flats and lofts the haunts of urbanites, gays, creative types, families and professionals.

It's these bourgeois bohemians who keep alive a burgeoning scene of world-cuisine restaurants, trendy bars, cultural venues, designer boutiques and *bio* (organic) supermarkets. Berliners may whisper behind raised palms that Prenzlauer Berg is losing its edge but that isn't stopping them from coming here.

The district is best explored on a gentle meander (see p22 for suggestions). Along the way, you'll likely be dodging an astonishing number of BMWs. No, we're not talking cars but 'baby moving wagons' – vintage

PRENZLAUER BERG

◉ SEE
Café Achteck 1 B5
Jüdischer Friedhof 2 B4
Kollwitzplatz 3 C4
Mauerpark 4 A3
Synagoge Rykestrasse 5 C4
Wasserturm 6 C4

◫ SHOP
Biodrogerie Rosavelle ...7 B5
Flohmarkt am
    Arkonaplatz 8 A4
Flohmarkt am
    Mauerpark 9 A3
Goldhahn &
    Sampson 10 C3
Luxus International 11 B3
Ta(u)sche 12 C3

Vamp Star Salon 13 B4
VEB Orange 14 A3
Zwischenzeit 15 C3

◫ EAT
Fellas 16 B2
Hans Wurst 17 C3
I Due Forni 18 B5
Konnopke's Imbiss 19 B3
Oderquelle 20 B3
Sasaya 21 C2
Schlemmerbuffet 22 A5
Schusterjunge 23 B3
Si An 24 C4
W-Imbiss 25 A4

▼ DRINK
Anna Blume 26 C4
Bar Gagarin 27 C4
Bonanza Coffee
    Heroes 28 A3
Deck 5 ....29 B2
Klub der Republik 30 B3
Marietta 31 C2
Prater 32 B3
Rote Lotte 33 A3
Wohnzimmer 34 C3
Zum Schmutzigen
    Hobby 35 C4

★ PLAY
Bassy 36 B5
Icon 37 B2
Kulturbrauerei 38 B3
Magnet 39 D5

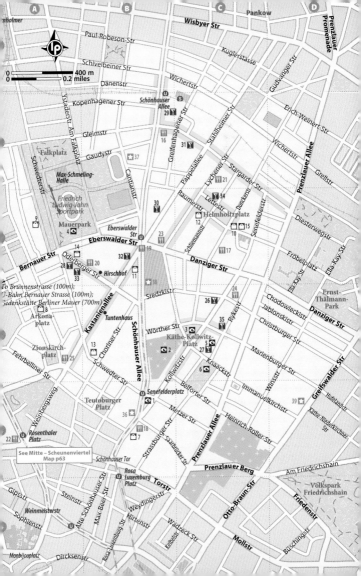

prams to high-tech strollers. Turns out Prenzlauer Berg is one of the most family-friendly districts in town: safe, quiet and with plenty of infrastructure, from playgrounds to baby boutiques and cafes.

SEE

JÜDISCHER FRIEDHOF

Jewish Cemetery; ☎ 441 9824; Schönhauser Allee 22; admission free; ⏱ 7.30am-5pm Mon-Thu, to 2.30pm Fri, 8am-5pm Sun Apr-Sep, 7.30am-4pm Mon-Thu, to 2.30pm Fri, 8am-4pm Sun Oct-Mar; ⊖ Senefelderplatz; ♿

Berlin's second Jewish cemetery opened in 1827 and, behind a thick wall, hosts such famous dearly departed as the artist Max Liebermann and the composer Giacomo Meyerbeer. WWII brought vandalism and bomb damage but it's still a pretty place with dappled light filtering through big old trees. Men must cover their heads (free skullcaps by the entrance).

KOLLWITZPLATZ

⊖ Senefelderplatz

This parklike triangular square was ground zero of Prenzlauer Berg's revitalisation. Grab a cafe table and watch the leagues of tattooed mamas, designer-jean hipsters and gawking tourists on parade. Kids burn energy on the big playground next to a bronze sculpture of the square's namesake, artist Käthe Kollwitz. A great time to visit is during the Thursday or Saturday farmers markets.

MAUERPARK & BERNAUER STRASSE

⊖ Eberswalder Strasse; ♿

The Berlin Wall ran north–south along Schwedter Strasse through today's Mauerpark, then continued west on Bernauer Strasse. Some of the best-known escape attempts took place along here, including the leap across barbed wire of a 19-year-old German Democratic Republic (GDR) border guard, Conrad Schumann, famously captured in a photograph by Peter Leibing (go to http://iconicphotos.files .wordpress.com and enter Schumann into the search box). Four multilingual panels set up along this fateful street vividly retell the escape of Schumann and three others. For additional background, keep going to the **Gedenkstätte Berliner Mauer** (☎ 464 1030; Bernauer Strasse 111; ⏱ 10am-6pm Apr-Oct, to 5pm Nov-Mar) about 1km west of the Mauerpark. For more on the Wall, see p160.

SYNAGOGE RYKESTRASSE

☎ 8802 8316; www.synagoge-rykestrasse .de; Rykestrasse 53; adult/concession €3/2, with German tour €5/3, with English tour €7/5; ⏱ 2-6pm Thu, 11am-4pm Sun, guided tours on the hour, English tour 4pm Thu; ⊖ Senefelderplatz; ♿

PRETTY PISSOIRS

We don't usually go around pointing out public toilets as tourist attractions, but the octagonal Christmas-tree-green hut outside the Senefelderplatz U-Bahn station is worth a special mention. It's one of about two dozen remaining public urinals that popped up all over Berlin in the late 19th century when the municipal sanitation system couldn't keep up with the exploding population. Inspired by their distinctive shape, Berliners nicknamed these relief stations **Café Achteck** (Café Octagon). Most were torn down when indoor plumbing became commonplace, but the survivors are gradually being restored and modernised. The Cadillac models — such as the new one on Gendarmenmarkt — can even accommodate women. But you still can't get coffee...

This rambling red-brick, neo-Romanesque pile is Berlin's largest synagogue and one of the few Jewish houses of worship that didn't go up in flames during the 1938 Kristallnacht pogroms. Now fully restored, it hosts services, cultural events and tours.

☉ WASSERTURM

Water Tower; cnr Knaackstrasse & Rykestrasse; ☉ **Senefelderplatz**
Nicknamed 'Dicker Hermann' (Fat Hermann), this 1873 brick water tower was an improvised concentration camp under the Nazis. After the war the tower was converted into flats. A lively row of restaurants and bars has sprung up on Knaackstrasse opposite.

🛍 SHOP

Indie boutiques hold forth around Helmholtzplatz and along Kastanienallee, Oderberger Strasse and Stargarder Strasse. There are also some interesting boutiques mixed in among the bargain stores along Schönhauser Allee. For everyday needs, stop by Schönhauser Allee Arcaden mall right by the eponymous U-/S-Bahn station.

🛍 BIODROGERIE ROSAVELLE
Cosmetics
☎ **4403 3475; www.rosavelle.de, in German; Schönhauser Allee 10-11;** ☉ **10am-8pm;** ☉ **Rosa-Luxemburg-Platz**
This candy store of cosmetics will have you looking fabulous in no time. Products are all natural, all the time. Favourite Euro-lines such as Dr Hauschka and Logona sell for a lot less here than overseas, and you can also get manicures and beauty treatments.

🛍 FLOHMARKT AM ARKONAPLATZ *Flea Market*
Arkonaplatz; ☉ **10am-5pm Sun;** ☉ **Bernauer Strasse**
This small market feeds the retro frenzy with plenty of groovy furniture, accessories, clothing, vinyl

NEIGHBOURHOODS

PRENZLAUER BERG

and books, including lots of GDR memorabilia.

FLOHMARKT AM MAUERPARK *Flea Market*

Bernauer Strasse, Mauerpark; 🕐 **10am-5pm Sun;** 🚇 **Eberswalder Strasse**

Easily combined with the nearby Arkonaplatz flea market, this park-adjacent contender draws all sorts of vendors, from T-shirt designers and families who've cleaned out their closets to down-at-heelers hawking trash. Follow up with a drink at the outdoor Mauersegler cafe or a nap in the Mauerpark.

GOLDHAHN & SAMPSON *Food*

☎ **4119 8366; http://goldhahnund sampson.de, in German; Dunckerstrasse 9;** 🕐 **10am-8pm Mon-Sat, 1-4pm Sun;** 🚇 **Eberswalder Strasse**

Pink Himalayan salt, Moroccan argan oil and crusty German breads are among the temptingly displayed delicacies at this posh food shop. Sasha and Andreas hand-pick all items, most of them rare, organic and from small suppliers. For inspiration, nose around the cookbook library or book a class at the on-site cooking school.

Cutesy handbags for sale at the Flohmarkt am Mauerpark treasure trove

🛍 LUXUS INTERNATIONAL
Gifts & Souvenirs

☎ 4432 4877; Kastanienallee 101;
⏰ 11am-8pm Mon-Fri, to 4pm Sat;
🚇 Eberswalder Strasse

With no shortage of creative spirits in Berlin – not many of whom are able to afford their own store – in comes Luxus International, which rents them a shelf or two to display everything from Berlin serviettes, witty souvenir T-shirts, silly jokes and Trabi-embossed tote bags (all Berlin originals).

🛍 TA(U)SCHE *Bags*

☎ 4030 1770; www.tausche-berlin.de;
Raumerstrasse 8; ⏰ 11am-8pm Mon-Fri,
to 6pm Sat; 🚇 Eberswalder Strasse

Heike Braun and Antje Strubels, both landscape architects by training, hand-make cool bags in various sizes that are practical, durable and stylish. Best of all, they're kitted out with exchange-able logo flaps that zip on and off in seconds.

🛍 VAMP STAR SALON *Fashion*

☎ 4057 6960; Schwedter Strasse 22;
⏰ 1-8pm Mon-Sat; 🚇 Senefelderplatz

Japanese-born and Berlin-based designer Endo showcases his eccentric designs, including a line of psychedelic tees, alongside stylish Japanese organic-cotton denim and down jackets by Dope & Drakkar.

🛍 VEB ORANGE *Vintage*

☎ 9788 6886; www.veborange.de;
Oderberger Strasse 29; ⏰ 10am-8pm
Mon-Sat; 🚇 Eberswalder Strasse

Viva retro! With its selection of the most beautiful things from the '60s and the '70s, this place will re-mind you of how colourful, plastic and fun home decor used to be. All kinds of furnishings, accesso-ries, lamps and fashions, much of it reflecting that irresistibly campy GDR spirit.

🛍 ZWISCHENZEIT *Vintage*

☎ 4467 3371; Raumerstrasse 35;
⏰ 2-7pm Mon-Fri, 11am-5pm Sat;
🚇 Eberswalder Strasse

Berlin's retro-rage finds its perfect expression at this small but scintillating store, where you can rummage through a rainbow assortment of crockery, furniture, board games, Krautrock vinyl and other vintage treats – all in better-than-good condition and sold at reasonable prices.

🍴 EAT

🍴 FELLAS *German* €€

☎ 4679 6314; www.fellas-berlin.de,
in German; Stargarder Strasse 3;
⏰ 10am-1am; 🚇 🚆 Schönhauser
Allee; 📶 Ⓥ

This unhurried neighbourhood resto employs a kitchen staff surely destined for fancier places.

Gordon W

W-Imbiss (p96) chef and designer, tiki worshipper, thereminist and neois

You came to Berlin from Canada. Why did you stay? Because of the vivid ar
and alternative scenes, general tolerance, drinking, smoking, staying up late
and general misbehaviour. **Where do you go for great food?** I enjoy Sasaya
(opposite), especially the grilled sepia with wasabi mayo. **Do you think Berlin
is a better city for romance or for sex?** There are bordellos everywhere. As
for romance, I was lucky once. Then there's the KitKatClub (p61) for the kinky.
How has Berlin changed since you moved here? Berlin is the last stand of
the avant-garde, but now big money is buying the buildings, gentrifying and
pushing the artists out when it was the artists who made the neighbourhood.
Why are you learning to tango? Tango infected my spirit and uses my body.
Berlin is number two in the world for tango; first is Buenos Aires.

The regular menu has great salads and schnitzel, but we've found that the most creativity goes into the big-flavoured weekly specials. Or come just for a snack and wine.

HANS WURST
Vegan €
☎ 4171 7822; Dunckerstrasse 2a; noon-midnight Tue-Sun; 🚇 Prenzlauer Allee; ✂ Ⓥ

The name is a bit of a tease, for the one thing you definitely won't find on the menu at this stylish boho cafe is Wurst (sausage) nor any other animal products. Owner-chef Michael Ristock is a veritable genius when it comes to coaxing maximum flavour out of organic and fair-trade ingredients. Perks: great music, relaxed crowd and pizza, too.

I DUE FORNI
Italian €
☎ 4401 7373; Schönhauser Allee 12; noon-midnight; 🚇 Senefelderplatz; ✂

In this hectic, graffiti-decorated hall run by a crew of Italian punks, the pizza is king, not you. Service can be slow and rude, but tattooed scenesters and boho families are not deterred: the pies are just that good. Make reservations if you hope to get fed after 8pm. Nice terrace.

KONNOPKE'S IMBISS
German €
☎ 442 7765; www.konnopke-imbiss.de, in German; Schönhauser Allee 44a; 6am-8pm Mon-Fri, noon-7pm Sat; 🚇 Eberswalder Strasse

This legendary sausage kitchen below the elevated U-Bahn tracks has been serving some of the best *Currywurst* (curried sausage) in town since 1930. Eat 'em while they're hot.

ODERQUELLE *German* €€
☎ 4400 8080; Oderberger Strasse 27; 6pm-1am; 🚇 Eberswalder Strasse; ✂

If this woodsy resto wasn't so darn popular, you'd just pop in for a beer and a well-crafted German meal. But, alas, without a reservation, chances of scoring a table after 8pm are practically nil, although the bar stools might do in a pinch. Good *Flammekuche* (Alsatian pizza), too.

SASAYA *Asian* €€
☎ 4471 7721; Lychener Strasse 50; noon-3pm & 6-10.30pm Thu-Tue; 🚇 Schönhauser Allee

Whatever you order at this minimalist space has perfect pitch – sushi to salads, tempura to fish. Tables fill quickly with Japanese expats and plugged-in locals, so it's best to make reservations several days ahead.

SCHLEMMERBUFFET
Middle Eastern €
☎ 283 2153; Torstrasse 125; ⏲ 24hr;
Ⓜ Rosenthaler Platz; ✕
The best doners in town. Enough
said.

SCHUSTERJUNGE *German* €
☎ 442 7654; Danziger Strasse 9;
⏲ 11am-midnight; Ⓜ Eberswalder
Strasse; ✕
This rustic corner joint doles out
authentic Berlin charm with as
much abandon as the delish home
cooking. Big platters of goulash,
pork roast and *Sauerbraten*
(vinegar-marinated beef pot roast)
feed both tummy and soul, and so
do the locally brewed Bürgerbräu
and Bernauer Schwarzbier.

SI AN *Vietnamese* €
☎ 4050 5775; www.sian-berlin.de;
Rykestrasse 36; ⏲ noon-midnight;
Ⓜ Eberswalder Strasse; ✕
For some of the sharpest Vietnamese food in town, grab a stool at
this stylish nosh spot that welcomes a steady stream of tousled
hipsters, yoga mamas and even
the occasional superceleb such as
Tom Cruise. Service could be more
snappy, less snippy.

W-IMBISS *Fusion* €
☎ 4849 2657; Kastanienallee 49;
⏲ noon-midnight; Ⓜ Rosenthaler
Platz; ✕

This steamy, hanky-sized kitchen
prepares eccentric Indian-Italian-
Californian fusion, which translates
into delicious naan pizzas, black-
bean quesadillas and tandoori-fish
rice bowls. The apple juice laced
with spirulina is a great hangover
cure.

🍸 DRINK

🍸 ANNA BLUME *Cafe*
☎ 4404 8749; www.cafe-anna-blume.de;
Kollwitzstrasse 83; ⏲ 8am-2am;
Ⓜ Eberswalder Strasse; ✕
Named for a Kurt Schwitters
poem, this is the living room of the
Prenzlauer Berg digital bohemians
and the stroller mafia. Potent java,
homemade cakes and flowers
from the attached shop perfume
the art nouveau interior, but in
fine weather the big terrace is the
perfect people-watching base.

🍸 BAR GAGARIN *Cafe-Bar*
☎ 442 8807; Knaackstrasse 22-24;
⏲ 10am-2am; Ⓜ Senefelderplatz
Prepare for lift-off with vodka, Russian beer and borscht at this retro
lounge dedicated to Soviet space
pioneer Yuri Gagarin. This is the
more low-key cousin of Pasternak
next door, with a spacey mural,
crouched conversationalists and
friendly staff. Good breakfast,
Russian grub, Sunday brunch and
full assortment of toiletries in the
ladies' loo.

⅄ BONANZA COFFEE HEROES
Cafe

☎ 0178 144 1123; Oderberger Strasse 35; 🕑 8.30am-7pm Mon, Tue & Fri, 10am-7pm Sat & Sun; ⊝ Eberswalder Strasse; ✗

If Synesso Cyncra and 'third wave coffee' are not mere gobble-dygook to you, you speak the language of Kiduk and Yumi, owners of this pocketsize shrine for javaholics. It's especially crowded on Sunday when the Mauerpark flea market is in session.

⅄ DECK 5
Beach Bar

www.freiluftrebellen.de, in German; Schönhauser Allee 80; 🕑 10am-midnight; ⊝ 🚊 Schönhauser Allee

Soak up the city light at this hidden beach bar in the sky while sinking your toes into tonnes of sand lugged to the top parking deck of the Schönhauser Arkaden mall. Take the lift (elevator) from within the mall or enter via a never-ending flight of stairs on Greifenhagener Strasse.

Decisions, decisions… Sunday brunch buffet at Bar Gagarin

☒ KLUB DER REPUBLIK *Bar*
**Pappelallee 81; ☽ from 10pm;
🚇 Eberswalder Strasse**
There's no sign at this popular
ballroom-turned-bar: just look up
till you see steamy windows, then
teeter up the staircase. Inside it's
pure GDR Ostalgie (nostalgia for
East Germany): well-worn armchairs, psychedelic wallpaper and
giant ball lamps. Join hormone-
happy hipsters for electronic
music, wall projections and cheap
fuel for the long night ahead.

☒ MARIETTA *Cafe-Bar*
**☎ 4372 0646; www.marietta-bar.de, in
German; Stargarder Strasse 13; ☽ from
10am; 🚇 🚆 Schönhauser Allee**
Retro is now at this neighbourly
self-service retreat where you
can check out passing eye candy
through the big window or lug
your beverage to the dimly lit
back room for quiet bantering. On
Wednesday nights it's a launch
pad for the local gay party circuit.

☒ PRATER *Beer Garden*
**☎ 448 5688; www.pratergarten.de;
Kastanienallee 7-9; ☽ from noon Apr-
Sep; 🚇 Eberswalder Strasse**
Berlin's oldest beer garden
(since 1837) has kept much of its
traditional charm and is a fun spot
for guzzling a cold one beneath
the chestnut trees. Kids can romp
around the small play area.

☒ ROTE LOTTE *Bar*
**☎ 0172 318 6868; Oderberger Strasse 38;
☽ 7pm-2am; 🚇 Eberswalder Strasse**
Named after a Nazi resistance
fighter, tiny Lotte's plush velvet
sofas, boudoir lighting and mellow indie sounds are great for
deep conversation and civilised
cocktails. The eponymous house
potion is made with strawberry-
lime liqueur and vodka.

☒ WOHNZIMMER *Cafe-Bar*
**☎ 445 5458; www.wohnzimmer-bar.de,
in German; Lettestrasse 6; ☽ from 9am;
🚇 🚆 Schönhauser Allee**
Bask in the vintage vibe of this cult
'living room', where talkative types
hang out for organic breakfast,
cakes and beer on mismatched
sofas and armchairs. It's great at
night, but daytime can be slow.

☒ ZUM SCHMUTZIGEN HOBBY *Gay Bar*
**www.ninaqueer.com, in German;
Rykestrasse 45; ☽ from 5pm;
🚇 Senefelderplatz**
Local trash drag deity Nina Queer
presides over this louche den
of kitsch and glam with decor,
clientele and goings-on that aren't
for the faint-of-heart (check out
the porno wallpaper in the men's
room). Test your celebrity gossip
IQ on Wednesdays at 9pm when
it's standing-room only for Nina's
'glamour trivia quiz'.

⭐ PLAY

⭐ BASSY Club
☎ 281 8323; www.bassy-club.de, in German; Schönhauser Allee 176a; cover varies; ⏰ from 10pm Fri & Sat; Ⓜ Senefelderplatz

A den of darkness for the post-uni crowd. Small and cosy with sofas for lounging and making out, it champions up-and-coming local bands and has a dance floor heaving with anything pre-1969. On Thursdays, drag diva Chantal brings in her House of Shame gay parties. Bassy also hosts Boheme Sauvage Roaring Twenties theme parties (www.boheme-sauvage.de, in German).

⭐ ICON Club
☎ 4849 2878; www.iconberlin.de; Cantianstrasse 15; cover €3-10; ⏰ from 11.30pm Tue, Fri & Sat; Ⓜ Eberswalder Strasse

This labyrinthine cellar of a former brewery is Berlin's holy grail of drum and bass – Recycle on Saturday is an eardrum-rinsing local institution. Friday is generally given over to special events, with some very strong nu-skool breakbeat and downtempo nights. International DJ royalty such as Grooverider and Nightmares on Wax occasionally head the line-up here.

⭐ KULTURBRAUEREI Cultural Centre
☎ 4431 5151; www.kulturbrauerei-berlin.de; Schönhauser Allee 36-39; Ⓜ Eberswalder Strasse

The fanciful red and yellow brick buildings of this 19th-century brewery are now a cultural powerhouse with a small village worth of venues, from concert and theatre halls to restaurants, nightclubs, galleries and a multiscreen cinema.

⭐ MAGNET Live Music
☎ 4400 8140; www.magnet-club.de, in German; Greifswalder Strasse 212-213; cover €1-15; ⏰ concerts 8pm, parties 11pm; 🚋 M4; ✗

Small, cheap and dingy, this indie bastion is known for bookers with an astronomer's vision for detecting stars in the making. LCD Soundsystem and The Presets had early performances here. After the show, the rambling, multifloor venue morphs into a dance club with DJs going wild with punk to pop to electro.

>EASTERN KREUZBERG & KREUZKÖLLN

Eastern Kreuzberg gets its street cred from being delightfully edgy, bipolar, wacky and, most of all, unpredictable. Still called SO36 after its pre-reunification postal code, the area is a multicultural mosaic where *dönerias* (doner kebab shops) rub up against Brazilian cafes, headscarf-wearing mamas push prams past punks with metal-penetrated faces, and black-haired Goths draped in floor-length leather coats chill next to bright-faced students at an outdoor cinema.

SO36's alternative spirit has its roots in the Cold War years. Then boxed in by the Berlin Wall on three sides, West Berlin's poorest district became a countercultural catch basin for students, punks, draft dodgers and squatters, (in)famous for its violent May Day brawls with police. The fall of the Wall catapulted it from the city's edge to its centre, eventually entailing rising rents and tendrils of gentrification.

As a result, students, artists and creatives are now pushing the frontier into the northern reaches of 'bad-rap' Neukölln. Christened

EASTERN KREUZBERG & KREUZKÖLLN

🏠 SHOP
Die Imaginäre
  Manufaktur 1 B2
Jumbo Second Hand 2 C2
Killerbeast 3 E2
Overkill 4 D2
UKO Fashion 5 B3
UVR Connected 6 A1

🍴 EAT
Burgermeister 7 E2
Café Jacques 8 B3
Defne 9 A3
Hartmanns 10 A4
Hasir 11 B2
Henne 12 A1

Horváth 13 B3
Il Casolare 14 A3
Major Grubert 15 B4
Musashi 16 B3
Rissani 17 C2
Spindler & Klatt 18 C1
Türkenmarkt 19 B3
Yellow Sunshine 20 C2

🍸 DRINK
Ankerklause 21 B3
Bellmann 22 D3
Freischwimmer 23 F3
Luzia 24 A2
Madame Claude 25 D2
Möbel Olfe 26 A2
Monarch Bar 27 B2

Orient Lounge 28 B2
Raumfahrer 29 B4
Rosa Bar 30 C2
Roses 31 B2
San Remo Upflamör 32 B2
Silverfuture 33 C4
Würgeengel 34 A2

⭐ PLAY
Badeschiff 35 F3
Club der Visionäre 36 F3
Dot Club 37 E2
Lido 38 E2
SO36 ....39 B2
Watergate 40 E2
Wild at Heart 41 C3

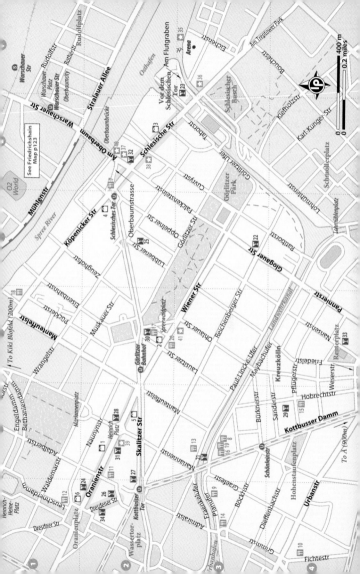

'Kreuzkölln', the area along Reuterstrasse, Hobrechtstrasse and Weserstrasse is the ever-burgeoning home of a funky antiscene teeming with improvised, trashy-cool hang-outs.

🛍 SHOP

🛍 DIE IMAGINÄRE MANUFAKTUR *Gifts*
☎ 2850 3012; www.geschenkesos.de, in German; Oranienstrasse 26; ⏰ 10am-7pm Mon-Fri, 11am-4pm Sat; ⊕ Kottbusser Tor or Görlitzer Bahnhof
Blind and sight-impaired artisans have been hand-making traditional brooms and brushes in this retro minifactory-cum-store for over a century. These days products also include ceramics, wicker goods and wooden toys, although the Berlin bear brush is still a perennial bestseller (and unusual gift).

🛍 JUMBO SECOND HAND *Vintage*
Wiener Strasse 63; ⏰ 11am-7.30pm Mon-Sat; ⊕ Görlitzer Bahnhof
Packed to the rafters, this musty thrift shop is where you could pocket a pair of platform boots, a GDR-era tee and a braided leather belt for less than €50. Not a bad place if you're a DIY vintage fashionista on a pauper's budget.

🛍 KILLERBEAST *Fashion*
☎ 9926 0319; www.killerbeast.de, in German; Schlesische Strasse 31; ⏰ 3-7.30pm Mon, noon-7.30pm Tue-Fri, 11am-4pm Sat; ⊕ Schlesisches Tor

'Kill uniformity' is the motto of this unique boutique where Claudia and her colleagues make new clothes from old ones right in the back of the store. No two pieces are alike and prices are very reasonable, so pick up one of her creations if you're a fan of that dressed-down Berlin look.

🛍 OVERKILL *Fashion*
☎ 107 33; www.overkill.de, in German; Köpenicker Strasse 195a; ⏰ 11am-8pm Mon-Sat; ⊕ Schlesisches Tor
What started as a graffiti magazine back in 1992 has evolved into one of Germany's top spots for streetwear. Now with four times the space, there's a mind-boggling selection of limited-edition sneakers by Onitsuka Tiger, Converse and Asics alongside import threads by cult labels Stüssy, Carhartt and Rocksmith.

🛍 UKO FASHION *Fashion*
☎ 693 8116; www.uko-fashion.de, in German; Oranienstrasse 201; ⏰ 11am-8pm Mon-Fri, to 4pm Sat; ⊕ Görlitzer Bahnhof
High quality at low prices is the magic formula that has garnered this uncluttered clothing store a loyal clientele. It's a veritable gold mine for the latest girl threads by Pussy Deluxe and Muchacha,

second-hand items from Esprit to Zappa and hot-label samples by Vero Moda, only and boyco.

UVR CONNECTED
Fashion

☎ 614 8125; www.uvrconnected.de, in German; Oranienstrasse 36; ⏰ 11am-8pm Mon-Sat; ◉ Kottbusser Tor or Görlitzer Bahnhof

This deceptively large space holds what seems to be 1001 local and international streetwear labels by and for bright young things. Kit yourself out from top to bottom – the range includes hats, hoodies, T-shirts, dresses, jeans, shoes and jewellery, much of it with an edge or a twist.

🍴 EAT

🍴 BURGERMEISTER
American   €

☎ 2243 6493; Oberbaumstrasse 8; ⏰ 11am-2am or later; ◉ Schlesisches Tor

You have to admire the gumption it takes to open a burger joint inside a century-old public toilet on a traffic island below the U-Bahn tracks. Don't fret, don't shudder, it works. The patties are big, delicious and eaten standing up.

🍴 CAFÉ JACQUES
International   €€

☎ 694 1048; Maybachufer 8; ⏰ 6pm-midnight; ◉ Schönleinstrasse; ✗

Fresh flowers, flattering candlelight, delicious wine – this intimate cafe might just be the perfect date spot. But, frankly, you only have to be in love with good food to enjoy this boho den where supper choices are rooted in French or North African cuisine. If in doubt, just ask charismatic owner Ahmad for advice. Reservations are de rigueur or hope for a no-show.

🍴 DEFNE *Turkish*   €€

☎ 8179 7111; www.defne-restaurant.de; Planufer 92c; ⏰ 4pm-1am; ◉ Kottbusser Tor or Schönleinstrasse

If you thought Turkish cuisine stopped at the doner kebab, Defne will teach you otherwise, and quick. The appetiser platter alone is a divine mix of hummus, garlicky carrot, walnut-chilli paste and other treats. The canalside location is idyllic, the decor warmly exotic and the service top notch.

🍴 HARTMANNS
Mediterranean   €€€

☎ 6120 1003; www.hartmanns-restaurant.de, in German; Fichtestrasse 31; ⏰ 6pm-midnight Mon-Sat; ◉ Südstern; ✗

Stefan Hartmann is the shooting star on Berlin's culinary firmament, lassoing the Chef of the Year title in 2008, a mere year after opening this romantic basement restaurant. The emphasis is on innovative French-Mediterranean cuisine, which translates into such offerings as fried halibut with tarragon asparagus or quail with carrot tortellini.

🍴 HASIR Turkish €€
☎ 614 2373; www.hasir.de; Adalbert-strasse 10; ⏰ 24hr; Ⓜ Kottbusser Tor; ✗

This is the mother ship of a small chain whose owner, Mehmed Aygün, invented the Berlin-style doner kebab back in 1971. Tables at this cheerfully decorated restaurant are packed at all hours with patrons lusting after spicy lamb kebab or the filling appetiser platter with tangy hummus, stuffed grape leaves and other exotic morsels.

🍴 HENNE German €
☎ 614 7730; www.henne-berlin.de, in German; Leuschnerdamm 25; ⏰ from 7pm Tue-Sat, from 5pm Sun; Ⓜ Kottbusser Tor or Moritzplatz; ✗

Don't like mile-long menus? Well, you won't have that problem at this woodsy Old Berlin institution, whose name *is* the menu: chicken it is, roasted to moist yet crispy perfection. It's a concept that's been a cult since 1907, so who are we to argue? There's garden seating in summer. Reservations are highly advised.

🍴 HORVÁTH *International* €€€
☎ 6128 9992; www.restaurant-horvath.de, in German; Paul-Lincke-Ufer 44a; ⏰ 6pm-1am Tue-Sun; Ⓜ Kottbusser Tor; ✗

At this jewel on bistro row along the Landwehrkanal (Landwehr canal), Wolfgang Müller slots influences from Asia, Germany and the Mediterranean into something uniquely his own. Foie gras with scallops and orange-vanilla leeks is a typical outcome. To truly test his talents, order the 10-course small-plate menu (€63).

🍴 IL CASOLARE *Italian* €
☎ 6950 6610; Grimmstrasse 30; ⏰ noon-midnight; Ⓜ Kottbusser Tor or Schönleinstrasse

This hectic place has a long-standing reputation for rude servers but on our last few visits it seemed as though they'd gotten a serious talking to. Just as well, for the pizzas here are truly dynamite – thin, crispy, cheap and wagon-wheel-sized – and the canalside beer garden an idyllic spot to gobble 'em up.

🍴 MAJOR GRUBERT *French* €
☎ 0176 6421 5251; Hobrechtstrasse 57; ⏰ from 4pm Tue-Sun; Ⓜ Schönleinstrasse

The time-travelling character created by French comic artist Moebius inspired the name of this colourful bistro-pub combo. It's only fitting then that the food, too, is French. Feast on crêpes, quiches, salads and robust stews, have a glass of wine and get away with less than €10.

🍴 MUSASHI *Japanese* €
☎ 693 2042; Kottbusser Damm 102; ⏰ noon-10.30pm Mon-Sat, 2-10pm Sun; ⓤ Schönleinstrasse; ✗
Sushi purists rejoice: you won't find any truffle-oil-infused wasabi nonsense at this tiny parlour with a massive following. From dark red tuna to marbled salmon, it's all fresh, expertly cut by Nippon natives and affordably priced to boot. Come at off-hours to snag a table, or get it to go and source a picnic spot by the canal.

🍴 RISSANI *Middle Eastern* €
☎ 6162 9433; Spreewaldplatz 4; ⏰ noon-3am Sun-Thu, to 5am Fri & Sat; ⓤ Görlitzer Bahnhof; ✗
Exotically painted and tiled, this salon makes some of the freshest falafel and *shwarma* (slivered meat stuffed into pita bread with lettuce, tomato and garlic sauce) in town. The complimentary palate-cleansing tea is a pleasant perk, or try the carrot-orange juice vitamin bomb.

🍴 SPINDLER & KLATT *Fusion* €€
☎ 319 881 860; www.spindlerklatt.com, in German; Köpenicker Strasse 16/17; ⏰ 8pm-1am daily May-Oct, Wed-Sat Nov-Apr; ⓤ Schlesisches Tor; ✗
Summers on the terrace are magical in this Prussian bread factory turned trendy nosh and party spot. Sit at a long table or lounge on a platform bed while sipping a Watermelon Man or tucking into creative Asian fusion fare. The interior is just as spectacular and morphs into a dance club after 11pm on Friday and Saturday.

🍴 TÜRKENMARKT *Market* €
Turkish Market; Maybachufer; ⏰ noon-6.30pm Tue & Fri; ⓤ Schönleinstrasse
Berlin goes Bosporus during this lively canalside farmers market where you can stock up on olives, feta spreads, loaves of fresh bread and mountains of fruit and vegetables, all at bargain prices. Grab your loot and head west along the canal to carve out your picnic spot in the little park by the Urbanhafen.

🍴 YELLOW SUNSHINE *Vegetarian* €
☎ 6959 8720; www.yellow-sunshine.de, in German; Wiener Strasse 19; ⏰ noon-midnight Mon-Thu, to 1am Fri & Sat; ⓤ Görlitzer Bahnhof; ✗ 🛜 Ⓥ

It's no longer a bread factory, but Spindler & Klatt (p105) still requires dough

Healthy fast food is not an oxymoron, as the folks at this certified organic meat-free diner are demonstrating. Their veggie burgers are slobberingly yummy and the seitan steak and tofu *Currywurst* (curried sausage) might even get hard-core carnivores salivating.

Y DRINK

Oranienstrasse and Schlesische Strasse are both established tipple drags, while Wiener Strasse and Skalitzer Strasse belong in the up-and-coming category. In Kreuzkölln, Hobrechtstrasse and

Weserstrasse are currently the most promising.

Y Ä *Pub*

☎ 0177 406 3837; www.ae-neukoelln.de, in German; Weserstrasse 40; ⏰ from 5pm; ⊕ Rathaus Neukölln

This *Kiez* (neighbourhood) pioneer is a fine place to feed your party animal an appetiser or wrap up a long night on the razzle. Or maybe just claim one of the colourful chairs and camp out for the night. There are DJs and concerts but once a month it's wall-to-wall with people for the live *Schmusetiersoap* starring cast-off stuffed animals.

▼ ANKERKLAUSE *Pub*

☎ 693 5649; www.ankerklause.de, in German; Kottbusser Damm 104; ⏰ from 4pm Mon, from 10am Tue-Sun; 🚇 Kottbusser Tor; ✗

Ahoy there! This nautical kitsch tavern with the best jukebox in town is in an old harbour-master's shack and great for quaffing and waving to the boats puttering along the Landwehrkanal. On Thursdays DJs shower attitude-free party patrons with an alchemy of sounds spun from disco, indie rock, electro et al.

▼ BELLMANN *Pub*

☎ 6953 7189; Reichenberger Strasse 103; ⏰ from 6pm; 🚇 Görlitzer Bahnhof

This funky glamour bar is always packed, mostly with low-key, talkative local folks. 'Glamour' because of the high ceiling, stucco ornamentation, great cocktails and candlelight. Funky because of the plain tables, DIY ambience, unembellished walls and…candlelight. If you get the munchies, pick from the small but satisfying menu.

▼ FREISCHWIMMER *Cafe-Bar*

☎ 6107 4309; www.freischwimmer -berlin.de, in German; Vor dem Schlesischen Tor 2a; ⏰ from 2pm Mon-Fri, from 11am Sat & Sun, check for winter hours; 🚇 Schlesisches Tor

Few places are more idyllic than this rustic ex-boathouse with a

sunny terrace floating above a little canal. Come just for drinks, a bite from the global snack menu or Sunday brunch.

▼ KIKI BLOFELD *Beach Bar*

www.kikiblofeld.de, in German; Köpenicker Strasse 48/49; ⏰ from 2pm Mon-Fri, from noon Sat & Sun; 🚇 Heinrich -Heine-Strasse

A Spree-side rendezvous with Kiki will have you swinging in a hammock, lounging on natural grassy benches, chilling on the riverside beach, waving to passing boats from the wooden deck, catching an offbeat flick or shaking it in an East German army boat patrol bunker. To find it, look for the sign DAZ 48/49, go past the car dealer, look for the gap in the construction fence and you're there.

▼ LUZIA *Bar*

☎ 6110 7469; www.luzia.tc; Oranienstrasse 34; ⏰ from 9am; 🚇 Kottbusser Tor; ✗ 📶

Tarted up nicely with vintage furniture, baroque wallpaper and whimsical wall art by Chin Chin, Luzia draws its crowd from SO36's more sophisticated urban dwellers. Some punters have derided it as Mitte-goes-Kreuzberg but it's still a comfy spot with lighting that gives even pasty-faced hipsters a glow.

☿ MADAME CLAUDE *Bar*

Lübbener Strasse 19; 🕓 **from 7pm;** 🚇 **Schlesisches Tor or Görlitzer Bahnhof;** ✂

Nope, it's not a bad acid trip, it's Madame's. Gravity is literally upended at this living-room-style booze burrow where tables, chairs and teapots dangle from the ceiling. Don't worry, there are still comfy sofas for slouching and entertaining your posse, plus Wednesday's music quiz night and other suitably wacky events.

☿ MÖBEL OLFE *Pub*

☎ **6165 9612; www.moebel-olfe.de, in German; Reichenberger Strasse 177;** 🕓 **from 6pm Tue-Sun;** 🚇 **Kottbusser Tor**

An old furniture store has been recast as an always-busy drinking den with cheap libations and a friendly crowd that's mixed in every respect. Watch out: those animal skeletons above the bar get downright trippy after a few Polish beers or high-octane vodkas. The entrance is on Dresdener Strasse.

☿ MONARCH BAR *Bar*

Skalitzer Strasse 134; 🕓 **from 9pm Tue-Sat;** 🚇 **Kottbusser Tor**

Bonus points if you can find this upstairs bar right away. Tip: the unmarked entrance is next to the doner kebab shop east of the Kaiser's supermarket. Behind steamed-up windows awaits

an ingenious blend of trashy sophistication infused with bouncy electro, strong drinks and a relaxed vibe.

☿ ORIENT LOUNGE *Bar*

☎ **6956 6762; www.orient-lounge.com, in German; Oranienstrasse 13;** 🕓 **from 5pm;** 🚇 **Görlitzer Bahnhof**

Heed the call of the kasbah at this classy nightspot infused with ambient Arabic sounds and the sweet aroma of apple and honey. Find your favourite cushion in the sultry *shisha* (water pipe) lounge or reserve a private niche to sip your cocktails behind a tinkling pearl curtain. The entrance is through the Rote Harfe pub.

☿ RAUMFAHRER *Bar*

Hobrechtstrasse 54; 🕓 **from 7pm Mon-Sat;** 🚇 **Schönleinstrasse**

You can't help but see 'red' in this out-there space capsule where drinks may quickly whisk you into never-never land. It's a lo-fi neighbourhood corner of the world, where the beer is cold, the vibe whispers good times and there's an easygoing crowd to match.

☿ ROSA BAR *Bar*

☎ **7007 1910; Spreewaldplatz 2;** 🕓 **from 8pm;** 🚇 **Görlitzer Bahnhof**

With only a pink 'Bar' sign and a bell to beckon you in, this basement den of liquidity lures mostly clued-in locals with a cocktail menu that's as long as a Tolstoy novel. Sippers chill on white beanbags or in semiprivacy in one of three coveted niches.

☗ ROSES *Gay Bar*
☎ 615 6570; Oranienstrasse 187; ⏲ from 9pm; ⊖ Kottbusser Tor
The ultimate in camp and kitsch (check out the plastic Virgin Marys), Roses is a glittery cult fixture on the lesbigay Kreuzberg booze circuit. Bartenders pour with a generous elbow, making this a great warm-up or wrap-up spot for nights on the razzle.

☗ SAN REMO UPFLAMÖR *Cafe-Bar*
☎ 7407 3088; www.sanremo-upflamoer .de, in German; Falckensteinstrasse 46; ⏲ 10am-2am; ⊖ Schlesisches Tor
Gather your posse at this laid-back hang-out next to Oberbaum-brücke (bridge) before heading out into the long Kreuzberg night. If easygoing clientele, nice waiters, DJ sessions and cold beers won't get you into party mood, what will? Coffee and cake in the day-time. No smoking until 8pm.

☗ SILVERFUTURE *Bar*
Weserstrasse 206; ⏲ from 5pm; ⊖ Hermannplatz
Dressed in rich purple, burgundy and silver, Kreuzkölln's favourite

gay – though thoroughly heter-ofriendly – bar is as charmingly over-the-top as a playful grope from your favourite drag queen. There's Madonna on the jukebox, Polish and Czech beer in the fridge and enough smiling faces for a dependably good time.

☗ WÜRGEENGEL *Bar*
☎ 615 5560; www.wuergeengel.de, in German; Dresdener Strasse 122; ⏲ from 7pm; ⊖ Kottbusser Tor; ✗
For a swanky night out, point the compass at this dimly lit cocktail cave. The interior is pure '50s with a striking glass ceiling, chandeliers and shiny black tables. The name, by the way, pays homage to the surreal 1962 Luis Buñuel movie *Exterminating Angel*.

⭐ PLAY
Oranienstrasse, Kottbusser Tor and Schlesische Strasse are the main party zones but there's also stuff going on along Köpenicker Strasse and Skalitzer Strasse.

☆ BADESCHIFF *Pool*
☎ 533 2030; www.arena-berlin.de, in German; Eichenstrasse 4; admission May-Oct €3, Nov-Apr €12; ⏲ varies, usually from 8am-open end May-Sep or Oct, noon-midnight Nov-Apr; ⊖ Schlesisches Tor
Take an old river barge, fill it with water, moor it in the Spree River

and – voila – an urban lifestyle pool is born, with bods bronzing in the sand and a bar to fuel the fun. On scorching days come before noon or risk a long wait. After-dark action includes parties, bands, movies and simply hanging out. In winter a plastic membrane covers up the pool and there's a deliciously toasty chill zone with saunas and lounge bar (men-only Mondays).

⭐ CLUB DER VISIONÄRE
Bar & Club
☎ 6951 8942; www.clubdervisionaere .com, in German; Am Flutgraben 1; cover free–€10; ☽ from 2pm Mon-Fri, from noon Sat & Sun; ⊙ Schlesisches Tor
This summertime chill and party playground in an old canalside boatshed is great for a drink or two at any time of day or night. Hang out beneath the weeping willows or claim a spot on the planks above the water. On weekends it practically never closes, making it one of the best afterparty spots in town.

⭐ DOT CLUB *Live Music*
☎ 7676 6267; www.liveatdot.com; Falckensteinstrasse 47; cover varies; ☽ most days; ⊙ Schlesisches Tor
If you want to catch tomorrow's bands today, head to this newish club, which does triple duty as concert hall, recording studio and

restaurant. It books an eclectic alchemy of sounds and also does party nights and jam sessions, all amid superb acoustics and decor teetering somewhere between kitsch and cult.

⭐ LIDO
Live Music
☎ 6956 6840, tickets 6110 1313; www .lido-berlin.de, in German; Cuvrystrasse 7; cover varies; ⊙ Schlesisches Tor
A 1950s cinema has been recycled into a rock-indie-elektropop mecca with mosh-pit electricity and a crowd that cares more about the music than about looking good. Global DJs and talented upwardly mobile live noisemakers pull in the punters.

⭐ SO36
Club & Live Music
☎ 6140 1306; www.so36.de, in German; Oranienstrasse 190; cover €3-8; ☽ most nights; ⊙ Kottbusser Tor
Check your attitude at the door at scruffy 'Esso', still the epicentre of Kreuzberg's alternative scene. The Dead Kennedys and Die Toten Hosen played gigs here when many of today's patrons were still in nappies (diapers). Overall, though, who goes when depends on what's on that night: a 'solidarity' concert, a lesbigay theme party, a night flea market, anything goes at SO36.

Lose yourself at edgy 'Esso' (S036), where anything goes

⭐ WATERGATE *Club*

☎ 6128 0394; www.water-gate.de;
Falckensteinstrasse 49a; cover €6-12;
🕐 from midnight Wed, Fri & Sat;
🚇 Schlesisches Tor

It's a short night's journey into day at this high-octane riverside club with panoramic windows and a floating terrace overlooking the Oberbaumbrücke and Universal Music building. Key events, promoters and top international spin-meisters keep the two dance floors packed and sweaty with a head-spinning mix of techno, breakbeat, house, and drum and bass.

⭐ WILD AT HEART
Live Music

☎ 611 9231; www.wildatheartberlin.de;
Wiener Strasse 20; cover €3-10; 🕐 from 8pm; 🚇 Görlitzer Bahnhof

Named after a David Lynch road movie, this one-room kitsch-cool dive is a raging orgy of live punk, rock, ska and rockabilly. Touring bands, including big names such as Girlschool and Dick Dale, bring in the tattooed set several times weekly. If your ears need a break, head to the tiki-themed restaurant-bar next door.

>WESTERN KREUZBERG

Despite its bohemian roots, western Kreuzberg feels sedate and upmarket compared with its eastern cousin around Kottbusser Tor. Nudging against Mitte in the north and Schöneberg in the west, you'll find such heavy-weight attractions as Checkpoint Charlie and the Jewish Museum. The historic Tempelhof airport meanwhile, which had its finest hour during the 1948 Berlin Airlift (see boxed text, p114), was finally closed in 2008.

Over the past 10 years, gentrification has arrived in this area with a vengeance, resulting in cleaner streets, prettier buildings, fancier restaurants and relaxed neighbourly flair. The best strips for a casual saunter are Mehringdamm and especially Bergmannstrasse, both teeming with fun cafes, indie boutiques and speciality stores. Bergmannstrasse runs into Marheinekeplatz square, where yoga mamas and digital bohemians stock up on organic gourmet food in a recently modernised historic market hall.

The hill that gave Kreuzberg (literally 'cross hill') its name is now a rambling park topped by a memorial celebrating Prussia's 1815 victory over Napoleon. Lawns for sunning, a beer garden and an artificial waterfall make this a great summertime play zone. Another fine spot for whiling away a lazy hour or two is along the Landwehrkanal, the canal that links western and eastern Kreuzberg.

WESTERN KREUZBERG

SEE
Berlinische Galerie 1 D2
Checkpoint Charlie 2 C1
Deutsches Technik-
museum 3 A3
Haus am Checkpoint
Charlie
(Mauermuseum) 4 C1
Jewish Museum 5 C2
Martin-Gropius-Bau 6 B1
Schwules Museum 7 B4
Spectrum Science
Centre 8 A3
Topographie des
Terrors 9 B1

SHOP
Faster, Pussycat! 10 B4
Herrlich 11 B5
Sameheads 12 C4
Space Hall 13 C5

EAT
Curry 36 ....14 B4
Foodorama 15 C5
Tomasa 16 A5

DRINK
Golgatha 17 A5
Haifischbar 18 B5
Solar 19 B2

PLAY
English Theatre Berlin ..20 B5
Liquidrom 21 B2
Schwuz ....(see 7)
Yorckschlösschen 22 B4

A

B

C

D

Trabi Safari

Zimmerstr

2

Niederkirchner Str

9

Ad.-Springer-Str

Section of
Berlin
Wall

Kochstr

4

Peter
Fechter
Memorial

Oranienstr

6

Kochstr

Charlottenstr

Lindenstr

Alte Jakobstr

Askanischer
Platz

Anhalter Str

19

1

Ritterstr

Mendelssohn-
Bartholdy-
Platz

Wilhelmstr

Schöneberger Str

Dessauer Str

Anhalter
Bahnhof

Stresemannstr

5

Friedrichstr

Franz-Künstler-Str

Anhalter
Bahnhof

21

Franz-Klühs-Str

Neuenburger Str

Alexandrinenstr

Trebiner Str

3

Möckernstr

Halleschestr Ufer

Mehringplatz

Tour Boat
Landing

Prinzenstr

Möckernbrücke

Böckler
Park

8

Hallesches Tor

Gitschiner Str

Tempelhofer Ufer

Obentrautstr

Blücherstr

Blücher
Platz

Möckernstr

Grossbeerenstr

Mehringdamm

Kirchhof
Jerusalem

Urbanstr

Hornstr

22

Baruther Str

Blücherstr

Yorckstr

14

Gneisenaustr

Nostitzstr

Solmstr

Zossener Str

Gneisenaustr

Brachvogelstr

Schleiermacherstr

Baerwaldstr

Hagelberger Str

10

12

13

7

Riemannstr

Mehringdamm

Methfesselstr

Kreuzbergstr

15

Bergmannstr

11

Marheineke
Markthalle

16

Marheinekeplatz

Bergmannstr

Viktoriapark

18

Arndtstrasse

Chamissoplatz

Monumentenstr

Kreuzberg
Memorial

17

20

Fidicinstr

Cemeteries

Katzbachstr

Schwiebusser Str

Jüterboger Str

Dudenstr

Friesenstr

Platz der
Luftbrücke

Columbiadamm

Zützhauer Str

Kaiserko so

Platz
der Luftbrücke

Luftbrückendenkmal

Tempelhofer Damm

Former
Flughafen
Tempelhof

To Insomnia
(1.8km)

400 m

0.2 miles

◉ SEE

◉ BERLINISCHE GALERIE

**Berlin Gallery; ☎ 7890 2600; www
.berlinischegalerie.de; Alte Jakobstrasse
124-128; adult/under 18/concession
€6/free/3; ⏱ 10am-6pm Wed-Mon;
◉ Kochstrasse; ♿**

Discover what the Berlin art scene
has been up to for, oh, the past
century or so in this converted
glass warehouse near the Jewish Museum. On view are fine
examples from such genres as
secessionism, Dada and Fluxus,
expressionism, Nazi art and contemporary art, presented on two
floors ingeniously linked by a pair
of intersecting floating stairways.

◉ CHECKPOINT CHARLIE

**cnr Friedrichstrasse & Zimmerstrasse;
◉ Kochstrasse**

Checkpoint Charlie was the
principal gateway for Allies,
other non-Germans and diplomats
between the two Berlins from
1961 to 1990. Unfortunately, this
potent symbol of the Cold War has
become a tacky tourist trap where
uniformed actors pose for tips
in front of a replica guardhouse.
The one redeeming aspect is the
free temporary open-air exhibit
chronicling Cold War history along
Friedrichstrasse, Zimmerstrasse
and Schützenstrasse.

◉ DEUTSCHES TECHNIKMUSEUM

**German Museum of Technology; ☎ 902
540; www.dtmb.de; Trebbiner Strasse 9;
adult/concession €4.50/2.50, under 18
after 3pm free; ⏱ 9am-5.30pm Tue-Fri,
10am-6pm Sat & Sun; ◉ Möckernbrücke;
♿ ♿**

Fantastic for kids, this giant shrine
to technology counts the world's
first computer, an entire hall of
vintage locomotives and extensive
exhibits on aviation and naviga-
tion among its top attractions. At
the adjacent **Spectrum science centre**
(enter from Möckernstrasse 26; admission in-

THE BERLIN AIRLIFT

The Berlin Airlift was a triumph of determination and a glorious chapter in the city's post-
WWII history. On 24 June 1948, the Soviets cut off all rail and road traffic to Berlin to force the
Western allies to give up their sectors and bring the entire city under their control. The British
and American military responded by flying in food, fuel and other supplies to the western city
24/7 for the next 11 months, mostly landing at Tempelhof airport. By the time the Soviets
backed down, they had made 278,000 flights, logged a distance equivalent to 250 round
trips to the moon and delivered 2.5 millions tons of cargo. The **Luftbrückendenkmal** (Airlift
Memorial) outside the airport honours the effort and those who died carrying it out.

WESTERN KREUZBERG > SEE

Checkpoint Charlie, where East and West once faced off

cluded) you can participate in more than 200 hands-on experiments.

HAUS AM CHECKPOINT CHARLIE (MAUERMUSEUM)

Berlin Wall Museum; ☎ 253 7250; www
.mauermuseum.de; Friedrichstrasse 43-45;
adult/concession €12.50/9.50; ⌚ 9am-
10pm; ⊖ Kochstrasse; partly ⟁
The Cold War years, especially
the history and horror of the
Berlin Wall, are well-meaningly, if
haphazardly, traced in this private
museum. The best bits are about
ingenious escapes to the West
in hot-air balloons, tunnels,

concealed car compartments and
even a one-person submarine.

JEWISH MUSEUM

Jüdisches Museum; ☎ 2599 3300; www
.juedisches-museum-berlin.de; Lindenstrasse 9-14; adult/concession/family
€5/2.50/10; ⌚ 10am-10pm Mon, to 8pm
Tue-Sun; ⊖ Hallesches Tor; ⟁
The history of German Jews and
their contributions to culture, art,
science and other fields are crea-
tively chronicled in this sprawling
museum in a spectacular building
by Daniel Libeskind. See p17 for
further details.

🄲 MARTIN-GROPIUS-BAU

☎ 254 860; www.gropiusbau.de;
Niederkirchner Strasse 7; admission
varies; 🕓 hours vary; 🚇 🚉 Potsdamer
Platz; ♿

Designed by the great-uncle of
Bauhaus guru Walter Gropius, this
Italian Renaissance–style exhibition hall next to a short stretch of
the Berlin Wall presents travelling
shows of international stature.
Across the street is the Abgeord-
netenhaus, the seat of Berlin's
state parliament.

🄲 SCHWULES MUSEUM

Gay Museum; ☎ 6959 9050; www
.schwulesmuseum.de, in German;
Mehringdamm 61; adult/concession €5/3;
🕓 2-6pm Wed-Fri, Sun & Mon, to 7pm
Sat; 🚇 Mehringdamm

Museum, archive and community
centre all in one, the nonprofit
Gay Museum is a great place to
learn about Berlin's queer history.
Special exhibits often focus on
gay icons such as Greta Garbo or
Oscar Wilde. The entrance is in
the courtyard behind the Melitta
Sundström cafe.

🄲 TOPOGRAPHIE DES TERRORS

Topography of Terror; ☎ 2548 6703;
www.topographie.de; Niederkirchner
Strasse 8; admission free; 🕓 10am-8pm
May-Sep, to dusk Oct-Apr; 🚇 🚉 Potsdamer Platz

Niederkirchner Strasse was once
the home of such feared institutions of Nazi Germany as the
Gestapo headquarters and the
SS central command. Since 1997
a harrowing open-air exhibit has
documented the impact of these
brutal organisations. In 2010 an
expanded version is expected to
open in a proper documentation
centre on the site.

🛍 SHOP

Mehringdamm, Bergmannstrasse
and Zossener Strasse are the
main drags for everything from
vintage fashions to music and
home accessories.

🄲 FASTER, PUSSYCAT! *Fashion*

☎ 6950 6600; Mehringdamm 57;
🕓 11am-8pm Mon-Fri, to 7pm Sat;
🚇 Mehringdamm

Russ Meyer's 1965 camp classic
about go-go dancers gone bad
inspired the store's name, and
fashions here definitely teeter towards the outlandish. But there's
also plenty of smart streetwear
and accessories by Skunkfunk,
Gsus, Pace, Alprausch and other
label-bunny favourites.

🄲 HERRLICH *Gifts*

☎ 6784 5395; www.herrlich-online.de,
in German; Bergmannstrasse 2; 🕓 10am-
8pm Mon-Sat; 🚇 Gneisenaustrasse

Next time you're looking for a gift for 'Him', peruse the racks of this fun store stocked with carefully culled men's delights. From retro alarm clocks to futuristic espresso machines – even a walking stick with hidden whisky flask – it's all here without a single sock or tie in sight.

SAMEHEADS *Fashion*
☎ 6950 9684; www.myspace.com/sameheads; Nostizstrasse 11; ⏰ noon-8pm Mon-Sat; ◉ Gneisenaustrasse

The Sameheads, that's Nathan, Leo and Harry, are three 20-something brothers from Britain keen on carv-

ing out a spot for true subculture through their fashion and music network. Their basement shop is a portal for around 30 up-and-coming local designers from around the globe. While there, probe them for details on their next underground party.

SPACE HALL *Music*
☎ 694 7664; www.space-hall.de; Zossener Strasse 33; ⏰ 11am-8pm Mon-Thu, to 10pm Fri & Sat; ◉ Gneisenaustrasse

This galaxy for electronic-music gurus has four floors filled with everything from acid to techno by way of drum and bass, neotrance,

Space Hall: heaven on earth for electronic-music disciples

dubstep and whatever other genres take your fancy. A dozen or so players stand by for easy prepurchase listening. Nirvana for DJs.

🍴 EAT

You'll find plenty of decent cafes and restaurants along Mehringdamm and Bergmannstrasse and around Marheinekeplatz.

🍴 CURRY 36 *German* €
☎ 251 7368; Mehringdamm 36;
🕐 9am-4am Mon-Sat, 11am-3am Sun;
🚇 Mehringdamm

One of the top *Currywurst* (curried sausage) purveyors in town, with round-the-clock queues to prove it.

🍴 FOODORAMA
International €€
☎ 6900 1100; www.foodorama.de;
Bergmannstrasse 94; 🕐 10am-11pm;
🚇 Mehringdamm

What looks like a stylish school cafeteria is actually Germany's first certified climate-neutral restaurant. Pop by for organic spins on local faves such as *Currywurst* and potato salad or travel the globe via yakitori and Viennese schnitzel. Quality is uneven but your conscience will be clear, at least as long as you don't order the bottled water from Norway or Scotland.

🍴 TOMASA
International €€
☎ 8100 9885; www.tomasa.de,
in German; Kreuzbergstrasse 62;
🕐 9am-1am Sun-Thu, to 2am Fri & Sat;
🚇 Mehringdamm

A charming 19th-century villa is the latest outpost of this popular local minichain, the menu of which is as long and confusing as a Dostoyevsky novel. Never mind. You can't really go wrong, no matter whether you go for breakfast, international tapas, the pizzalike *Flammkuchen* or a meaty main. Bargain alert: the daily €5 lunch specials.

🍸 DRINK

🍸 GOLGATHA *Beer Garden*
☎ 785 2453; www.golgatha-berlin.de,
in German; Dudenstrasse 48-64,
Viktoriapark; 🕐 10am-6am Apr-Sep;
🚇 🚉 Yorckstrasse

The pilgrimage to this beer garden in the Viktoriapark is a beloved summer ritual. Kick back with a foamy lager in a deck chair downstairs or catch the day's final rays on the rooftop terrace. After 10pm a DJ hits the decks. Many paths lead to Golgatha but it's easiest to find by entering the park from Katzbachstrasse, corner of Monumentenstrasse, then take your first right.

🍸 HAIFISCHBAR *Bar*
☎ 691 1352; www.haifischbar-berlin
.de, in German; Arndtstrasse 25; ⏱ from
7pm; ♿ ⓡ Yorckstrasse
With two sharks above the
entrance portal to beckon you
in, this unassuming thirst parlour
plays it cool for cocktail lovers. The
bartender wields the shaker with
confidence, there are tapas on the
menu in the back room and the
toilets get a 10 on the kitsch meter.

🍸 SOLAR *Bar*
☎ 0163 765 2700; www.solar-berlin.de;
Stresemannstrasse 76; ⏱ 6pm-2am
Sun-Thu, to 4am Fri & Sat; ⓡ Anhalter
Bahnhof
The door's tight, service slow and
the cocktails only so-so but the
views – oh, the views – really are
worth the vertigo-inducing trip
aboard an exterior glass lift to this
17th-floor Manhattan wannabe.
The entrance is off-street in an
ugly high-rise behind the Pit Stop

auto shop. Ignore the overpriced
restaurant.

⭐ PLAY
ENGLISH THEATRE BERLIN
Theatre
☎ 691 1211; www.etberlin.de; Fidicin-
strasse 40; tickets €9-18; ♿ Platz der
Luftbrücke; ♿
The repertoire of Berlin's oldest
English-language stage includes
classics, physical theatre, comedy
and works by emerging writers and
directors, many based in Berlin.

LIQUIDROM *Pool*
☎ 258 007 820; www.liquidrom-berlin
.de; Möckernstrasse 10; 2hr/4hr/day pass
€17.50/20.50/22.50; ⏱ 10am-midnight
Sun-Thu, to 1am Fri & Sat; ⓡ Anhalter
Bahnhof
Feel your daily cares slip away at
this stylishly minimalist day spa
that's the perfect mood enhancer
on a rainy day. Besides saunas,

SEX & THE CITY
For a night of hedonistic pleasure, travel to far-flung Tempelhof, south of Schöneberg, the home of **Insomnia** (☎ 0177 233 3878; www.insomnia-berlin.de; Alt-Tempelhof 17-19; cover varies; ⏱ Tue-Sun; ♿ Alt-Tempelhof). This late-19th-century ballroom has been reincarnated as a classy playground of passion presided over by SM and fetish queen Dominique (see our interview with Dominique on p120). Besides the dance floor and big-screen Andrew Blake porn, there are performances and various pleasure pits, including a whirlpool, a bondage room and gynaecological chair. Saturday's Circus Bizarre is good for first-timers; Sundays are reserved for couples and their playmates. The special-themed sex parties during the week are for more advanced players; many require preregistration.

⭐ Dominique
Dominatrix, performer and owner of Insomnia erotic night club (p119)

How did you get started in the erotic business? I've always been interested in sex. My mother was a dominatrix and I opened my own SM studio just before turning 18. Later I ran SM seminars, parties at the KitKatClub and erotic performances with Double Trouble (www.doubletrouble-berlin .de). **What makes Insomnia special?** It's a stylish and safe place that brings together night owls, clubbers, swingers and fetish and SM people. **Any tips for first-timers?** Be open, friendly and communicative. Watching is OK but clumsily grabbing strangers is not. With guys it's often, the fuller the pants, the emptier the brain. **What's so great about your job?** I love it when people tell me that I've made a positive difference in their lives. **What do you do to relax?** Definitely no partying! I take my son cycling in the forest, get together with friends or read a good book.

dipping pools and lounge areas, the star of the show is the darkened domed hall where you float in a saltwater pool while being showered with soothing sounds and psychedelic light projections. Pure bliss.

⭐ SCHWUZ *Gay Club*
☎ 629 0880; www.schwuz.de, in German; Mehringdamm 61; cover €3-8; ☽ Fri & Sat; ◉ Mehringdamm

This party palace is a good place to ease into the lesbigay scene. Fortify yourself in the Melitta Sundström cafe out front, then head to the basement dance floors to grind shoulder to shoulder with friendly locals. The party roster ranges from retro hits to alternative and classic rock, drawing a wide variety of punters. On the fourth Friday it's lesbians only during L-Tunes.

⭐ YORCKSCHLÖSSCHEN
Live Music
☎ 215 8070; www.yorckschloesschen.de; Yorckstrasse 15; ☽ 10am-3am; ◉ Mehringdamm; ✗ ⦿

This knick-knack-laden watering hole has plied an all-ages, all-comers crowd of jazz and blues lovers with tunes and booze for over a century. There's live music on Wednesday and weekends (in winter also on Thursday and Friday), pub grub till 1am, a pool table out the back and a garden in summer.

>FRIEDRICHSHAIN

Friedrichshain, in the former East Berlin, is a shape-shifter, a slippery creature, fluid in identity and defiant of all standard labels. In many ways, it's the 'anti-Mitte', still unsettled in its world view and offering a rambunctious stage for good times and DIY surprises. It celebrates its underground-punk-squatter roots in the derelict industrial outposts along Revaler Strasse and the graffiti-slathered funkytown around Ostkreuz. Mere steps away, Simon-Dach-Strasse is a bar-laden stumbling zone where the young and the restless drink, dance and flirt with all the mad exuberance of a stag party.

Meanwhile, over on socialist-era Karl-Marx-Allee, a postcollege crowd gets liquefied on martinis – pinkie raised, and all – at swish German Democratic Republic–vintage bars before drifting off into the utopia of the Berghain/Panoramabar techno temple. Not far from here, the gleaming O2 World entertainment arena signals that not even Friedrichshain will forever remain immune to gentrification.

Conventional tourist sites are limited to the East Side Gallery, the longest remaining stretch of the Berlin Wall, and the Karl-Marx-Allee, the epitome of Stalinist pomposity. Pockets of pleasantness include the Volkspark Friedrichshain, a wonderland of tamed wilderness filled with trails, tennis courts, a half-pipe, an outdoor cinema and lots of greenery for sunning, grilling and picnicking.

FRIEDRICHSHAIN

⊙ SEE
Café Sybille 1 C1
East Side Gallery 2 B3
Sammlung Haubrok 3 A1

🏠 SHOP
Antikmarkt am
  Ostbahnhof 4 B2
Flohmarkt am
  Boxhagener Platz 5 E2
Mondos Arts 6 F1

🍴 EAT
Meyman 7 E2
Miseria & Nobiltà 8 E2
Papaya 9 E2
Schneeweiss 10 E3
Schwarzer Hahn 11 F3

🍸 DRINK
CSA 12 C1
Eastern Comfort
  Hostel Boat 13 C4
Habermeyer 14 E3
Hops & Barley 15 E2

Kaufbar 16 E3
Kptn A Müller 17 E3
Strandgut Berlin 18 C3

★ PLAY
Berghain/
  Panoramabar 19 C2
Cassiopeia 20 E3
Maria am
  Ostbahnhof 21 B2
Monster Ronson's
  Ichiban Karaoke 22 D4
Radialsystem V 23 B2
Rosi's 24 F3

◉ SEE

◉ EAST SIDE GALLERY

www.eastsidegallery.com; Mühlen-strasse; admission free; ⏱ 24hr; ◉ ⓡ Ostbahnhof or Warschauer Strasse

Between Oberbaumbrücke and Ostbahnhof, this is the longest, best-preserved and most interesting remaining stretch of the Berlin Wall. Paralleling the Spree, the 1.3km section was turned into an open-air gallery in 1990. It was completely restored in 2009, in time for the 20th anniversary of the Wall's demise. Also see p15.

◉ KARL-MARX-ALLEE

btwn Alexanderplatz & Frankfurter Tor; ◉ Strausberger Platz, Weberwiese or Frankfurter Tor

This monumental boulevard is one of the most impressive relics from the GDR era. At 90m wide, it was built between 1952 and 1960 and runs for 2.3km between Alexanderplatz and Frankfurter Tor. A source of considerable national pride, it provided modern flats for thousands of comrades and also served as a backdrop for vast military parades. The exhibit at **Café Sybille** at No 72 has more background.

What better way to spend a Sunday? Trash and treasure trawling at Flohmarkt am Boxhagener Platz

🔵 VOLKSPARK FRIEDRICHSHAIN
Am Friedrichshain & Friedenstrasse;
🚌 **200**
Berlin's oldest public park (since 1840) provides treasured relief from urbanity. Besides expansive lawns, it has playgrounds, tennis courts, a free half-pipe for skaters, the Märchenbrunnen (Fairytale Fountain; popular with gay cruisers after dark) and various socialist monuments. Its two hills are actually piles of wartime debris. Summer events include a popular outdoor film series.

🛍 SHOP
Not yet a shopping mecca, Friedrichshain is nevertheless growing an interesting crop of design and indie boutiques. Have a look at what's happening in the side streets around Boxhagener Platz.

📷 ANTIKMARKT AM OSTBAHNHOF
Flea Market
Ostbahnhof, Erich-Steinfurth-Strasse 1;
🕐 **9am-5pm Sun;** 🚇 **Ostbahnhof**
Exit the S-Bahn station's northern side and plunge onto a cheerful line of antiques and collectibles (such as old coins and banknotes, Cold War relics, gramophone vinyl, books, stamps and jewellery). Snack vendors stand by to assuage hunger pangs.

📷 BERLINOMAT
Fashion & Accessories
☎ **4208 1445; www.berlinomat.com; Frankfurter Allee 89;** 🕐 **11am-8pm Mon-Sat;** 🚇 🚋 **Frankfurter Allee**
This minidepartment store presents the latest visions from a pool of Berlin creatives working in fashion, accessories, furniture and jewellery. Showered by electronic beats, you can inspect sassy jeans by Hasipop, cult GDR-era-style sneakers by Zeha, messenger bags by MilkBerlin and other *Zeitgeist*-savvy stuff you won't find on the high street back home.

📷 FLOHMARKT AM BOXHAGENER PLATZ
Flea Market
Boxhagener Platz; 🕐 **10am-6pm Sun;** 🚇 🚋 **Warschauer Strasse;** 🚇 **Frankfurter Tor**
Wrapped around leafy Boxhagener Platz, this fun flea market is just a java whiff away from scads of nearby Sunday brunch cafes. It's easy to sniff out the pros from the regular folks here to unload their spring-cleaning detritus for pennies.

📷 MONDOS ARTS
Ostalgiana
☎ **4202 0225; www.mondosarts.de, in German; Schreinerstrasse 6;** 🕐 **10am-7pm Mon-Fri, 11am-4pm Sat;** 🚇 **Samariterstrasse**

WORTH THE TRIP – STASI SIGHTS IN THE DEEP EAST

Anyone interested in German Democratic Republic history, and the Stasi in particular, should head out to these two chilling sites. The former head office of the Ministry of State Security is now the **Stasi Museum** (☎ 553 6854; www.stasimuseum.de; House 1, Ruschestrasse 103; adult/concession €3.50/3; ⏰ 11am-6pm Mon-Fri, 2-6pm Sat & Sun; ⊙ Magdalenenstrasse), where you can see cunningly low-tech surveillance devices (hidden in watering cans, rocks, even neckties) and the obsessively neat offices of Stasi chief Erich Mielke. From the U-Bahn station, turn north on Ruschestrasse, then right after about 100m and walk another 50m across a parking lot towards the building straight in front of you.

Victims of Stasi persecution often ended up in the grim **Stasi Prison** (☎ 9860 8230; www.stiftung-hsh.de; Genslerstrasse 66, Hohenschönhausen; tours adult/concession €4/2, Mon free; ⏰ tours 11am & 1pm Mon-Fri, also 3pm Mar-Dec, hourly 10am-4pm Sat & Sun; ⊕ M5), now a memorial site. Tours (in English at 2pm Saturday and occasionally during the week), sometimes led by former prisoners, reveal the full extent of the terror and cruelty perpetrated by the Stasi upon thousands of suspected regime opponents, many of them utterly innocent. If you've seen the Academy Award–winning film *The Lives of Others*, you'll recognise many of the original settings. To get there, ride tram M5 from Alexanderplatz to Freienwalder Strasse, then walk 10 minutes along Freienwalder Strasse.

Cult and kitsch seem to be the GDR's strongest survivors at this funky little shop, named after Mondos, a brand of condoms. It's fun to have a look even if you didn't grow up drinking Red October beer, falling asleep to the *Sandmännchen* (Little Sandman) TV show or listening to rock by the Puhdys.

🍴 EAT

For demanding foodies, Friedrichshain is still a blank spot on the map, but when it comes to all-you-can-eat Sunday brunch buffets, you'll find a great selection around Boxhagener Platz.

🍴 MEYMAN *Middle Eastern* €
☎ 0163 806 1363; Krossener Strasse 11a; ⏰ noon-2am; ⊙ ⊕ Warschauer Strasse; ⊕ Frankfurter Tor; ✗
The name is Kurdish for 'happy person' and happy you will be after filling your tummy with fresh felafel, *shwarma* (slivered meat stuffed into pita bread with lettuce, tomato and garlic sauce), couscous and other balance-restoring munchies. It's perennially popular with scenesters on a bar hop.

🍴 MISERIA & NOBILTÀ *Italian* €€
☎ 2904 9249; Kopernikusstrasse 16; ⏰ 5.30pm-midnight Tue-Thu & Sun, to 1am Fri & Sat; ⊙ ⊕ Warschauer Strasse

When Eduardo Scarpetta penned the comedy *Poverty and Nobility* in 1888, he had no idea that it would one day inspire the name of this popular trattoria. Thanks to the gracious owners, you'll definitely feel more king than pauper when digging into their deftly prepared and daily-changing southern Italian compositions.

PAPAYA *Thai* €
☎ 2977 1231; Krossener Strasse 11; ✆ noon-midnight; ◉ ⓡ Warschauer Strasse; ◉ Frankfurter Tor; ✗
It's a bit bright and the decor is less than inspired, but at least there will be few distractions from the prettily presented tom ka soups, pad Thai noodles and Thai basil chicken streaming from the open kitchen. The spiciness is pitched to German palates, so tell your server if you want the cooks to turn up the heat.

SCHNEEWEISS
German €€
☎ 2904 9704; www.schneeweiss-berlin .de, in German; Simplonstrasse 16; ✆ 10am-1am; ◉ ⓡ Warschauer Strasse
Friedrichshain grunge gets a New York glam makeover at the aptly named 'Snow White' whose chilly-chic decor – awesome 'ice' chandelier – was inspired by the Alps. Same goes for the menu,

which is big on southern German and Austrian classics executed with a fresh postmodern twist.

SCHWARZER HAHN
German €€
☎ 2197 0371; Seumestrasse 23; ✆ 10am-10pm Mon-Sat; ⓡ Ostkreuz; ◉ Warschauer Strasse; ✗
The small menu (cutely presented in a picture frame) at this personable slow-food bistro is stocked with oldies but goodies updated for the 21st century. Service is impeccable and the friendly owner knows a thing or two about wine and will happily give you a taste before you commit.

▽ DRINK
Simon-Dach-Strasse has 'bar crawl' written all over it, especially if you like it loud and lively and don't yet draw a big pay check. Look for classier libation stations in the side streets and along socialist-surreal Karl-Marx-Allee.

CSA *Bar*
☎ 2904 4741; www.csa-bar.de; Karl-Marx-Allee 96; ✆ from 8pm May-Oct, from 7pm Nov-Apr; ◉ Weberwiese
Friedrichshain's fanciest bar has been carved out of the offices of the former Czechoslovakian national airline and sports clean lines and a wonderfully self-ironic Soviet vintage vibe. Dim lights and strong

MOGULS, MAYHEM, MEDIASPREE

The Spree River banks are bracing for change. A small army of developers wishes to build offices, residential buildings, hotels and other commercial structures along a 3.6km stretch south of Jannowitz bridge. It's a €3 billion to €5 billion investment that comes with the promise of creating between 20,000 and 50,000 jobs. Some say it's a smart thing in a city that's €60 million in debt and saddled with high unemployment, but it depends on who you ask. More than 30,000 residents of the district of Kreuzberg-Friedrichshain, through which the territory in question runs, expressed their opposition in a 2008 referendum. They're concerned about insensitive construction, rising rents, restricted public access to the riverfront and the loss of beloved party venues such as **Maria am Ostbahnhof** (p130). As of this writing, the situation is mired in a stand-off, but in the end it seems to be only a matter of time before Berlin's skyline will again be changing dramatically.

Not your standard beach scene: Berlin Wall remnant decorating a Spree River beach

classic cocktails make it a favourite of the grown-up set. Check out the tables with built-in ashtrays.

☿ HABERMEYER *Bar*
☎ 2977 1887; www.habermeyer-bar.de, in German; Gärtnerstrasse 6; ☾ from 7pm; ❻ 🚇 Warschauer Strasse
Habermeyer isn't about seeing and being seen – it's too dark for that. Funky GDR-era furniture, a pinball machine and endearing self-crafted decor (check out the 'pipe grotto' out the back) bring in local hipsters who avoid Simon-Dach-Strasse like the plague. DJs hit the decks most nights.

☿ HOPS & BARLEY *Pub*
☎ 2936 7534; www.hopsandbarley -berlin.de, in German; Wühlischstrasse 38; ☾ from 5pm Sun-Fri, from 3pm Sat; ❻ 🚇 Warschauer Strasse
Conversation flows as freely as the mild and malty beer (and cider) produced right at this congenial microbrewery inside a former butcher shop. Share a table with low-key locals swilling post-work pints and munching rustic *Treberbrot,* a hearty bread made with a natural by-product from the brewing process.

☿ KAUFBAR *Cafe-Bar*
☎ 2877 8825; www.kaufbar-berlin.de, in German; Gärtnerstrasse 4; ☾ 10am-1am; ❻ 🚇 Warschauer Strasse; ✗

The name is the concept at this sweet, unhurried cafe where everything is *'kaufbar'* (for sale): the sofa you're sitting on, the cup you're drinking from, the vases decorating the table. Tousled students, young mums and local artists invade for the mix-and-match breakfast (until 5pm), coffee, cakes, drinks and light snacks. Nice garden, too.

☿ KPTN A MÜLLER *Pub*
☎ 5473 2257; www.kptn.de, in German; Simon-Dach-Strasse 32; ☾ from 6pm; ❻ 🚇 Warschauer Strasse; ✗ 📶
Arrgh matey, the captain's in town, bringing much-needed relief from this strip's cookie-cutter cocktail-lounge circuit. Pretensions do not fly at this self-service bar where drinks are cheap (such as a half-litre of beer or 200mL glass of wine for €2) and there's no charge for table foosball or wi-fi.

☿ STRANDGUT BERLIN *Beach Bar*
☎ 7008 5566; www.strandgut-berlin .com, in German; Mühlenstrasse 61-63; ☾ from 10am; 🚇 Ostbahnhof; 📶
Drink a toast to Berlin at the chicest of the East Side Gallery sand pits where the beer is cold, the cocktails strong, the crowd grown-up and the DJs tops (André Galluzzi celebrated his birthday party here in 2008).

⭐ PLAY

⭐ BERGHAIN/PANORAMABAR
Club

www.berghain.de; Am Wriezener Bahnhof; cover €14; ⌚ **Fri & Sat;** 🚇 🚉 **Ostbahnhof**

It's the best club in the world, according to Britain's well-regarded *DJ Mag*, and we have no problem seconding the hype. Only vinyl masters such as André Galluzzi and Ricardo Villalobos heat up this hedonistic bass junkie hellhole inside a labyrinthine ex-power plant. The upper floor (Panorambar, aka 'Pannebar') is all about house; the gay-leaning big factory hall below (Berghain) pounds with minimal techno beats. Strict door and no cameras. In summer there's a beer garden for daytime chilling.

⭐ CASSIOPEIA *Club*

☎ **2936 2966; www.cassiopeia -berlin.de; Revaler Strasse 99; cover €4-6;** ⌚ **varies, always Wed-Sat;** 🚇 🚉 **Warschauer Strasse**

An old-time train-repair shop has been given a new life by being turned into an urban playground that includes a skate hall, a beer garden, a climbing tower and an attitude-free, two-floor party den. The crowd defines the word eclectic and so does the music, which covers the spectrum from vintage hip hop to hard funk, roots, reggae and punk.

⭐ MARIA AM OSTBAHNHOF
Club

☎ **2123 8190; www.clubmaria.de, in German; Stralauer Platz 33-34; cover €10;** ⌚ **from 11pm Thu, from midnight Fri & Sat;** 🚇 🚉 **Ostbahnhof**

This cavernous club by the Spree River has been a long-time rave fixture and often brings in top DJs from the US and the UK alongside Berlin royalty such as Modeselektor, Apparat and T. Raumschmiere. If you like it more mellow, head to Maria's little brother, the club-within-the-club called Josef.

BERLIN'S BOAT OF BABBLE

A fun and easy way to meet friendly locals over beer and bratwurst is at the World Language Party, which takes over the retro lounge of the floating **Eastern Comfort Hostel Boat** (☎ 6676 3806; Mühlenstrasse 73-77; 🚇 🚉 Warschauer Strasse) every Wednesday from 7pm. It brings together an easygoing, all-ages international crowd, including lots of regulars, but don't be shy – people are friendly and eager to welcome newcomers. Admission, which is added to your first drink, is €1 until 8.30pm, €2 after that. Also check MC Charles' website, www.english-events-in-berlin.de, for updates and additional goings-on.

⭐ MONSTER RONSON'S ICHIBAN KARAOKE *Karaoke*

☎ 8975 1327; www.karaokemonster
.com, in German; Warschauer Strasse 34;
😊 from 7pm; ⊕ 🚇 Warschauer Strasse

Knock back a couple of brewskis if you need to loosen your nerves before belting out your best J Lo or Justin at this mad, great karaoke joint. *Pop Idol* wannabes can pick from thousands of songs and hit the stage; shy types may prefer music and mischief in a private party room (per hour €12).

⭐ RADIALSYSTEM V
Performance Space

☎ 288 788 588; www.radialsystem.de;
Holzmarktstrasse 33; admission varies;
⊕ 🚇 Ostbahnhof; ✂ 📶

Contemporary dance meets medieval music, poetry meets pop tunes, painting meets digital. This progressive performance space in an old riverside pump station blurs the boundaries between music, dance, fine arts, new media and other art forms to nurture new forms of creative expression. Nice riverside cafe-bar from 10am (noon on weekends).

⭐ ROSI'S *Club*

www.rosis-berlin.de; Revaler Strasse 29;
cover €6; 😊 Thu-Sat; 🚇 Ostkreuz

This derelict house-cum-garden-lounge next to the railway tracks catches the Friedrichshain vibe spot on – dim lighting, dank concrete, mismatched furniture and an alchemy of sounds (surf music to Latin, breakbeat to dancehall) that gets a punky-funky crowd fired up for extended dance-a-thons. Live acts and the relaxed beer garden are bonuses.

>CHARLOTTENBURG

During the Cold War, ritzy Charlottenburg was the glittering heart of West Berlin. This is where the jet set wallowed in the fruits of capitalism, gorging on steak and lobster in chic restaurants, debating politics in smoke-filled cafes and disco-foxing at cocaine-addled parties in glamorous Ku'damm haunts.

Alas, after reunification, the district almost instantly lost its edge as artists and the avant-garde moved on to uncharted terrain once trapped behind the Wall. The City West, meanwhile, was left to give off the self-satisfied air of middle-aged burghers content with the status quo. Experimentation is elsewhere.

City planners hope that two mega-projects coming online soon will bring the spotlight back on Charlottenburg. The world's largest Ferris wheel should be making its merry rounds by the time you're reading this. And nearby, construction is underway on a skyline-changing 118m high-rise called the Zoofenster.

Fortunately, Charlottenburg's main draws have never been in danger of disappearing. You can still catch a cabaret at Bar jeder Vernunft, star-soprano Anna Netrebko at the Deutsche Oper or international jazz greats at A-Trane. Shopaholics can get their kicks on Kurfürstendamm, 'royal' groupies continue to delight in Schloss Charlottenburg and, though now fully grown, polar bear Knut still delights with his antics at the Berlin Zoo.

CHARLOTTENBURG

☉ SEE
Aquarium 1 F2
Berlin Zoo – Budapester
   Strasse Entrance 2 F2
Berlin Zoo –
   Hardenbergplatz
   Entrance 3 E1
Kaiser-Wilhelm-
   Gedächtniskirche 4 F2
Käthe-Kollwitz-
   Museum 5 D3
Museum für
   Fotografie 6 E2
Story of Berlin 7 D3

⌂ SHOP
Galerie Michael Schultz 8 A2
Hautnah 9 D3
Stilwerk 10 D2

⍾ EAT
Bond 11 D1
Brel 12 D2
Café Wintergarten im
   Literaturhaus 13 D3
Moon Thai 14 C2
Mr Hai & Friends 15 D2

☷ DRINK
Café Richter 16 B3
Galerie Bremer 17 D4
Puro Skylounge 18 F2
Schleusenkrug 19 F1

★ PLAY
A-Trane 20 C2
Bar jeder Vernunft 21 E4
Deutsche Oper Berlin ..22 B1
Schiller Theater 23 C1

NEIGHBOURHOODS

CHARLOTTENBURG

SEE

BERLIN ZOO & AQUARIUM

☎ 254 010; www.zoo-berlin.de; Hardenbergplatz 8; adult/child/student zoo or aquarium €12/6/9, zoo & aquarium €18/9/14, family tickets available; ⏰ 9am-7pm mid-Mar–mid-Sep, 9am-6pm mid-Sep–mid-Oct, 9am-5pm mid-Oct–mid-Mar; ⊕ ⓡ Zoologischer Garten; ♿

Germany's oldest animal park opened in 1844 with furry and feathered critters from the royal family's private reserve. Today some 14,000 creatures from all continents, 1500 species in total, make their home here. Knut, the polar bear born in the zoo in 2006, and Bao Bao, a giant panda from China, are among the biggest celebrities. At the adjacent **Aquarium** (www.aquarium-berlin.de; enter at Budapester Strasse 32) dancing jelly fish, iridescent poison frogs and real-life 'Nemo' clownfish thrill even the most Playstation-jaded youngsters.

OLYMPICS UNDER THE SWASTIKA

When the International Olympics Committee awarded the 1936 Games to Germany in 1931, the gesture was supposed to welcome the country back into the world community after its defeat in WWI and the humiliating 1920s. No one could have known that only two years later, in 1933, the fledgling democracy would be helmed by a megalomaniacal dictator with an agenda to take over the world.

As Hitler opened the Games on 1 August in Berlin's Olympic Stadium, prisoners were putting the finishing touches on the first large-scale Nazi concentration camp at Sachsenhausen just north of town. Only while the Olympic flame was flickering were political and racial persecution suspended and anti-Semitic signs taken down.

Even though it was put through a total modernisation for the 2006 FIFA World Cup, it's hard not to remember the Nazi legacy when visiting the **Olympic Stadium** (☎ 2500 2322; www.olympiastadion-berlin.de; Olympischer Platz 3; self-guided tour adult/concession/family €4/3/8, guided general tours in German €8/7/16, Hertha BSC tour €10/8.50/24; ⏰ 9am-8pm Jun–mid-Sep, 9am-7pm mid-Mar–May & mid-Sep–Oct, 9am-4pm Nov–mid-Mar on nonevent days; ⊕ ⓡ Olympiastadion; ♿). The bombastic bulk of the Colosseum-like structure undoubtedly remains, although it's now softened by the addition of a spidery oval roof. These days, the more than 74,000 seats are often filled with fans cheering on the local Hertha BSC football (soccer) team, the Pope or Madonna. Call ahead to make sure the stadium is open for touring. Multilingual audioguides are available for an additional €2.50.

For stunning bird's-eye views of the stadium, head to 77m-high **Glockenturm** (Clock Tower; ☎ 305 8123; adult/concession €3.50/1.50; ⏰ 9am-6pm; ⓡ Pichelsberg), which also has a fascinating exhibit about the 1936 Olympic Games and the history of the grounds.

'Rotten tooth': Kaiser-Wilhelm-Gedächtniskirche

⊙ KAISER-WILHELM-GEDÄCHTNISKIRCHE

Emperor-William-Memorial-Church; ☎ 218 5023; www.gedaechtniskirche-berlin.de; Breitscheidplatz; ⏰ 9am-7pm; ⊙ Kurfürstendamm; ♿
The bombed-out tower of this landmark church serves as an anti-war memorial, standing quiet and dignified amid the roaring traffic. It was once a real beauty as you'll be able to tell from the before and after pictures on the ground floor. Also duck into the modern annexe with its incredible midnight-blue glass walls and giant floating Jesus.

⊙ KÄTHE-KOLLWITZ-MUSEUM

☎ 882 5210; www.kaethe-kollwitz.de; Fasanenstrasse 24; adult/concession €5/2.50; ⏰ 11am-6pm; ⊙ Uhlandstrasse
This exquisite museum is devoted to Käthe Kollwitz, one of the greatest German female artists, whose social and political awareness lent a tortured power to her work. After losing both her son and grandson on the battlefields of Europe, death and motherhood became recurring themes. Also see Neue Wache (p48) and Kollwitzplatz (p90).

⊙ MUSEUM FÜR FOTOGRAFIE

Museum of Photography; ☎ 3186 4825; www.smb.spk-berlin.de/mf; Jebensstrasse 2; adult/under 16/concession incl same-day admission to Museum Berggruen & Sammlung Scharf-Gerstenberg €8/free/4, last 4hr Thu free; ⏰ 10am-6pm Tue, Wed & Fri-Sun, to 10pm Thu; ⊙ ⊛ Zoologischer Garten; ♿
Built as a Prussian officers' casino and later used as an art library, this imposing neoclassical building now houses a museum of photography. Changing exhibits of international stature are presented upstairs in the Kaisersaal (Emperor's Hall), a barrel-vaulted banqueting hall, while the ground floor is dedicated to the works of Helmut Newton, the Berlin-born *enfant terrible* of fashion photography.

SCHLOSS CHARLOTTENBURG & AROUND

The grandest of Berlin's surviving nine former royal residences is **Schloss Charlottenburg** (Charlottenburg Palace; ☎ 320 911; www.spsg.de; Spandauer Damm; day pass €12/9; 🚇 Richard-Wagner-Platz, then 🚌 145). It consists of the main palace and two outbuildings in the lovely Schlossgarten (park). Each building charges separate admission, but it's best to invest in the *Tageskarte*, which gives you an entire day to see everything except the Neuer Flügel (New Wing). To avoid the worst crowds, come early on weekends and in summer. A palace visit is easily combined with a spin around the trio of nearby museums, described below.

The Schloss (palace) began as the summer residence of Sophie Charlotte, wife of King Friedrich I. Their baroque living quarters in the palace's oldest section, the **Altes Schloss** (Old Palace; ☎ 320 911; adult/concession incl guided tour or audioguide €10/7; ⌚ 10am-6pm Tue-Sun Apr-Oct, to 5pm Nov-Mar; ♿), are an extravaganza in stucco, brocade and overall opulence. Admission includes access to the upstairs apartment of Friedrich Wilhelm IV.

The most beautiful rooms, though, are the flamboyant private chambers of Frederick the Great in the **Neuer Flügel** (☎ 320 911; adult/concession incl audioguide €6/5; ⌚ 10am-6pm Wed-Mon Apr-Oct, to 5pm Nov-Mar; ♿), designed by starchitect du jour Georg Wenzeslaus von Knobelsdorff in 1746. The austere neoclassical ones of his successor, Friedrich Wilhelm II, in the same wing, pale in comparison. Adjacent to the Neuer Flügel, the Schinkel-designed **Neuer Pavillon** (New Pavilion; ☎ 3209 1443) served as a summer retreat of Friedrich Wilhelm III and now houses paintings from the Romantic and Biedermeier periods. Closed for renovation during our visit, it should have reopened by now.

In fine weather, a spin around the sprawling **palace park** with its shady walkways, flower beds and manicured lawns is a must. In the northeast corner, you'll stumble upon the pint-sized palace called **Belvedere** (☎ 3209 1445; adult/concession €3/2.50; ⌚ 10am-6pm Tue-Sun Apr-Oct, noon-4pm Tue-Sun Nov-Mar), now an elegant setting for porcelain masterpieces by the royal manufacturer KPM.

Across the carp pond, the marble sarcophagi in the sombre **Mausoleum** (☎ 3209 1446; adult/concession €2/1.50; ⌚ 10am-5pm Tue-Sun Apr-Oct) are the final pad of big-shot royals such as Emperor Wilhelm I and his wife. For more on Schloss Charlottenburg, see p12.

South of the palace, the **Museum Berggruen** (☎ 3269 5815; www.smb.museum/mb; Schlossstrasse 1; adult/under 16/concession €8/free/4, last 4hr Thu free; ⌚ 10am-6pm Tue-Sun; ♿) exhibits major classical modern art with a special focus on Picasso, Klee, Matisse and Giacometti.

The Berggruen ticket is also good for same-day admission to the **Sammlung Scharf-Gerstenberg** (☎ 3435 7315; www.smb.museum/ssg; Schlossstrasse 70; adult/under 16/concession €8/free/4, last 4hr Thu free; ⌚ 10am-6pm Tue-Sun; ♿), and vice versa. This stellar museum trains the spotlight on surrealist artists with an impressive body of works by Magritte, Max Ernst, Dalí, Dubuffet and their 18th-century precursors such as Goya and Piranesi. (Note that you can also use the ticket to get into the Museum für Fotografie, p135.)

Also pop by the **Bröhan Museum** (☎ 3269 0600; www.broehan-museum.de; Schlossstrasse 1a; admission €6; ⌚ 10am-6pm Tue-Sun; ♿) for an outstanding collection of furniture and decorative objects from the art nouveau, art deco and functionalism periods.

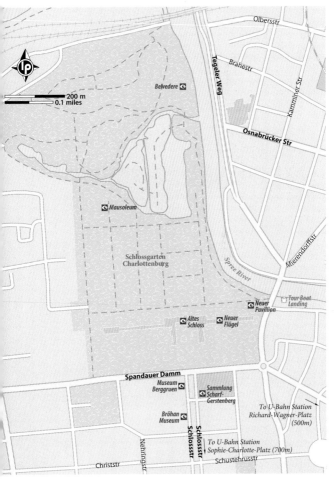

Römer + Römer
Artists, represented by Galerie Michael Schultz (opposite)

You both studied with AR Penck at the Düsseldorf Art Academy. Why did you move to Berlin? The structures here are not so rigid. There's more movement, more international impulses and a multicultural population. **What's your favourite district?** Kreuzberg, where we live. It's the most artistic neighbourhood where many different lifestyles flourish and there's still a gritty vibe left from the punk and squatter days. **Do the arts get support in Berlin?** Yes, there are galleries willing to take on young artists and also many unconventional spaces where you can show your art. **Many of your paintings depict scenes in Berlin. How do you choose your motifs?** We look for scenes that reflect daily life but are not clichéd. They have to have a certain scurrility and intensity. **What are your favourite places for viewing art?** Hamburger Bahnhof (p78), Martin-Gropius-Bau (p116) and Haus der Kulturen der Welt (p79).

STORY OF BERLIN
☎ 8872 0100; www.story-of-berlin.de;
Kurfürstendamm 207-208; adult/
concession/family €9.80/8/21; ⏰ 10am-
8pm, last admission & bunker tour 6pm;
Ⓜ Uhlandstrasse; ♿
This multimedia museum breaks
down 800 years of Berlin history
into bite-sized chunks that are
easy to swallow but still sub-
stantial enough to be satisfying.
The Cold War era comes creep-
ily to life during a tour of a still
fully functional atomic bunker
beneath the building. You'll find
the entrance inside the Ku'damm
Karree mall.

🛍 SHOP
Charlottenburg's shopping spine
is Kurfürstendamm and its eastern
extension, Tauentzienstrasse.
Kantstrasse, meanwhile, is the
go-to zone for home designs.
Connecting side streets such as
Bleibtreustrasse and Fasanenstrasse have their share of upscale
indie and designer boutiques,
bookstores and galleries.

🏠 FLOHMARKT STRASSE DES 17 JUNI *Flea Market*
Strasse des 17 Juni; ⏰ 10am-5pm Sat &
Sun; 🚊 Tiergarten
Some people think this big market
west of the Tiergarten S-Bahn sta-

tion is the cat's pyjamas but we're
not impressed by the fact that
bargains here are as rare as tulips
in Tonga. Still, it's one of the best
places for quality Berlin memorabilia, stuff from granny's closet
and jewellery.

🏠 GALERIE MICHAEL SCHULTZ *Art Gallery*
☎ 319 9130; www.galerie-schultz.de;
Mommsenstrasse 34; ⏰ 11am-7pm
Mon-Fri, 10am-2pm Sat;
🚊 Charlottenburg
This well-established gallery
represents such contemporary
German hot shots as AR Penck
and Georg Baselitz. It also works
with internationally well-known
Berlin-based figurative painters
of the next generation, includ-
ing Cornelia Schleime, SEO and
Römer + Römer, a Russian-
German artist couple that we've
interviewed (see opposite).

🏠 HAUTNAH *Erotica*
☎ 882 3434; www.hautnahberlin.de,
in German; Uhlandstrasse 170;
⏰ noon-8pm Mon-Fri, 11am-4pm Sat;
Ⓜ Uhlandstrasse
Those who like to worship at the
altar of hedonism should check
out this three-floor emporium of
erotica. Fetishistas can stock up on
latex bustiers, rubber bodysuits,

NEIGHBOURHOODS

CHARLOTTENBURG

sex toys, themed get-ups and vertiginous footwear, along with an interesting wine selection (Marquis de Sade champagne anyone?).

⬚ **STILWERK** *Interior Design*
☎ 315 150; www.stilwerk.de, in German; Kantstrasse 17; ⏰ 10am-7pm Mon-Sat; 🚇 Savignyplatz
If this four-floor temple of good taste doesn't get your decorative juices flowing, nothing will. Everything for home and hearth is here, from sugar bowls to chairs and kitchens, all by such top names as Alessi, Bang & Olufsen, Philippe Starck, Ligne Roset et al.

🍴 **EAT**
🍴 **BOND** *International*   €€
☎ 5096 8844; www.bond-berlin.de; Knesebeckstrasse 16; ⏰ noon-3pm & 6pm-midnight Mon-Fri, 6pm-midnight Sat, 10am-11pm Sun; 🚇 Savignyplatz
If you're in Berlin *On Her Majesty's Secret Service,* you'll impress *The Living Daylights* out of your date at this chill designer den decked out in sensuous royal purple, ebony and gold. The standard menu is heavy on, well, standards such as grilled meats, club sandwiches and burgers. All are capably executed, and the specials are worth trying, too. Cheap

it ain't, but remember, *You Only Live Twice*.

🍴 **BREL** *Belgian*   €€
☎ 3180 0020; www.cafebrel.de, in German; Savignyplatz 1; ⏰ 9am-1am; 🚇 Savignyplatz; ✗ 🛜
Belgian cult crooner Jacques Brel is the namesake of this smart-existentialist corner bistro located in a former bordello. During the day, bleary-eyed boho regulars place orders for coffee and croissants, while suits and tourists take advantage of the three-course €9 lunches. During *moules et frites* (mussels and French fries) season (September to February) the place is often packed with Belgian expats. Breakfast is available until 6pm.

🍴 **CAFÉ WINTERGARTEN IM LITERATURHAUS**
Cafe   €€
☎ 882 5414; www.literaturhaus -berlin.de, in German; Fasanenstrasse 23; ⏰ 9.30am-1am; 🚇 Uhlandstrasse; ✗ 🅅
You don't have to be the literary type in order to enjoy a coffee or light lunch at this genteel art nouveau villa. Get a dose of Old Berlin flair in the gracefully stucco-ornamented rooms or, in fine weather, repair to the idyllic garden. Breakfast till 2pm.

🍴 MOON THAI
Thai €€

☎ 3180 9743; www.moonthai-restau rant.com, in German; Kantstrasse 32; ⏱ noon-midnight; 🚇 Savigny-platz; 🍴 V

This is our favourite Thai nosh spot in the western city. Sunset-coloured walls with exotic art create an upbeat ambience that's a perfect foil for dishes so perky they might get you off your Pro-zac. Anything revolving around duck or squid gets top marks.

🍴 MR HAI & FRIENDS
Vietnamese €€

☎ 3759 1200; www.mrhai.de; Savigny-platz 1; ⏱ 11am-midnight; 🚇 Savigny-platz; 🍴 V

Watch the chef hats bob up and down through the window of the show kitchen at this stylish restau-rant that usually gets jam-packed with trendy locals lusting after soups, spring rolls, satays, wok combinations and other tasties, all made fresh and treated with an aromatic balm of spices. Reserva-tions advised.

🍸 DRINK
🍸 CAFÉ RICHTER
Cafe

☎ 324 3722; Giesebrechtstras-se 22; ⏱ 7am-7pm Mon-Sat, 9am-7pm Sun; 🚇 Adenauerplatz; 🍴

It may look like your grandma's cafe but a quick scan of the crowd reveals the cross-generational appeal of Richter's jazzy java and homemade cakes. Truly an authentic throwback to the West Berlin of yesteryear.

🍸 GALERIE BREMER *Bar*
☎ 881 4908; www.galerie-bremer.de, in German; Fasanenstrasse 37; ⏱ from 8pm Mon-Sat; 🚇 Spichernstrasse

Entering this tiny bar tucked behind an art gallery feels like slip-ping into a swanky '20s speakeasy. The air, though, is rather genteel, grown-up and completely devoid of debauchery. Vintage fans will adore the original interior by Ber-liner Philharmonie architect Hans Scharoun.

🍸 PURO SKYLOUNGE
Bar-Club

☎ 2636 7875; www.puro-berlin.de, in German; Tauentzienstrasse 11; ⏱ from 8pm Tue-Sat; 🚇 Kurfürstendamm

Puro has quite literally raised the bar in Charlottenburg – by moving it to the 20th floor of the Europa Center, that is – with predictably fabulous views. It's a great place if you want to trade classic Berlin funky-trash for a high-heeled Chanel world. Mind-erasers of choice are Moët, martinis and cosmos. Dress up, or forget about it.

☷ SCHLEUSENKRUG
Beer Garden

☎ 313 9909; www.schleusenkrug.de, in German; Müller-Breslau-Strasse; ⏱ from 10am; ⊙ ☷ Zoologischer Garten; ✗

Watch the riverboats slip into the lock that gives this canalside beer garden its name. From morn' to midnight, punters from all walks of life share pints of Pils and simple, filling treats beneath the shady beech trees. Smoking OK outside.

★ PLAY

☆ **A-TRANE** *Jazz Club*

☎ 313 2550; www.a-trane.de, in German; Bleibtreustrasse 1; cover €5-20; ⏱ 9pm-2am Sun-Thu, open end Fri & Sat; ☷ Savignyplatz; ✗

Herbie Hancock and Diana Krall have anointed the stage of this intimate jazz club but mostly it's emerging talent bringing their A-game to the A-Trane. Entry is free on Monday when local boy Andreas Schmidt shows off his dexterous skills, and after 12.30am

What's on at Bar jeder Vernunft? Posters entice with gigs past and present

on Saturday for the late-night jam session.

⭐ BAR JEDER VERNUNFT
Cabaret
☎ 883 1582; www.bar-jeder-vernunft
.de, in German; Schaperstrasse 24; tickets
vary; Ⓢ Spichernstrasse; ✗
Life's still a cabaret at this intimate
1912 art nouveau mirrored tent,
which puts on song-and-dance
shows, comedy and *chanson*
evenings plus intermittently the
famous *Cabaret* cult musical itself. If
you just want to see the place, have
a postshow drink in the piano bar
(opening hours depend on what's
on). Enter via the parking lot.

⭐ DEUTSCHE OPER BERLIN
Opera
☎ 343 8401; www.deutscheoperberlin
.de; Bismarckstrasse 35; tickets €14-120;
Ⓤ Deutsche Oper
Berlin's largest opera house may
look unsightly but its acoustics are
the stuff of every tenor's dreams.
Its first-ever female boss, Kirsten
Harms, has helped update its
image and even generated a little
controversy with a production of
Mozart's *Idomeneo* that featured
the severed heads of Mohammed,
Jesus, Buddha and Neptune…
All operas are performed in the
original language.

>SCHÖNEBERG

Residential Schöneberg has a radical pedigree rooted in the squatter days of the '80s but now flaunts a relaxed middle-class identity. There are no major conventional sights in this former West Berlin borough, but the KaDeWe department store – Berlin's equivalent of London's Harrods and New York's Bloomingdale's – is a key attraction. Schöneberg's laid-back character best reveals itself on a stroll from Nollendorfplatz to Hauptstrasse, via Maassenstrasse, Goltzstrasse and Akazienstrasse, which are lined with indie boutiques, comfy cafes and smooth bars. The route skirts Winterfeldtplatz square, which draws eager throngs to its bountiful Saturday farmers market.

Near Nollendorfplatz, the gay crowd has partied on Motzstrasse and Fuggerstrasse since the 1920s, cheered on by the ghost of Anglo-American author Christopher Isherwood who lived nearby. One local gal who liked to party with the 'boyz' was Marlene Dietrich. She's buried not far from Rathaus Schöneberg, the town hall where John F Kennedy gave his morale-boosting *Ich bin ein Berliner!* speech back in 1963. Schöneberg shows its most multiculti face around Hauptstrasse 155, northeast of the Rathaus, where David Bowie and Iggy Pop shared a flat in the late '70s.

SCHÖNEBERG

🛍 SHOP			🍸 DRINK			⭐ PLAY		
KaDeWe	1	A2	Green Door	6	B3	Connection	9	A2
			Heile Welt	7	B2			
🍴 EAT			Mutter	8	B3			
Habibi	2	C3						
More	3	B2						
Renger-Patzsch	4	B5						
Trattoria á Muntagnola	5	A2						

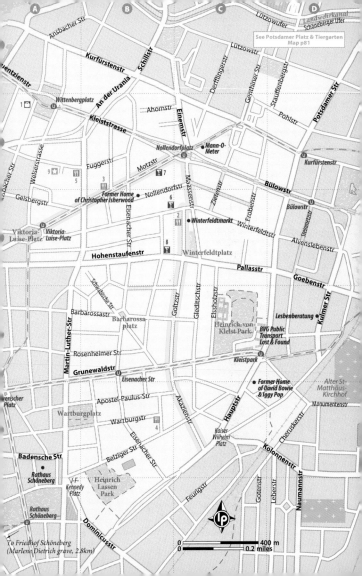

A
B
C
D

Ansbacher Str

Kurfürstenstr
Schillstr

Lützowufer
Lützowstr

Schöneberger Ufer
Landwehrkanal

See Potsdamer Platz & Tiergarten
Map p81

Derfflingerstr
Genthiner Str
Staufenbergstr

Potsdamer Str

1 🏛
Wittenbergplatz
An der Urania
Kleiststrasse
Ahornstr
Einemstr

Pohlstr

entzienstr

...bacher Str

Welserstrasse
Fuggerstr
9 📮
5 🍴
3 🍴
Motzstr
7 🍴

Nollendorfplatz
Mann-O-
Meter

Maaßenstr

Kurfürstenstr

Bülowstr

Bülowstr

Geisbergstr

Former Home
of Christopher Isherwood
Nollendorfstr
Eisenacher Str
6 🍴

Zietenstr
Frobenstr

Steinmetzstr

Viktoria-
Luise-Platz
Viktoria-
Luise-Platz
2 🍴
• Winterfeldtmarkt

Winterfeldtstr

Alvenslebenstr

Hohenstaufenstr
8 🍴
Winterfeldtplatz

Pallasstr

Goebenstr

Schwäbische Str
Barbarossastr
Barbarossa-
platz

Golzstr
Gleditschstr
Elßholzstr

Heinrich-von-
Kleist-Park

Kulmer Str
• Lesbenberatung

BVG Public
Transport
Lost & Found

Martin-Luther-Str

Rosenheimer Str

Kleistpark

Grunewaldstr
Eisenacher Str

Former Home
of David Bowie
& Iggy Pop

Hauptstr

Alter St-
Matthäus-
Kirchhof
Monumentenstr

...erischer
Platz

Apostel-Paulus-Str
Wartburgplatz
Wartburgstr
4 🍴

Akazienstr

Eisenacher Str

Kaiser
Wilhelm
Platz

Cheruskerstr

Naumannstr

Badensche Str

Belziger Str
Eisenacher Str

Kolonnenstr

Gotenstr
Leberstr

Rathaus
Schöneberg

J-F-
Kennedy
Platz

Heinrich
Lassen
Park

Feurigstr

Rathaus
Schöneberg

To Friedhof Schöneberg
(Marlene Dietrich grave, 2.8km)

Dominicusstr

LP

0   400 m
0   0.2 miles

SHOP

KADEWE *Department Store*
☎ 212 10; www.kadewe-berlin.de;
Tauentzienstrasse 21-24; ⏱ 10am-8pm
Mon-Thu, to 9pm Fri, 9.30am-8pm Sat;
🚇 Wittenbergplatz

This century-old department
store has an assortment so vast
that a pirate-style campaign is the
best way to plunder its bounty. If
pushed for time, at least hurry up
to the legendary gourmet food
hall on the 6th floor.

EAT

HABIBI *Middle Eastern*　€
☎ 215 3332; Goltzstrasse 24;
⏱ 11am-3am Sun-Thu, to 5am Fri &
Sat; 🚇 Nollendorfplatz

This perennially popular snack
shack makes soul-sustaining
felafel that pairs perfectly with a
freshly pressed carrot juice.

MORE
International　€€
☎ 2363 5702; www.more-berlin.de;
Motzstrasse 28; ⏱ 9am-midnight;
🚇 Nollendorfplatz

Finally, a designer den with
substance. Sip a Prosecco on the
rocks while casually scanning
the crowd for pretty boyz and
anticipating platters of perfectly
prepared beef olives with truffled
mashed potato or a succulent
rump steak dressed with gorgon-
zola. Always busy, and for good
reason.

KaDeWe mega-department store: Berlin's answer to Harrods and Bloomingdale's

🍴 **RENGER-PATZSCH**
German €€
☎ 784 2059; www.renger-patzsch.com; Wartburgstrasse 54; ⏲ 6-11.30pm; Ⓔ Eisenacher Strasse

Named for an early-20th-century German photographer, this off-the-beaten-path restaurant exudes a refreshing earthiness that matches its robust menu. Try big-hunger mains such as red-wine-braised ox cheeks or snack on flawless *Flammekuche* (Alsatian-style pizza).

🍴 **TRATTORIA Á MUNTAGNOLA** *Italian* €€
☎ 211 6642; www.muntagnola.de; Fuggerstrasse 27; ⏲ 5pm-midnight; Ⓔ Wittenbergplatz; ♿

Everybody feels like family at this convivial trattoria where dishes burst with the feisty flavours of southern Italy's sun-baked Basilicata region. Many ingredients are imported straight from the Boot and turned into crispy pizzas, homemade pastas and rustic offerings such as garlic-braised rabbit. Nice touch: the olive oil trolley.

🍸 **DRINK**
🍸 **GREEN DOOR** *Bar*
☎ 215 2515; www.greendoor.de; Winterfeldtstrasse 50; ⏲ 6pm-3am Mon-Thu, to 4am Fri & Sat; Ⓔ Nollendorfplatz

A long line of renowned mixologists has tended at this oh-so-stylish establishment. They make

you ring the doorbell to gain entry, but once inside you may find it hard to leave the comfy surrounds.

🍸 **HEILE WELT** *Gay Bar*
☎ 2191 7507; Motzstrasse 5; ⏲ from 6pm; Ⓔ Nollendorfplatz

Chic yet laid-back, the 'Perfect World' gets high marks for its international flair, flirt factor and sensuous fur-covered walls. It's a great first stop before launching into a raunchy night on the razzle.

🍸 **MUTTER** *Cafe-Bar*
☎ 216 4990; Hohenstaufenstrasse 4; ⏲ from 10am; Ⓔ Eisenacher Strasse; ✗

'Mother', as this tavern is named, does indeed take good care of its children. Most are chatty students and older locals who keep the two gold-tinted rooms perennially packed. There's Thai and sushi on the menu, but you'll find better eateries on nearby Goltzstrasse.

⭐ **PLAY**
⭐ **CONNECTION** *Gay Club*
☎ 218 1432; www.connection-berlin.de, in German; Fuggerstrasse 33; cover varies; ⏲ Fri & Sat; Ⓔ Wittenbergplatz

This classic gay disco was a techno pioneer way back in the '80s and it hasn't lost a beat. The labyrinth of underground darkrooms is legendary, while upstairs resident DJ Serge Laurent and guests heat up two floors of dance action.

Are you a clubber, a history nut, an architecture aficionado, an art collector, a foodie or a hunter of the quirky and bizarre? Berlin is a veritable palimpsest of discoveries no matter whether your interests run to the highbrow or the gutter. Just keep an open mind and enjoy.

> Accommodation	150
> Food	152
> Gay & Lesbian	154
> Galleries	156
> Jewish Berlin	158
> The Berlin Wall	160
> Back to the GDR	162
> Clubbing	163
> Drinking	164
> Fashion	165
> Kids	166
> Museums	167
> Music	168
> Sex & Fetish	169
> Shopping	170

Remembering the Nazi horrors of Jewish Berlin (p158): memorial at Grunewald station's platform 17

ACCOMMODATION

Berlin boasts more than 100,000 beds and more are scheduled to come online. Just about every international chain has a flagship in Berlin but more interesting options abound – you can sleep in a former bank, boat or factory, in the home of a silent-movie diva, in a 'flying bed' or even a coffin. Standards are high but fierce competition keeps prices low compared with other capital cities. In fact, Berlin is nirvana for budget travellers. The hostel scene is the most vibrant in Europe and consists of both classic backpacker hostels with alternative flair, and modern 'flashpacker' hostels catering for lifestyle-savvy city-breakers with greater needs for privacy and security.

Of late, hostels have been getting competition from budget designer hotels, such as the Motel One chain. In response, hostel owners have opened their own versions, such as the Circus Hotel in Mitte and the Meininger City Hostel & Hotel in Prenzlauer Berg.

Design-minded travellers with deeper pockets can choose from plenty of lifestyle and boutique hotels as well as *Kunsthotels* (art hotels), which are either designed by artists and/or liberally sprinkled with original art.

Nostalgic types seeking unique 'Old Berlin' flavour should check into a charismatic B&B, called *Hotel-Pension* or simply *Pension*. They typically occupy one or several floors of historic residential buildings and offer local colour and personal attention galore. Amenities, room size and decor vary; many have been updated and feature wi-fi, cable TV and other mod cons.

Also increasingly popular among short-term visitors are furnished flats that give you the benefit of space, privacy and independence, making them especially attractive to families and self-caterers.

Hotels & Hostels

Need a place to stay? Find and book it at lonelyplanet.com. Over 363 properties are featured for Berlin – each personally visited, thoroughly reviewed and happily recommended by a Lonely Planet author. From hostels to high-end hotels, we've hunted out the places that will bring you unique and special experiences. Read independent reviews by authors and other travellers, and get practical information including amenities, maps and photos. Then reserve your room simply and securely via Hotels & Hostels – our online booking service. It's all at lonelyplanet.com/hotels.

WHERE TO STAY

Berlin's excellent public transport puts you within easy reach of everything, so you don't have to be too fussy about where to stay. However, if you enjoy being within walking distance of the trophy sights, find a place in Mitte or around Potsdamer Platz, although you'll pay for the privilege. The high-end international chains cluster around Gendarmenmarkt and Potsdamer Platz, while their smaller arty cousins and a few hostels prefer the quiet side streets north of Unter den Linden and in the Scheunenviertel.

Charlottenburg generally offers excellent value and the greatest concentration of midrange abodes. This is where traditional Old Berlin *Pensionen* rub shoulders with urban-hipster temples, with a sprinkling of four-star business hotels thrown in. Kreuzberg, Mitte, Friedrichshain and Prenzlauer Berg are all good areas to pitch yourself if you want to be close to nightlife.

WEB RESOURCES

Berlin has lots of beds but the best ones often sell out, so make reservations, especially around major holidays and events. A good place to start is Lonely Planet's accommodation service (see boxed text, opposite). Locally try **Berlin Tourismus Marketing** (☎ 250 025; www.visitberlin.de), which books rooms at partner hotels for free. For last-minute bargains check www.hrs.de, for hostels try www.hostelworld.com, www.gomio.com or www.hostel-berlin.de, and for holiday flats check out www.tc-apartments-berlin.de or www.all-berlin-apartments.com.

BEST FOR CHARM & ROMANCE
> Hotel Askanischer Hof (www.askanischer-hof.de)
> Honigmond Garden Hotel (www.honigmond-berlin.de)
> Ackselhaus & Blue Home (www.ackselhaus.de)

BEST LUXE ESCAPES
> Hotel de Rome (www.hotelderome.com)
> Mandala Hotel (www.themandala.de)
> Louisa's Place (www.louisas-place.de)

BEST ART & DESIGNER DENS
> Arte Luise Kunsthotel (www.luise-berlin.com)
> Arcotel John F (www.arcotel.at)
> Propeller Island City Lodge (www.propeller-island.de)

BEST HOSTELS
> Circus Hostel (www.circus-berlin.de)
> East Seven Hostel (www.eastseven.de)
> Meininger City Hostel & Hotel (www.meininger-hostels.de)
> Wombat's City Hostel Berlin (www.wombats-hostels.com)

FOOD

If you crave traditional comfort food, you'll certainly find plenty of places to indulge in roast pork knuckles, smoked pork chops or calves liver in Berlin. These days, though, 'typical' local fare is lighter, healthier, creative and more likely to come from gourmet kitchens, organic eateries and a UN worth of ethnic restaurants.

Even those finicky Michelin testers have confirmed that Berlin is ripe for the culinary big league by awarding coveted stars to 11 chefs, including those helming the stoves at Weinbar Rutz (p71) and Facil (p86). Fortunately, you don't need deep pockets to put your tummy into a state of contentment. In fact, some of the best eating is done in neighbourhood restaurants such as Café Jacques (p103) that feel as snug and comfortable as a warm mitten.

Berlin's multicultural tapestry has brought the world's foods to town, from Austrian schnitzel to Zambian zebra steak. Even finding decent sushi has become quite easy, and vegetarian (even vegan) restaurants are sprouting as fast as alfalfa, as are *bio* eateries where dishes are prepared from organic and locally sourced ingredients. In fact, Berlin is home to Germany's first organic fast-food restaurant, Yellow Sunshine (p105), and first climate-neutral restaurant, Foodorama (p118).

Two more hot trends have emerged in recent times. First, Asian lifestyle eateries. The concept – steaming soups plus a few daily changing specials served in designer ambience – was pioneered a few years back by Monsieur Vuong (p70) and has since been copied *ad nauseum*. Also popular is 'guerrilla dining': secret supper clubs held in private homes for just a few weeks or at irregular intervals and often accessible by invitation only. At the time of writing, one semipublic venue was the **Shy Chef** (http://theshychef .wordpress.com).

Berliners are big on breakfast and many cafes serve them until well into the afternoon. All-you-can-eat Sunday brunch buffets are a social institution in their own right and provide the ideal excuse to recap Saturday night's shenanigans at leisure.

International fast-food chains are ubiquitous, of course, but the most beloved home-grown snack is the humble *Currywurst* – a slivered, subtly spiced pork sausage swimming in tomato sauce and sprinkled with curry powder. Another local invention is the *döner* (doner kebab), a lightly toasted bread pocket stuffed with thinly shaved veal or chicken and salad and doused with garlicky yoghurt sauce.

BEST QUICK EATS
> Burgermeister (p103)
> Curry 36 (p118)
> Dolores (p60)
> Schlemmerbuffet (p96)

BEST HEALTHY EATS
> Hans Wurst (p95)
> Monsieur Vuong (p70)
> Yellow Sunshine (p105)

BEST TRADITIONAL FARE
> Henne (p104)
> Oderquelle (p95)
> Schusterjunge (p96)
> Schwarzwaldstuben (p70)
> Zur Letzten Instanz (p60)

BEST INVENTIVE FARE
> Fellas (p93)
> Hartmanns (p103)
> Horváth (p104)
> Uma (p53)

Top left Mmmm...*döner* (doner kebab): the more garlic, the better

GAY & LESBIAN

Berlin's legendary liberalism has spawned one of the world's biggest, most fabulous and diverse gay, lesbian, bisexual and transgender (GLBT) playgrounds. Anything goes in 'Homopolis' (and we *do* mean anything), from the highbrow to the hands-on, the bourgeois to the bizarre, the mainstream to the flamboyant.

The closest Berlin comes to a 'gay ghetto' is Schöneberg, where the rainbow flag has proudly flown since the heady 1920s, especially on Motzstrasse (Map p145, B2) and Fuggerstrasse (Map p145, B2). Prenzlauer Berg has the hippest gay scene in eastern Berlin, even though it's fairly well spread out across the entire district. Hubs include Greifenhagener Strasse (Map p89, B2), Gleimstrasse (Map p89, B2) and Schönhauser Allee (Map p89, B2). Kreuzberg has more of an alt-flavoured feel (check out Oranienstrasse, Map p101, A2; and Mehringdamm, Map p113, B4), while Friedrichshain's small but up-and-coming scene is still predominantly student-driven.

Berlin's gayscape runs the entire spectrum from mellow cafes, campy bars and cinemas to saunas, cruising areas, clubs with darkrooms and all-out sex venues. In fact, sex and sexuality are entirely everyday matters to the unshockable city folks and there are very few, if any, itches that can't be quite openly and legally scratched. As elsewhere, gay men have more options for having fun, but grrrrls – from lipstick lesbians to hippie chicks to bad-ass dykes – won't feel left out either.

Except for the hard-core places, gay spots get their share of opposite-sex and straight patrons, drawn by gay friends, the fabulousness of the venues, abundant eye candy and, for women in gay bars, a nonthreatening atmosphere.

The freezine *Siegessäule* (www.siegessaeule.de, in German) is the Berlin bible for all things GLBT and also publishes the free English/German booklet *Out in Berlin* (www.out-in-berlin.de), available at the Berlin Infostores (p188). *Blu Magazine* (www.blue.fm, in German) comes in print and online versions and has searchable up-to-the-minute location and party listings. The bimonthly *L-Mag* (www.l-mag.de, in German) caters for lesbians.

Berlin's queer scene suffered tremendously under the Nazis. Gays were socially ostracised and often sent to concentration camps where the Pink Triangle identified their sexual orientation. A memorial on Ebertstrasse

(Map p43, A3) commemorates their suffering. There's also a plaque outside the Nollendorfplatz U-Bahn station (Map p145, C2).

Since 2001 Berlin has been governed by an openly gay mayor, Klaus Wowereit, who outed himself by saying 'I'm gay, and that's OK', which has since become a slogan in the community. To learn more about Berlin's queer history, visit the Schwules Museum (p116).

The annual festival calendar kicks off with **Easter in Berlin** (www.blf.de), a six-day mega-party that whips tens of thousands of leather, rubber, skin and military fans out of the dungeons and into the streets of Berlin. It culminates with the crowning of the 'German Mr Leather'.

In June the **Lesbisch-Schwules Strassenfest** (Lesbigay Street Festival; www.regenbogenfonds.de) takes over the queer *Kiez* (neighbourhood) in Schöneberg with nonstop bands, food, information booths and merriment. It's basically a warm-up for Christopher Street Day (p28) later that month. The leather crowd returns in September for another weekend of kinky partying during **Folsom Europe** (www.folsomeurope.com).

For advice and information, gay men should swing by **Mann-O-Meter** (Map p145, C2; ☎ 216 8008; www.mann-o-meter.de; Bülowstrasse 106; ☼ 9am-8pm Mon-Fri; ☻ Nollendorfplatz). For lesbians there's the **Lesbenberatung** (Lesbian Support Centre; Map p145, D4; ☎ 215 2000; www.lesbenberatung-berlin.de, in German; Kulmer Strasse 20a, Schöneberg; ☼ 10am-7pm Mon, Tue & Thu, to 5pm Wed & Fri; ☻ ☒ Yorckstrasse).

For customised gay lifestyle tours (nightlife, shopping, culinary) contact **Berlinagenten** (☎ 4372 0701; www.berlinagenten.com).

BEST OF THE PARTY CIRCUIT
> Berlin Hilton (www.berlinhilton.net)
> Chantals House of Shame (www.siteofshame.com)
> Gayhane (www.so36.de, in German)
> GMF (www.gmf-berlin.de)
> Irrenhaus (www.ninaqueer.com)

BEST BARS
> Heile Welt (p147)
> Möbel Olfe (p108)
> Roses (p109)
> Zum Schmutzigen Hobby (p98; pictured)

GALLERIES

Since the collapse of the Wall in 1989, Berlin has become a hotshot in the art world, boasting a flourishing gallery scene, its own annual art fair (Art Forum Berlin; p29) and the biannual Biennale exhibit of cutting-edge works. Creative synergies, a free-spirited climate and cheap rents have turned the German capital into a major magnet for artists from around the globe. International collectors, meanwhile, have their radar firmly trained on what's coming out of local studios. Works by Berlin-based artists Olafur Eliasson, Elmgreen & Dragset, Thomas Scheibitz, Isa Genzken, Jonathan Meese and Norbert Bisky enjoy feverish demand worldwide.

With more than 400 galleries spread across town, there's always some fantastic show going on somewhere. Berlin has no designated gallery quarter, but you'll find concentrations of them on Auguststrasse in Mitte (Map p63, C3; see www.rundumin-auguststrasse.de); along Brunnen-strasse (off Map p89) in northern Mitte; and around Checkpoint Charlie (p114) on Zimmerstrasse, Kochstrasse, Charlottenstrasse and, a bit further east, on Lindenstrasse. The galleries below Jannowitzbrücke (Map p57, E4) and at the Halle am Wasser (Hall by the Water; p78) are also well worth a visit. Charlottenburg has established scenes along the Kur-fürstendamm (Map p133, C3) and such side streets as Mommsenstrasse (Map p133, B2) and Fasanenstrasse (Map p133, D3).

In addition, a few private collectors are also sharing their treasures with the public. Examples include **Sammlung Hoffmann** (Map p63, D3;

www.sammlung-hoffmann.de), Sammlung Boros (p66) and **Sammlung Haubrok** (Map p123, A1; www.sammlung-haubrok.de).

Berlin's art museum landscape is also among the richest in the country. You can admire more Rembrandts than anywhere else at the Gemälde-galerie (p82), and an exceptional collection of German expressionist works at the Neue Nationalgalerie (p85). The premier space for contemporary art is the Hamburger Bahnhof (p78), while Picasso fans gravitate to the Museum Berggruen (p136) and Caspar David Friedrich gets quite a bit of play at the Alte Nationalgalerie (p44). Art created in 20th-century Berlin is the focus of the Berlinische Galerie (p114), while at the Sammlung Scharf-Gerstenberg (p136) the spotlight is on surrealist works.

To find out what's on where, turn to the listings magazines *Tip* (www .tip-berlin.de, in German) or *Zitty* (www.zitty.de, in German) or check http://berlin.art49.com. Other German-language options include www .indexberlin.de, www.art-in-berlin.de, www.berliner-galerien.de and www .kunstmagazinberlin.de. The book *Berlin Art Now* by Mark Gisbourne engagingly profiles 19 of Berlin's major current artists (in English), while *Berlin Contemporary 2008/2009* by Angela Hohmann and Imke Ehlers por-trays 75 of the most important galleries for contemporary art (in German).

For the inside scoop on the gallery scene, you could also join a guided tour such as those offered by **Berlin Entdecken** (www.berlin-entdecken.de/junge _kunst.php, in German; tour €10; ☺ 11am Sat) and **Go Art** (www.goart-berlin.de).

BEST FOR BIG NAMES
> Alte Nationalgalerie (p44)
> Gemäldegalerie (p82)
> Martin-Gropius-Bau (p116)
> Neue Nationalgalerie (p85)

BEST NICHE COLLECTIONS
> Berlinische Galerie (p114)
> Emil Nolde Museum (p47)
> Käthe-Kollwitz-Museum (p135)
> Museum Berggruen (p136)

BEST FOR CUTTING-EDGE ART
> Contemporary Fine Arts (p51)
> Hamburger Bahnhof (p78)
> Kunst-Werke Berlin (p64)
> Temporäre Kunsthalle (p50)
> Sammlung Boros (p66)

BEST FOR STYLISH SETTINGS
> Sammlung Boros (p66)
> Daimler Contemporary (p82)
> Halle am Wasser (p78)
> Hamburger Bahnhof (p78)

Top left Women spinning yarns at Martin-Gropius-Bau (p116)

JEWISH BERLIN

Since reunification, Berlin has had the fastest growing Jewish community in the world, thanks largely to a steady influx of Russian Jewish immigrants. The ranks have also been swelled by German Jews who've returned home, Israelis who wish to escape the tumultuous homeland and American expats lured by Berlin's low cost of living and limitless creativity. Today there are about 13,000 active members of the Jewish community, including 1000 belonging to the Orthodox congregation Adass Yisroel. However, since not all Jews choose to be affiliated with a synagogue, the actual population is estimated to be at least twice as high.

The community supports eight synagogues, two mikvah ritual baths, several schools, numerous cultural institutions and a handful of kosher restaurants and shops. The golden-domed Neue Synagoge (New Synagogue; p65) on Oranienburger Strasse is the most visible beacon of Jewish revival, even though today it's not primarily a house of worship but a community centre and exhibition space. Across town in Kreuzberg, the Jewish Museum (Jüdisches Museum; p17 and p115), a spectacular structure by Daniel Libeskind, tracks the ups and downs of Jewish life in Germany for 2000 years.

Records show that Jews first settled in Berlin in 1295. Their presence, however, hinged on a religious technicality that allowed them to be moneylenders, a practice forbidden to Christians. Throughout the Middle Ages the community had to contend with being blamed for any kind of societal or economic woe. When the plague struck in 1348, rumours that Jews had poisoned the wells led to the first major pogrom. In 1510, 38 Jews were publicly tortured and burned for allegedly stealing the host from a church because a confession by the actual (Christian) perpetrator was deemed too straightforward to be true.

Financial interests, not humanitarian ones, motivated the Great Elector Friedrich Wilhelm to invite 50 Jewish families expelled from Vienna to settle in Berlin in 1671. To his credit, he later extended the offer to Jews in general and also allowed them to practice their faith – which was by no means common in Europe at the time. Berlin's oldest Jewish cemetery, the Alter Jüdischer Friedhof (p64) was founded during this period.

Among the people buried here is the great philosopher Moses Mendelssohn, who arrived in Berlin in 1743. His progressive thinking and lobbying paved the way for the Emancipation Edict of 1812, which made

Jews full citizens of Prussia with equal rights and duties. By the end of the 19th century, many of Berlin's Jews, numbering about 5% of the population, had become thoroughly German in speech and identity.

When a wave of Hasidic Jews escaping the pogroms in Eastern Europe arrived around that time, they found their way to today's Scheunenviertel, which was then essentially an immigrant slum. By 1933 the community had grown to around 160,000, or one-third of all Jews living in Germany. The well-known horrors of the Nazi years sent most into exile and left 55,000 dead. Only about 1000 to 2000 are believed to have survived the war years in Berlin, often with the help of their non-Jewish neighbours and friends.

The most prominent among Berlin's many monuments to the victims of those years is the enormous Holocaust Denkmal (Holocaust Memorial; p48) near the Brandenburg Gate. The open-air exhibit Topographie des Terrors (Topography of Terror; p116), soon to be in a permanent building, also goes a long way towards ensuring that the Third Reich years are not swept under the carpet of history.

Cultural events attended by Jews and non-Jews alike include the annual festival called **Jüdische Kulturtage** (Jewish Cultural Days; www.juedische-kulturtage .org, in German) held in late October since 1987. The Jewish theatre **Bamah** (www.bamah.de, in German) has presented plays, cabaret, *chansons* and readings since 2001. English-language tours of Jewish life in Berlin are offered by Berlin Walks (p187). For general information about the community, check out www.berlin-judentum.de.

Above The gleaming gold dome of the Neue Synagoge (p65), a symbol of Berlin's revitalised Jewish community

THE BERLIN WALL

It's more than a tad ironic that Berlin's most popular tourist attraction is one that no longer exists. For 28 years the Berlin Wall, the most potent symbol of the Cold War, divided not only the city but the world. Construction began shortly after midnight of 13 August 1961, when East German soldiers rolled out miles of barbed wire that would soon be replaced with prefab concrete slabs. The Wall was a desperate measure launched by the German Democratic Republic (GDR) government to stop the sustained brain and brawn drain it had experienced since its founding in 1949. Some 3.6 million people had already left for the West, putting the country on the verge of economic and political collapse.

Euphemistically called the 'Anti-Fascist Protection Barrier', the Wall was a 155km-long symbol of oppression that turned West Berlin into an island of democracy within a sea of socialism. Continually reinforced and refined over time, it eventually grew into a complex border-security system that included a 'death strip' riddled with trenches, floodlights, patrol roads, attack dogs, electrified fences and watchtowers staffed by trigger-happy guards.

The first would-be escapee was shot only a few days after 13 August, but the extent of the system's cruelty became blatantly clear on 17 August 1962 when 18-year-old Peter Fechtner was shot and wounded and then left to bleed to death while the East German guards looked on. There's a memorial in the spot where he died on Zimmerstrasse (Map p113, C1). Another Wall Victims Memorial is just south of the Reichstag, on the eastern end of Scheidemannstrasse (Map p43, A2).

The demise of the Wall came as unexpectedly as its creation. Once again the GDR was losing its people in droves, this time via Hungary, which had opened its borders with Austria. East Germans took to the streets by the hundreds of thousands, demanding improved human rights and an end to the Socialist Unity Party of Germany (Sozialistische Einheitspartei Deutschlands, SED) monopoly. On 9 November 1989 SED spokesperson Günter Schabowski made a surprise announcement on GDR TV: all travel restrictions to the West would be lifted. Immediately. Amid scenes of wild partying and mile-long parades of GDR-made Trabant cars (Trabi, for short), the two Berlins came together again. The dismantling of the hated barrier began almost immediately.

Only little more than 1.5km of the Berlin Wall still stands as a symbol of the triumph of freedom over oppression. The longest, best-preserved and most interesting stretch is the 1.3km-long section called East Side Gallery (p15 and p124) because of the many murals painted by international artists in 1990 and again in 2009.

Over the last 20 years, the two city halves have visually merged so perfectly that in many places it takes a keen eye to tell East from West. Fortunately, there's help in the form of a double row of cobblestones that guides you along 5.7km of the Wall's course.

Fat Tire Bike Tours (www.fattirebiketoursberlin.com) offers guided English-language Wall tours. If you're feeling ambitious, follow all or part of the 160km-long **Berliner Mauerweg** (Berlin Wall Trail; www.berlin.de/mauer/index.en.html), a signposted walking and cycling path along the former border fortifications with 40 multilingual information stations posted along the way.

A high-tech way to walk the Wall is with the **Mauerguide** (www.mauerguide.de; adult/concession per 4hr €8/5, per day €10/7), a nifty hand-held minicomputer that maps its course via GPS and provides intelligent commentary and historic audio and video. Call or check the website for rental locations.

For more background, swing by the **Gedenkstätte Berliner Mauer** (off Map p89; ☎ 464 1030; www.berliner-mauer-gedenkstaette.de; Bernauer Strasse 111; admission free; ⏲ 10am-6pm Apr-Oct, to 5pm Nov-Mar; Ⓜ Bernauer Strasse; Ⓡ Nordbahnhof), a memorial that combines a documentation centre, art installation, short section of original Wall, chapel and outdoor gallery. The Mauermuseum, aka Haus am Checkpoint Charlie (p115), also chronicles the Cold War period.

For the complete low-down, check out www.stadtentwicklung.berlin .de/denkmal (go to English, then Monuments, Berlin Wall) or www.berlin .de/mauer.

Above Berlin Wall remnants, complete with pretend communist soldier, at Potsdamer Platz (p80)

BACK TO THE GDR

The German Democratic Republic (GDR) may have been extinct for more than two decades, but in Berlin plenty of places still evoke the era so fascinatingly portrayed in the hit movies *Good Bye, Lenin!* and *The Lives of Others*. The small and delightfully interactive DDR Museum (p58) takes a mostly benign look at daily life behind the Iron Curtain. Lest you get the impression that life in the GDR was cute and wholesome, though, you might want to juxtapose a visit here with a trip out to the Stasi Museum (p126). This exhibit set up in the original Ministry of State Security makes it crystal clear that the East German leadership knew no limits when it came to controlling its own people. Suspected dissidents often ended up at the notorious Stasi Prison (p126) in Hohenschönhausen, where tours are sometimes led by former inmates.

Follow up with a stroll along Karl-Marx-Allee (p124), a monumental boulevard that's an open-air showcase of GDR architecture and a meta- phor for the inflated sense of importance and grandeur of that country's regime. For relief, pop into Mondos Arts (p125), which celebrates Ostalgie (nostalgia for the East) with a hilarious assortment of GDR-era knick- knacks. Another popular souvenir store is Ampelmann Galerie (p67), which specialises in products shaped like or adorned with the charming fellow on East Berlin pedestrian traffic lights. And speaking of traffic, if you want to know what driving was like back in those days, hop behind the wheel of an original Trabant car and take a Trabi Safari (p188).

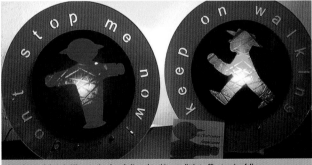

Ampelmann Galerie (p67): an entire shop dedicated to this cute, little traffic-stopping fellow

CLUBBING

Berlin is Germany's club capital, the city where techno came of age, the living heart of the European electronic scene and the spiritual home of the lost weekend. No matter whether you're into house, minimal techno, drum and bass, breakbeat, Britpop, dancehall, ska, reggae or ballroom, you'll find a place to party any night of the week. And with so many top DJs living in Berlin – and others happy to visit – the city is a virtual musical testing lab. Line-ups are often amazing. DJ royalty to watch out for includes André Galluzzi, Ellen Allien, Ricardo Villalobos, Paul Kalkbrenner, Modeselektor and Apparat.

Getting into clubs is easier here than in most European cities. Individual style beats Armani in most cases, and there's no need to worry about those little wrinkles either – if your attitude is right, age rarely matters.

Wherever you're going don't bother showing up before 1am. In fact, places such as Berghain/Panoramabar only start hitting their peak after 4am and, thanks to a growing number of afterparties and daytime clubs, not going home at all on weekends is definitely an option.

For the latest scoop, scan the listings magazines *Zitty*, *Tip* or *030* and sift through the myriad flyers in shops, cafes and bars. German readers should check into www.clubcommission.de. See also p13.

BEST PARTY ON...
Monday SO36 (p110)
Tuesday Cookies (p55)
Wednesday Watergate (p111)
Thursday Weekend (p61)
Friday Clärchens Ballhaus (p74)
Saturday Berghain/Panoramabar (p130)
Sunday Club der Visionäre (p110)

BEST CLUB FOR...
Afterparties Delicious Doughnuts (p74)
Big-time DJs Watergate (p111)
Celebrity sightings Cookies (p55)
Daytime parties Club der Visionäre (p110)
Hedonism Berghain/Panoramabar (p130)
Views Weekend (p61)

DRINKING

Berlin is a great place for boozers. From cosy pubs to riverside beach bars, chestnut-shaded beer gardens to underground dives, DJ bars to snazzy hotel lounges and designer cocktail temples, you're rarely far from a good time. Kreuzberg and Friedrichshain are currently the edgiest bar-hopping grounds, with swanky Mitte and Charlottenburg being more suited for date night than dedicated drinking. Style and atmosphere matter everywhere, and some proprietors have gone to extraordinary lengths to come up with unique design concepts.

The line between cafe and bar is often blurred, with many places changing stripes as the hands move around the clock. Alcohol is served pretty much all day in case you're keen on getting a head start. Dedicated bars open between 6pm and 8pm and keep pouring until the last tippler leaves. Beer continues to be a beloved libation, but you'll also see plenty of hipsters swilling cocktails, sparkling wine (often on the rocks), fancy vodkas or some wicked absinthe concoction.

A phenom that takes over the Scheunenviertel in the evening hours is the organised pub crawl. For about €12, you and a few dozen other global nomads can get wasted on free shots and cheap drinks at a handful of touristy bars and pubs. **Insider Tour** (☎ 692 3149; www.insidertour.com) and **New Berlin Tours** (☎ 0179 973 0397; www.newberlintours.com) are among the companies operating these drink-a-thons that seem to be especially popular with the 'triple A crowd' (Anglo-Saxons, Americans and Australians).

BEST FOR...

Beer garden setting Prater (p98)
Coffee Anna Blume (p96)
Daytime drinking Bar Gagarin (p96)
Expert cocktails Bebel Bar (p53)
Genteel ambience Galerie Bremer (p141)
Provocative decor Zum Schmutzigen Hobby (p98)
Retro flair Klub der Republik (p98)
Views Solar (p119)

BEST SIGNLESS BARS

> Monarch Bar (p108)
> Orient Lounge (p108)
> Tausend (p54)
> Würgeengel (p109)

FASHION

Forget Paris and Milan: Berlin's currently the hottest ticket on the fashion circuit. However, it's not the Pradas and Dolce & Gabbanas that are generating the buzz, but a growing league of innovative young designers with ideas that pick up on Berlin's idiosyncratic spirit. This is not stuffy, snob-value couture for fashion clones: the local look is down-to-earth, practical (even when painstakingly crafted), slightly irreverent and with a fresh edge.

Fashion-forward designers and labels such as talkingmeanstrouble, Kostas Murkudis, Bo van Melskens, Lala Berlin and presque fini are able to walk the fine line between originality and contemporary trends in a way that more mainstream labels are not. Often, these locals labels are more insistent on fair-trade practices and ethical manufacturing than other fashion brands. Caro-e and slomo are two leading contenders that work only with ethically sourced organic materials.

As in the arts, experimentation is the order of the day in Berlin, and with the recent streetwear boom (key local labels include Irie Daily, Hasipop and Butterfly Soulfire), Berlin has come to be a fertile zone for innovative young talent.

Despite a disturbing proliferation of global-brand flagship stores, the Scheunenviertel remains ground zero for concept stores, micro-boutiques and studio-stores selling local indie labels. Cool-hunters can quickly plug into the Berlin fashion scene via the internet platform **Berlinerklamotten** (www.berlinerklamotten.com). It represents about 140 local labels and also has a showroom at the Hackesche Höfe (see p67). Another excellent way to keep tabs on the Berlin fashion scene is the online mag *Modekultur* (www.modekultur.info). To buy Berlin fashions online, try www.styleserver.de.

BEST OF BERLIN FASHION
> Berlinerklamotten (p67)
> Berlinomat (p125)
> Killerbeast (p102)
> Lala Berlin (p68)
> Sameheads (p117)

BEST OF BERLIN ACCESSORIES
> Blush Dessous (p67)
> IC! Berlin (p68)
> Ta(u)sche (p93)

V

SNAPSHOTS

KIDS

(Tiny) hands down, travelling to Berlin with tots can be child's play, especially if you keep a light schedule and involve them in the day-to-day planning. There's plenty to do to keep tykes occupied. Imaginative playgrounds abound in all neighbourhoods as do parks such as the vast Tiergarten, which is great for picnics or paddling around the Neuer See lake.

Animal-lovers gravitate towards Berlin Zoo (p134), home to polar-bear celebrity Knut, a petting corral and an adventure playground. The adjacent aquarium has lots more crowd-pleasers, but to prevent exhaustion save a visit here for another day.

Finny friends also take centre stage at Sea Life Berlin (p59), the smaller size of which makes it suitable for the kindergarten set, as is the Legoland Discovery Centre (p83).

Kid-friendly museums include the Museum für Naturkunde (Museum of Natural History; p65) with its giant dinosaurs; the Deutsches Technikmuseum (German Museum of Technology; p114) with its planes, trains and automobiles; and the Haus am Checkpoint Charlie (p115) with its Cold War spy and escape exhibits.

Follow up a visit here with tooling around Berlin's 'Wild East' in a quaint GDR-era car on a Trabi Safari (p188). And your music-loving teens will think you're way cool if you take them on the Fritz Music Tour (p188).

For more ideas, see www.visitberlin.de or www.travelforkids.com.

Statue in Alexanderplatz (p56) welcomes a tot with open arms – ya can't get much more child-friendly than that

MUSEUMS

In the beginning there was the Altes Museum (p44). This Schinkel-designed 1830 temple to the muses was the germ cell of Berlin's extraordinary museum landscape that would be the envy of many a small country. From art deco to agriculture, sex to sugar, diamonds to dinosaurs, there is hardly a theme not covered in the city's 175 re-positories. And that number is still growing. Recent openings included the much-anticipated Neues Museum (p49), the surrealist Sammlung Scharf-Gerstenberg (p136) and the Emil Nolde Museum (p47). Coming online soon is the Topography of Terror documentation centre (p116).

More than 11 million visitors poke around Berlin's cultural riches each year. Ancient world treasures are particularly popular. Queen Nefertiti continues to turn heads at the Neues Museum (p49), while all eyes are on the Pergamon Altar and the Ishtar Gate at the nearby Pergamonmuseum (p50). Both are part of Museumsinsel (Museum Island), a Unesco World Heritage site since 1999, which is gradually being revamped to the tune of €1.5 billion, making it Europe's single largest cultural investment project.

Avid museum goers can save a bundle by buying the SchauLust Museen Berlin pass (p184). Museum nights, called 'Lange Nacht der Museen', take place twice a year (see www.lange-nacht-der-museen.de, in German). For the low-down on art museums, see p156.

ESSENTIAL MUSEUMS
> Haus am Checkpoint Charlie (p115)
> Jewish Museum (p115)
> Neues Museum (p49)
> Pergamonmuseum (p50)

BEST OFFBEAT MUSEUMS
> Ramones Museum (p66)
> Berliner Medizinhistorisches Museum (p78)
> DDR Museum (p58; pictured)
> Stasi Museum (p126)

MUSIC

Just like the city itself, Berlin's music scene is a shape-shifter, a dynamic and restlessly inventive creature fed by the city's appetite for diversity and change. Berlin has long held a fascination for musicians. Iggy Pop, David Bowie, Depeche Mode and U2 all recorded seminal albums at the legendary Hansa Studios (Map p81, F3) or, as Bowie called it, the 'big hall by the Wall'.

There's no 'Berlin sound' as such but many parallel developments, from indie rock by the Beatsteaks to Peter Fox' upbeat reggae and the sugar-sweet melodies of 2raumwohnung, from Jazzanova's downtempo eclectic soul to the dark punk rock of Rammstein. And thanks to an ever-fluid mix of talents and visions, crossover genres are constantly invented, deconstructed, reinvented and combined more quickly than anyone can define them.

With at least 2000 active bands and dozens of indie labels, including Bpitch Control (techno), Shitkatapult (crossover electro), Chicks on Speed (pop), DNS (pop), Piranha (world music) and !K7 (electro), Berlin is Germany's undisputed music capital. About 60% of the country's music revenue is generated here, up from a paltry 8% in 1998. Universal Music and MTV have their European headquarters here and Popkomm, one of the world's top music trade fairs, is also held in Berlin.

For upcoming gigs check *Zitty* or *Tip*.

BEST FOR CATCHING UP-AND-COMERS
> Dot Club (p110)
> Magnet (p99)
> SO36 (p110; pictured)

BEST FOR CATCHING TOURING BANDS
> Lido (p110)
> Wild at Heart (p111)

SEX & FETISH

A steep flight of stairs spills into a hall-like room bathed in red and gold and bordered by a long bar. Thumping house music keeps the dance floor throbbing. The ambience is relaxed, friendly, uninhibited. This could be just your average Berlin nightclub were it not for the patrons clad in rubber suits, cupless corsets, kilts, capes and other sexy outfits. Many are busy with foreplay, turned on by large-screen porn, live shows and their own imaginations. Others have retreated upstairs to open lounge beds or to back rooms outfitted with toys, tubs and even a gynaecological chair.

Welcome to Insomnia (p119), an erotic nightclub presided over by the statuesque Dominique (see p120). Yup, the decadence of the Weimar years is alive and kicking in a city long known for its libertine leanings. While full-on sex clubs are most common in the gay scene, places such as Insomnia and the KitKatClub (p61) allow straights, gays, lesbians, the bi-curious and polysexuals to live out their fantasies in a safe if public setting. Surprisingly, there's absolutely nothing seedy about this, but you do need to check your inhibitions – and much of your clothing – at the door. If fetish gear doesn't do it for you, wear something sexy or glamorous; men can usually get away with tight pants and an open (or no) shirt. No normal street clothes, no tighty whities. As elsewhere, couples and girl groups get in easier than all-guy crews. And don't forget: always practise safe sex.

Get cheeky and kinky at KitKatClub @ Sage (p61), Berlin's most (in)famous erotic nightclub

SHOPPING

Berlin is a great place to shop, and we're definitely not talking malls and chains. In fact, getting the most out of shopping here means venturing off the high street and into the neighbourhoods (known as *Kieze*). This is where you'll discover a cosmopolitan cocktail of indie boutiques stirred by the city's zest for life, envelope-pushing energy and entrepreneurial spirit.

Each *Kiez* comes with its own flair, identity and mix of stores calibrated to the needs, tastes and bank accounts of local residents. Shopping here is a benign diversion that's as much about visual and mental stimulus as it is about actually buying stuff. Whether you're a penny-pincher or a power-shopper, you'll find plenty of opportunities to drop some cash.

Go to Charlottenburg for antiques, art and fashions, Kreuzberg for vintage garb and to Schöneberg for home accessories. Cosmopolitan Friedrichstrasse has all the iconic international brands, while Mitte and Prenzlauer Berg are local designer hotbeds. Popular buys include anything made in Berlin, such as progressive streetwear, bags, chocolates, eyewear, candy and jewellery.

But brand-name bunnies need not worry. Of course Berlin also has the big-label boutiques, the high-street chains, the malls and the department stores. Kurfürstendamm (Map p133, C3) and Tauentzienstrasse (Map p133, E2) are major retail spines, the luxe KaDeWe (p146) department store has lured shoppers for a century and near Alexanderplatz the mega-mall Alexa (p59) provides an American-style shopping experience.

Note that many smaller stores do not accept credit cards.

BEST MARKETS
> Flohmarkt am Arkonaplatz (p91)
> Flohmarkt am Mauerpark (p92)
> Türkenmarkt (p105)
> Flohmarkt am Boxhagener Platz (p125)

BEST FOODS
> Bonbonmacherei (p68)
> Fassbender & Rausch (p52)
> Goldhahn & Sampson (p92)
> KaDeWe food hall (p146)

BEST QUIRK FACTOR
> 1. Absinth Depot Berlin (p67)
> Ausberlin (p59)
> Herrlich (p116)
> Mondos Arts (p125)
> VEB Orange (p93)

BEST BOOKSHOPS
> Berlin Story (p50)
> Dussmann – Das Kulturkaufhaus (p51)

>BACKGROUND

The Holocaust Denkmal (p48): a solemn and sobering graveyard-like memorial

BACKGROUND

HISTORY

MEDIEVAL BEGINNINGS

By German standards, Berlin entered the stage of history fairly late and puttered along in relative obscurity for centuries. Founded in the 13th century as a trading post, it merged with its sister settlement Cölln across the Spree River in 1307. The town achieved a modicum of prominence after the powerful Hohenzollern clan from southern Germany took charge in 1411, at least until the 17th century when it was ravaged during the Thirty Years War (1618–48). Only 6000 people (roughly half the population) survived the pillage, plunder and starvation.

The war's aftermath gave Berlin its first taste of cosmopolitanism. In a clever bit of social engineering, Elector Friedrich Wilhelm (called the 'Great Elector'; r 1640–88) decided to quickly raise the number of his subjects by inviting foreigners to settle in Berlin. Some Jewish families arrived from Vienna, but most of the new settlers were Huguenot refugees from France. By 1700 one in five locals was of French descent.

THE AGE OF PRUSSIA

Elector Friedrich III, the Great Elector's son, presided over a lively and intellectual court but was also a man of great political ambition. In 1701 he simply promoted himself to become King Friedrich I of Prussia, making Berlin a royal residence and capital of the new state of Brandenburg-Prussia.

His son, Friedrich Wilhelm I (r 1713–40), laid the groundwork for Prussian military might. Soldiers were this king's main obsession and he dedicated much of his life to building an army of 80,000, partly by instituting the draft (highly unpopular even then) and by persuading his fellow rulers to trade him men for treasure. History quite appropriately knows him as the Soldatenkönig (Soldier King).

Ironically, these soldiers didn't see action until his son Friedrich II (aka Frederick the Great; r 1740–86) came to power in 1740. Friedrich fought tooth and nail for two decades to wrest Silesia from Austria and Saxony. When not busy on the battlefield, 'Old Fritz', as he was also called, sought greatness through building and embracing the ideals of the Enlightenment. With some of the day's leading thinkers in town (Gotthold Ephraim Lessing and Moses Mendelssohn among them),

Berlin blossomed into a great cultural centre that some even called 'Athens on the Spree'.

Old Fritz' death sent Prussia on a downward spiral, culminating in a serious trouncing of its army by Napoleon in 1806. The French marched triumphantly into Berlin on 27 October and left two years later, their coffers bursting with loot. The post-Napoleonic period saw Berlin caught up in the reform movement sweeping through Europe. Since all this ferment brought little change from the top, in 1848 Berlin joined with other German cities in a bourgeois democratic revolution. Alas, the time for democracy wasn't yet ripe and the status quo was quickly restored.

WARS & REVOLUTIONS

Meanwhile, the Industrial Revolution had snuck up on Berliners, with companies such as Siemens and Borsig vastly spurring the city's growth and spawning a new working class and political parties like the Social Democratic Party (SPD) to represent them. Berlin boomed politically, economically and culturally, especially after becoming capital of the German Reich in 1871. By 1900 the population had reached two million.

Once again war, WWI in this case, stifled Berlin's momentum. In its aftermath, it found itself at the heart of a power struggle between monarchists, ultraleft Spartacists and democrats. Though the democrats won out, the Weimar Republic (1920–33) only brought instability, corruption and inflation. Berliners responded like there was no tomorrow and made their city as much a den of decadence as a cauldron of creativity (not unlike today…). Artists of all stripes flocked to this city of cabaret, Dada and jazz.

Hitler's rise to power put an instant damper on the fun. Berlin suffered heavy bombing in WWII and a crushing invasion of 1.5 million Soviet soldiers during the final, decisive Battle of Berlin in April 1945. During the Cold War, it became ground zero for hostilities between the US and the USSR. The Berlin Blockade of 1948 and the construction of the Berlin Wall in 1961 were major milestones in the stand-off. For 40 years East and West Berlin developed as two completely separate cities.

THE REUNITED CITY

With reunification, Berlin once again became the German capital in 1990 and the seat of the federal government in 1999. Mega-sized construction projects such as Potsdamer Platz and the government quarter eradicated the scars of division but did little to improve the city's balance sheet or unemployment statistics. Berliners compensated by turning their city into a hive of cultural cool, with unbridled nightlife, an explosive art scene and booming fashion and design industries. They showed off their legendary liberalism at the Love Parade and welcomed the global community to such events as the FIFA World Cup.

However, social woes continue to bedraggle Berlin. Poorly performing schools, violent racial attacks by right-wing groups and a spate of 'honour killings' of young Muslim women wishing to live a Western lifestyle have all captured the headlines in recent years.

Two decades after the rejoining of the city halves, Berlin is reaching a watershed moment. Districts such as Mitte and Prenzlauer Berg, once pioneers of progressiveness, are now firmly in the grip of gentrification and the boho-bourgeois class. Global developers are building up the banks of the Spree River, investors from Denmark to Ireland to America are snapping up bargain-priced apartments, and international chains are replacing homespun businesses.

All this begs the question: can Berlin remain the homeland of social freedom and experimentation while increasingly becoming a more corporate-driven, 'normal' metropolis? Governing mayor Klaus Wowereit famously called Berlin 'poor but sexy'. In 10 years it may no longer be poor. But will it still be sexy?

LIFE AS A BERLINER

Compared with other world capitals, daily life in Berlin moves to a less frantic rhythm. You rarely have to shoehorn your way inside buses or trains, street traffic tends to be light and moves quite smoothly, scoring a dinner reservation usually means calling the restaurant the same day and getting into a club doesn't require hustling your way onto the VIP list.

Berliners are refreshingly attitude-free and egalitarian, less impressed by Armani suits and Gucci bags than personal, individualistic style. Striving for material wealth and social status takes a back seat to living well, spending time with friends and enjoying the city's myriad cultural and natural offerings.

Many Berliners embrace life to the fullest, drinking a lot, smoking too much, partying late and often, and having a laissez-faire attitude towards sex and sexual orientation. No wonder the lesbigay, SM and fetish scenes here are among the biggest in Europe.

BERLIN BY THE NUMBERS

> Population: 3.416 million, including 477,000 non-Germans
> Gross Domestic Product (GDP): €87.5 billion
> Unemployment: 14%
> Number of playgrounds: 1824
> Per capita annual income: €14,738
> Total annual visitors: 7.9 million, including 2.75 million from abroad
> Total overnight stays: 17.8 million
> Number of museums: 175
> Average daily temperature: 9.7°C

Daily life is defined by activity, though this does not necessarily entail work. Berliners always seem to be heading to or from somewhere, be it the office, the gym, the shops, the bar, the cinema, the theatre or all of the above.

Perhaps because of their on-the-go lifestyle, family life is less of a priority. In fact, the singles' scene is intense here, with more than 50% of all people now living alone. Single parenthood is also common, and as many children now live with one parent as with two.

Overall, locals are accommodating and helpful towards visitors and will often volunteer assistance if you look lost. This politeness does not necessarily extend to friendliness, however, and in public people usually maintain a degree of reserve towards strangers – you won't find many impromptu conversations being struck up on the U-Bahn or in the supermarket checkout line.

On the other hand, in younger company it's easy to chat with just about anyone, particularly around the many student hang-outs (remember German students are generally older than elsewhere, often graduating at 28 rather than 21), and if you start frequenting a place you'll quickly get to know staff and regulars. You'll also probably find people very open after a relatively short time, discussing sex, relationships and life with equal candour.

In fact, many locals are relatively new in town too, having moved here from some other part of Germany or from another country. With people from 185 nations making up 14% of the population, Berlin is Germany's most multicultural city, with most immigrants hailing from Turkey, Poland, the former states of Yugoslavia and the old Soviet republics.

GOVERNMENT & POLITICS

Since 2001 Berlin has been governed by a coalition of the centre-left Sozialdemokratische Partei Deutschlands (SPD; Social Democratic Party of Germany) and the far left Die Linke.PDS (Party of Democratic Social-ism). Led by the SPD's Klaus Wowereit, who is the governing mayor, the new government inherited a fiscal storm that had been brewing since 1990. Following reunification Berlin lost the hefty federal subsidies it had received during the years of division. Also gone were 100,000 manufac-turing jobs, most of them through closures of unprofitable factories in East Berlin. The end result was a whopping debt of €60 billion.

Wowereit responded by making painful, across-the-board spending cuts, but with a tax base eroded by high unemployment and ever-growing welfare payments, these have done little to get Berlin out of the poorhouse. But Wowereit, who was re-elected in 2006, appears to remain undaunted. With his characteristic mix of substance and glamour, the openly gay mayor never tires of touting Berlin as a capital of cool. And with some success. Universal Music moved its German headquarters from Hamburg to Berlin, MTV followed in its wake and so did the music trade fair Popcomm. And in 2007 Berlin's first ever fashion week was inaugurated. Visitor numbers, meanwhile, have shot through the roof and more and more young creatives flock to town to share in Berlin's infectious spirit.

DOS
> Say 'Guten Tag' when entering a business.
> State your last name at the start of a phone call.
> Keep your hands above the table when eating.
> Carry some form of picture ID, an identity card or a passport – it's the law.
> Bring a small gift or flowers when invited to a meal.
> Bag your own groceries in supermarkets. And quickly!

DON'TS
> Talk about WWII with a victor's mentality.
> Be late for meetings and dinner invitations.
> Expect the bill to arrive automatically in a restaurant; you have to ask for it.
> Assume you can pay by credit card, especially when eating out.
> Immediately call people by their first name.

GREEN LIGHT FOR SMOKERS?

After years of foot-dragging, a total smoking ban in all gastronomic establishments was to take effect in Berlin on 1 July 2008. But less than a month later, Germany's highest court ruled the sweeping ban unconstitutional. Now smoking is again allowed, but only in single-room bars and clubs that are smaller than 75 sq metres, don't serve anything to eat and keep out customers under 18. Huh?

Never mind, it's as absurd as it sounds, which explains the current state of 'anarchy' in Berlin. Some places allow smoking, others don't, at some you can puff away after 10pm, at others in certain areas or outside only. In short, Berlin-style laissez-faire at its finest!

In practice, most restaurants do not allow smoking at all, but many bars and clubs have set up separate smoking rooms. In this book, listings sporting the nonsmoking icon (✗) do not allow smoking inside at all.

ARCHITECTURE

Berlin is essentially a creation of modern times. Only a few Gothic churches, most notably the Nikolaikirche (see Nikolaiviertel; p58) and Marienkirche (p58), bear silent witness to the days when today's metropolis was just a small trading town. As Berlin grew, so did the representational needs of its rulers, especially in the 17th and 18th centuries, when the baroque and neoclassical styles became all the rage. Fine examples of both architectural styles line the grand boulevard Unter den Linden (p42), which is one of the few areas offering a glimpse of Berlin's splendour during its Prussian heyday.

No single king foisted a more lasting legacy on central Berlin than Frederick the Great. Together with his childhood friend Georg Wenzeslaus von Knobelsdorff, he masterminded the Forum Fridericianum, an ambitious building project centred on today's Bebelplatz (p44). Not all structures were built, though, because the king's many war exploits had emptied his coffers.

Unter den Linden also boasts the neoclassical Altes Museum (Old Museum; p44) and Neue Wache (New Guardhouse; p48), both by Karl Friedrich Schinkel, who was Prussia's most prominent building master and defined the look of early-19th-century Berlin.

The grand boulevard is bookended by the Brandenburg Gate (p46), an early neoclassical work by Carl Gotthard Langhans. For 28 years the Berlin Wall ran right along this famous landmark. When the Iron Curtain was dismantled, however, it created a void as empty as a politician's promise and with it the challenge and opportunity to join the two city halves together architecturally. Today the former death strip is a splendid showcase of cutting-edge architecture created by the world's top architects, including Frank Gehry, Renzo Piano, Helmut Jahn and Rafael Moneo. Starting at the Hauptbahnhof (central train station), stroll south through the new government quarter (p76) to the rebuilt Pariser Platz (p49) and its immediate neighbour, the monumental Holocaust Denkmal (Holocaust Memorial; p48). Just beyond lies the Potsdamer Platz area (p80), an entire urban quarter that sprang up from a bleak no-man's-land in less than 10 years.

Long before the Wall turned Berlin into a tale of two cities, the clash of ideologies and economic systems between East and West also found expression in the architectural arena. East Germans looked to Moscow, where Stalin favoured a style that was essentially a socialist reinterpretation of good old-fashioned neoclassicism. This was in stark contrast to the modernist aspirations of the democratic West.

One of the most prominent construction projects in West Berlin is the Kulturforum, a cultural complex just west of Potsdamer Platz. Hans Scharoun's warped Philharmonie (p87) and Mies van der Rohe's Neue Nationalgalerie (New National Gallery; p85) are both formidable presences here. Elsewhere in the West, postwar reconstruction was not always as successful. A case in point is the area around the Zoologischer Garten (Zoo Station) in Charlottenburg. Once the glittering heart of West Berlin, it is largely characterised by drab 1960s high-rises such as the Europa Center. An attempt to spice up the blandness with bold contemporary buildings – such as Helmut Jahn's Neues Kranzler Eck (Map p133, E2), Josef Paul Kleihues' Kantdreieck (Map p133, D2) and Nicolas Grimshaw's armadillo-inspired Ludwig-Erhard-Haus (Map p133, E2) – has done little to improve the overall effect. Frankly, the most attractive buildings around here are the stately 19th-century residential town houses lining fashionable Kurfürstendamm and its side streets.

Back across the Wall, the East German leaders decided to create a showpiece road of their own, the Karl-Marx-Allee (p124) in Friedrichshain. Built by some of the finest German Democratic Republic (GDR) architects of the day, including Hermann Henselmann, this 'socialist boulevard' is 90m wide, 2.3km long and the epitome of Stalinist pomposity. It culminates at Alexanderplatz (p56), which is orbited by massive '60s-era buildings that flaunt a more modern socialist look that could only be partly tempered by a recent makeover.

FURTHER READING

Pavel & I (2008; Dan Vyleta) This novel explores the friendship between a US soldier and a German orphan in the aftermath of WWII during the bitterly cold winter of 1946/7.

Rift Zone (2004; Raelynn Hillhouse) A woman smuggler between the East and the West in 1989 becomes a pawn in a KGB agent's game.

Stasiland (2004; Anna Funder) Australian writer Funder documents the Stasi's vast domestic spying apparatus by letting both victims and perpetrators tell their stories.

After the Wall: Confessions from an East German Childhood and the Life That Came Next (*Zonenkinder*; 2002; Jana Hensel) Just 13 years old when the Wall fell, Hensel reflects upon the loss of identity and the challenges of adapting to a new culture in her best-selling memoir.

Berlin Blues (*Herr Lehmann*; 2001; Sven Regener) It's hard to imagine a Berlin novel where the fall of the Wall is almost incidental to the plot, but this cult story of Kreuzberg nights pulls it off nicely. It was made into a movie in 2003.

Russian Disco (*Russendisko*; 2000; Wladimir Kaminer) These stranger-than-fiction vignettes present an entertaining and unsentimental portrait of present-day Berlin from the perspective of one of the city's most famous Russian immigrants.

Heroes Like Us (*Helden Wie Wir*; 1998; Thomas Brussig) This tongue-in-cheek bestseller was one of the first reunification novels and offers poignant and humorous insight into a now-extinct society.

Berlin Rising: Biography of a City (1994; Anthony Read & David Fisher) An excellent social history tracing the life of the city from its beginnings to the post-Wall era.

Berlin Noir Trilogy (1994; Phillip Kerr) Kerr's compelling depictions of Berlin in the murky days before, during and after WWII follow private investigator Bernie Gunther through the city's seamy side.

Berlin Game, Mexico Set, London Match (1983, 1984, 1985; Len Deighton) There are more unexpected twists and turns than on a roller coaster ride in this classic spy trilogy set in '80s Berlin.

The Spy That Came in from the Cold (1964; John Le Carré) Graham Greene called the tale of British spook Alex Leamas in early Cold War Berlin the finest spy story ever written.

Divided Heaven (1964; Christa Wolf) Set against an industrial backdrop, this is the powerful story of a woman's love for a man who fled to the West.

Berlin Diary: Journal of a Foreign Correspondent (1941; William Shirer) One of the most powerful works of reportage ever written, Shirer's portrait of the city he loved, grew to fear and eventually fled is a giant of the genre.

Goodbye to Berlin (1939; Christopher Isherwood) A brilliant semi-autobiographical perspective on 1920s Berlin as seen through the eyes of a gay Anglo-American journalist.

Berlin Alexanderplatz (1929; Alfred Döblin) This stylised meander through the seamy 1920s is still an essential Berlin text and was made into a movie in 1931 and a 14-part miniseries by Rainer Werner Fassbinder in 1980.

FILMS

The Lives of Others (*Das Leben der Anderen;* 2006; Florian Henckel von Donnersmarck) This brilliant Academy Award winner reveals the absurdity, hypocrisy and destructiveness of the Stasi and one agent's personal journey to disillusionment.

Downfall (*Der Untergang;* 2004; Oliver Hirschbiegel) Chilling account of Hitler's last 12 days – from his birthday to his suicide – holed up in his Berlin bunker.

Rosenstrasse (2003; Margarete von Trotta) Tells the true story of German women who peacefully but tenaciously protested the planned deportation of their Jewish husbands, in a rare and courageous act of defiance against the Nazi regime.

Good Bye, Lenin! (2003; Wolfgang Becker) Hugely successful, this comedy tells the story of a young East Berliner replicating the GDR for his mother after the fall of the Wall.

Sun Alley (*Sonnenallee;* 1999; Leander Haussmann) This is the endearing and often hilarious story of the everyday reality of a feckless teen who grows up and falls in love on the wrong (eastern) side of the Wall.

Run Lola Run (*Lola rennt;* 1997; Tom Tykwer) Lola's quest to raise US$100,000 in 20 minutes to save her lover's life is an inventive, energetic MTV-generation movie.

Wings of Desire (*Der Himmel über Berlin;* 1987; Wim Wenders) Set in postwar Berlin, this is the story of an angel who decides to become human – and mortal – after falling in love with a beautiful trapeze artist.

Legend of Paul and Paula (*Die Legende von Paul und Paula;* 1973; Heiner Carow) This GDR cult film, which was censored shortly after its release for its honest (and thus unflattering) portrayal of daily life, is really about the troubled love between a married man and an unmarried woman with children.

Berlin: Symphony of a City (*Berlin: Sinfonie einer Grosstadt;* 1927; Walter Ruttmann) Ambitious for its time, this fascinating silent documentary captures a day in the life of Berlin in the '20s.

DIRECTORY
TRANSPORT
ARRIVAL & DEPARTURE
AIR

Berlin has two international airports: Tegel (TXL), about 8km northwest from the city centre, and Schönefeld (SFX), about 22km southeast. For information about either, go to www.berlin-airport .de or call ☎ 0180 500 0186. Schönefeld is currently being expanded into Berlin Brandenburg International (BBI), scheduled to start operation in late 2011. Once BBI is open, Tegel will close.

Tegel

Tegel airport is connected to Mitte by the JetExpressBus TXL (€2.10, 30 minutes) and to Zoologischer Garten (Bahnhof Zoo or Zoo Station) by express bus X9 (€2.10, 20 minutes). Bus 109 also goes to the western city but it is slower and most useful if you're headed somewhere along Kurfürstendamm. Tegel is not directly served by the U-Bahn, but both bus 109 and X9 stop at Jakob-Kaiser-Platz (U7), the station closest to the airport. Taxi rides into town cost between €20 and €25.

Schönefeld

Schönefeld airport is served twice hourly by the Airport-Express train from Zoologischer Garten (30 minutes), Friedrichstrasse (23 minutes), Alexanderplatz (20 minutes) and Ostbahnhof (15 minutes). Note that these are regular regional (RE or RB) trains designated as Airport-Express in the timetable. S9 trains run more frequently but are slower (40

AIR TRAVEL ALTERNATIVES

Flying has become second nature in this era of low-cost airlines and few of us stop to consider using alternative travel methods and doing our bit for the environment. Yet, depending on where you're based, getting to Berlin without an aeroplane is easier and more comfortable than you might think. Coming from London, for instance, you could catch the Eurostar around 3.30pm, arrive in Paris by 7pm, switch to a night train and be in Berlin for breakfast. There are also direct overnight trains from Warsaw, Vienna, Munich, Paris and Brussels as well as frequent daytime connections from many other cities. For the full low-down, check out **Rail Europe** (www.raileurope.com), or, if in the UK, call ☎ 0871 880 8066.

Buses are slower and less comfortable, but they're another option, especially if you're travelling at short notice or live in an area poorly served by air or train. **Eurolines** (www .eurolines.com) is the umbrella organisation of 32 European coach operators whose route network serves 500 destinations in 30 countries, including Berlin.

minutes from Alexanderplatz). The S45 line goes straight to the trade fairground.

A free shuttle bus links the airport train station to the terminals every 10 minutes. Walking takes about five to 10 minutes.

Buses 171 and X7 go directly from outside the terminals to the U-Bahn station Rudow (U7), with onward connections to central Berlin.

The fare for any of these trips is €2.80 (buy zones ABC ticket). Taxis to the centre cost between €30 and €40.

GETTING AROUND

Berlin's extensive and efficient public-transport system is operated by BVG and consists of the U-Bahn (underground, subway), S-Bahn (light rail), buses and trams. In this book, the nearest U-Bahn/S-Bahn/bus or tram station or stop is noted after the 🚇 🚆 🚌 and 🚊 icons in each listing. For trip planning and general information, call the 24-hour hotline at ☎ 194 49 or go online to www.bvg.de.

The network is divided into fare zones A, B and C, with tickets available for zones AB, BC or ABC. Unless you're venturing to Potsdam or Schönefeld airport, you need the AB ticket (€2.10), which is valid for two hours. The short-trip ticket (*Kurzstreckenticket*; €1.20) is good for three stops on any U-Bahn or S-Bahn or six on any bus or tram. Children aged six to 13 qualify for reduced (*ermässigt*) rates, while kids under six travel for free.

Buy tickets from vending machines in U- or S-Bahn stations and aboard trams, from bus drivers and at station offices, news kiosks and any vendor sporting the BVG logo. All tickets except those bought from bus drivers must be stamped before boarding. A €40 fine applies if you get caught without a valid ticket.

CLIMATE CHANGE & TRAVEL

Travel – especially air travel – is a significant contributor to global climate change. At Lonely Planet, we believe that all who travel have a responsibility to limit their personal impact. As a result, we have teamed with Rough Guides and other concerned industry partners to support Climate Care, which allows people to offset the greenhouse gases they are responsible for with contributions to energy-saving projects and other climate-friendly initiatives in the developing world. Lonely Planet offsets all staff and author travel.

For more information, turn to the responsible travel pages on www.lonelyplanet .com. For details on offsetting your carbon emissions and a carbon calculator, go to www .climatecare.org.

TRAVEL PASSES

One-day travel passes (*Tageskarte*) are valid for unlimited travel on all forms of public transport until 3am the following day. The cost for the AB zone is €6.10. Group day passes (*Kleingruppenkarte*) are valid for up to five people travelling together and cost €15.90. Individual seven-day passes (*Wochenkarte*) are €26.20 and transferable.

U-BAHN

The most efficient way to travel around Berlin is by U-Bahn, designated U1, U2 etc in this book. Trains operate from 4am until about 12.30am and throughout the night on Friday, Saturday and public holidays (all lines except the U4).

BUS & TRAM

Buses run frequently between 4.30am and 12.30am. From Sunday to Thursday, night buses take over in the interim at 30-minute intervals. Buses N2, N5, N6, N8 and N9 follow more or less the routes of the U2, U5, U6, U8 and U9.

Trams only operate in the eastern districts. The M10, N54, N55, N92 and N93 offer continuous service nightly.

S-BAHN

S-Bahn trains make fewer stops than U-Bahns and are therefore handy for longer distances, but they don't run as frequently.

Denoted as S1, S2 etc in this book, they operate from around 4am to 12.30am and all night on Friday, Saturday and public holidays.

BICYCLE

Bike lanes abound in flat Berlin. Bicycles (*Fahrräder*) may be taken aboard designated U-Bahn and S-Bahn cars (though not on buses) for the price of a reduced single ticket (€1.40). Many hostels and hotels hire bicycles to their guests or can refer you to an agency. Expect to pay around €10 to €15 per day and €50 per week. One reliable outfit with English-speaking staff and six branches throughout central Berlin is **Fahrradstation** (☎ central reservations 0180 510 8000; www.fahrradstation.de). Call for the location nearest to you.

The website www.bbbike.de is a handy route planner.

TAXI

Taxis line up outside airports, train stations and, at night, theatres, clubs and other venues. You can order one on ☎ 443 322, ☎ 202 020, ☎ 210 202 or ☎ 263 000.

Flag fall is €3.20, then it's €1.65 per kilometre up to 7km and €1.28 for each kilometre after that. A ride from Alexanderplatz to Zoologischer Garten costs about €16. For short hops (up to 2km) ask for the €4 *Kurzstreckentarif* (short-trip rate). You must flag down a moving taxi and request this special rate before the driver has activated the meter. If you want to continue past 2km, regular rates apply to the entire trip.

PRACTICALITIES
BUSINESS HOURS
Shops may set their own hours but typical core times are from 10am to 8pm Monday to Saturday. Some malls, supermarkets and department stores stay open until 9pm or 10pm, at least on some nights. Small boutiques tend not to open until noon and close as early as 6pm or 7pm and at 4pm on Saturdays.

For stocking up on basics after hours, head to a petrol station or the nearest *Spätkauf,* which are neighbourhood stores open until the wee hours. Supermarkets in the Hauptbahnhof, Ostbahnhof and Friedrichstrasse train stations do business until about 10pm, even on Sundays. Also see the Quick Reference guide on the inside front cover.

DISCOUNTS
Berlin WelcomeCard (www.berlin-welcome card.com; per 2/3/5 days for fare zones AB €16.50/22/29.50, for zones ABC €18.50/25/34.50) Entitles you to unlimited public transport within the AB fare zone and up to 50% discount to 140 sights, attractions and tours. Available at the Berlin Infostores (see Tourist Information, p188),

U-Bahn and S-Bahn ticket vending machines, BVG offices and many hotels.
CityTourCard (www.citytourcard.de; per 2/3/5 days for zones AB €15.90/20.90/28.90, for zones ABC €17.90/22.90/33.90) Works on same scheme as Berlin WelcomeCard and is a bit cheaper but offers fewer discounts. Available at some hotels and from U-Bahn and S-Bahn vending machines.
SchauLust Museen Berlin (adult/child €19/9.50) Unbeatable deal for culture vultures. Buys admission to permanent exhibits of about 70 museums on three consecutive opening days; available at Berlin Infostores and partici-pating museums.

ELECTRICITY
Standard voltage is 220V, 50Hz AC. Plugs are the Continental type, with two round pins.

EMERGENCIES
For emergency assistance call ☎ 110 for the police or ☎ 112 for the fire department/ambulance. Other useful phone numbers and addresses:
American Hotline (☎ 0177 814 1510) Despite the name, this is a crisis hotline and referral service for all English speakers, not just Americans.
BVG Public Transport Lost & Found (Map p145, C4; ☎ 194 49; Potsdamer Strasse 180/182; ⏰ 9am-6pm Mon-Thu, to 2pm Fri; 🚇 Kleistpark)
Call-a-Doc (☎ 01804 2255 2362) Non-emergency medical assistance and treatment referral.
International Helpline (☎ in English 4401 0607; ⏰ 6pm-midnight) Volunteer-run, anony-mous help for people in any crisis situation.

HOLIDAYS

Neujahrstag (New Year's Day) 1 January
Ostern (Easter) March/April – Good Friday, Easter Sunday and Easter Monday
Christi Himmelfahrt (Ascension Day) 40 days after Easter
Maifeiertag (Labour Day) 1 May
Pfingsten (Whit Sunday/Pentecost Sunday and Monday) May/June
Tag der Deutschen Einheit (Day of German Unity) 3 October
Weihnachtstag (Christmas Day) 25 December
2. Weihnachtstag (Boxing Day) 26 December

INTERNET

Many hostels, hotels and cafes offer wireless surfing (called W-LAN in German) and the entire Sony Center at Potsdamer Platz (Map p81, E2) is a free public hot spot. The website www.hotspot -locations.com can help you pin down others.

Internet cafes in Berlin have about the lifespan of a fruit fly, so it's best to ask at the tourist office or your hotel for the nearest one. Also look for coin-operated laptops by **Sidewalk Express** (www .sidewalkexpress.com; per hr €2), usually found in malls (eg Potsdamer Platz Arkaden, Alexa) and train stations (eg Friedrichstrasse, Alexanderplatz).

Also, do your homework and check out these sites so you can hit the ground running when you get to Berlin. All are in English.

3D Stadtmodell (www.3d-stadtmodell -berlin.de) Virtual Google Earth–powered journey through Berlin.
Berlin Hidden Places (www.berlin-hidden -places.de) Ideas for getting off the tourist track.
Berlin Tourismus Marketing (www .visitberlin.de, www.visitberlin.tv) Official tourist-office website.
Berlin Unlike (http://berlin.unlike.net) Hip guide with up-to-the-minute reviews and happenings; sign up for a free weekly newsletter.
Gridskipper (www.gridskipper.com/ travel/berlin) Urban travel guide to the useful, offbeat, naughty and nice.
I Heart Berlin (www.iheartberlin.de) Lifestyle blog with posts about parties, fashion, art and scene insiders.

LANGUAGE

BASICS

Hello.	*Guten Tag/Hallo.*
Goodbye.	*Auf Wiedersehen.*
Excuse me/ Sorry.	*Entschuldigung.*
Yes.	*Ja.*
No.	*Nein.*
Please.	*Bitte.*
Thank you (very much).	*Danke (schön).*
You're welcome.	*Bitte schön.*
Do you speak English?	*Sprechen Sie Englisch?*
I don't understand.	*Ich verstehe nicht.*
How much is it?	*Wieviel kostet es?*
That's too expensive.	*Das ist zu teuer.*

EATING & DRINKING

That was delicious!	*Das war sehr lecker!*
I'm a vegetarian. (m/f)	*Ich bin Vegetarier(in).*
Please bring the bill.	*Die Rechnung, bitte.*
curried sausages	*Currywurst*
pork roast	*Schweinebraten*
pike perch filet	*Zanderfilet*
thin-crust pizza-like dough topped with cream, bacon and onion	*Flammekuche*

EMERGENCIES

I'm sick.	*Ich bin krank.*
Help!	*Hilfe!*
Call the police!	*Rufen Sie die Polizei!*
Call an ambulance!	*Rufen Sie einen Krankenwagen!*

DAYS & NUMBERS

today	*Heute*
tonight	*Heute Abend*
tomorrow	*Morgen*
1	*eins*
2	*zwei*
3	*drei*
4	*vier*
5	*fünf*
6	*sechs*
7	*sieben*
8	*acht*
9	*neun*
10	*zehn*
11	*elf*
12	*zwölf*
13	*dreizehn*
20	*zwanzig*
21	*einundzwanzig*
22	*zweiundzwanzig*
30	*dreissig*
31	*einunddreissig*
40	*vierzig*
50	*fünfzig*
60	*sechzig*
70	*siebzig*
80	*achtzig*
90	*neunzig*
100	*hundert*
1000	*tausend*

MAGAZINES

Zitty (www.zitty.de, in German), *Tip* (www.tip-berlin.de, in German) and *Prinz* (www.prinz.de/berlin), in that order, are the dominant entertainment-listings magazines, although the freebie *030* (www.berlin030.de) is popular as well. The freezine *Siegessäule* (www.siegessaeule.de) is the city's lesbi-gay 'bible'. *ExBerliner* (www.exberliner.de) is a quality English-language magazine largely written by expats with features, essays and listings.

MONEY

Berlin is the western European capital where you can get the most bang for your buck. Reckon on spending around €120 to €170 per day for a short stay in three-star accommodation with three daily meals. Luxury lovers can easily double that figure, while the seriously cash-deficient could probably subsist on as little as €40.

The easiest way to access your money is via ATMs throughout the city, most of which are linked to international networks such as Star, Cirrus or Maestro. Credit cards are becoming more widely accepted in central Berlin, but it's best not to assume that you'll be able to use them – always inquire first.

For currency exchange rates, see the Quick Reference guide on the inside front cover.

ORGANISED TOURS

WALKING & CYCLING TOURS

Several companies offer both introductory city spins and themed tours (eg Third Reich, Cold War, Sachsenhausen, Potsdam), usually led by sharp-witted English-speaking guides. Tours don't require reservations – just show up at one of the meeting points. Since these change quite frequently, look for flyers in hotel or hostel lobbies or at the tourist offices or contact the companies directly. Some tours are free (well, the guides work for tips, so give what you can) but most cost between €10 and €15.

BARGAIN BUS

One of Berlin's best bargains is a self-guided city tour aboard public buses 100 or 200, the routes of which check off nearly every major sight in the city centre for the price of a standard bus ticket (€2.10, day pass €6.10).

Bus 100 travels from Zoologischer Garten (Bahnhof Zoo or Zoo Station) to Alexanderplatz, passing by the Gedächtniskirche, Tiergarten (with the Siegessäule), the Reichstag, the Brandenburg Gate and Unter den Linden. Bus 200 also links Zoologischer Garten and Alexanderplatz but takes a more southerly route via the Kulturforum and Potsdamer Platz. Without traffic, trips take about 30 minutes.

Companies include:

Berlin on Bike (☎ 4373 9999; www.berlinonbike.de)

Berlin Walks (☎ 301 9194; www.berlinwalks.de) The first English-language walking-tour company founded after the fall of the Wall and still tops.

Brewer's Berlin Tours (☎ 0177 388 1537; www.brewersberlintours.com) Home of the epic all-day Best of Berlin tour (foot massage not included) and shorter free tour.

Fat Tire Bike Tours (☎ 2404 7991; www.fattirebiketoursberlin.com)

Insider Tour (☎ 692 3149; www.insidertour.com) Also does bike tours and a pub crawl.

New Berlin Tours (☎ 0179 973 0397; www.newberlintours.com) Pioneered the concept of the 'free tour' and the notorious pub crawl.

BOAT TOURS

A lovely way to experience Berlin on a warm day is from the deck of a boat cruising along the city's rivers, canals and lakes. Tours range from one-hour spins around the historic centre (from €7) to longer trips to Schloss Charlottenburg and beyond (from €16). Most offer live narration in English and German. **Stern & Kreisschiffahrt** (www .sternundkreis.de) is one of the main operators. The season runs from April to mid-October. The maps in the Neighbourhoods chapters indicate embarkation points.

SPECIALITY TOURS

Berlinagenten (☎ 4372 0701; www.berlina genten.com) Get under the skin of Berlin's lifestyle scene with clued-in guides that whisk you off the beaten track and into unique bars, boutiques, restaurants and clubs, even private homes. For an insider's primer on the culinary scene, book its Gastro-Rallye, where you enjoy one course at each of three to five restaurant stops. Also see our interview with company founder Henrik Tidefjärd (p73).
Berliner Unterwelten (☎ 4991 0518; www.berliner-unterwelten.de; adult/ concession €9/7) Explore Berlin's dark and dank underbelly by picking your way past hospital beds, wartime helmets and filter systems on a tour of WWII-era underground bunkers.
Fritz Music Tours (☎ 3087 5633; www .musictours-berlin.com) Get the low-down on Berlin's legendary music history – from Iggy and Bowie to U2 and Depeche Mode, from cult clubs to the Love Parade – on this dynamic bus tour (€19). Private minibus

tours, walking tours and tours of the Hansa Studios are also available.
Trabi Safari (Map p113, B1; ☎ 2759 2273; www.trabi-safari.de; cnr Wilhelmstrasse & Zimmerstrasse; 1/2/3/4 passengers per person €60/40/35/30) Spend an hour exploring Berlin's Wild East behind the wheel, or as a passenger, of a GDR-era Trabant (Trabi for short). Live commentary is piped into your vehicle.

TELEPHONE

Mobile (cell) phones operate on GSM 900/1800. Check with your carrier about roaming charges. Most public pay phones only work with phonecards such as those issued by Deutsche Telekom or private companies. Buy them at newsagents or discount telephone-call shops.

For key phone numbers, see Quick Reference on the inside cover.

TIPPING

Porters €1 per bag
Restaurants 10%
Taxis 5% to 10%

TOURIST INFORMATION

The city tourist office, **Berlin Tourismus Marketing** (BTM; www.visitberlin.de), operates four walk-in offices called Berlin Infostores and a **call centre** (☎ 250 025; 8am-7pm Mon-Fri, 9am-6pm Sat & Sun) whose multilingual staff field general questions and make hotel and ticket bookings. From April to October hours at the following may be extended.

Berlin Infostore Alexa Shopping Center
(Map p57, D2; Grunerstrasse 20, near Alexan-
derplatz; ⏰ 10am-8pm Mon-Sat; 🚌 100)
Berlin Infostore Brandenburg Gate
(Map p43, A3; south wing; ⏰ 10am-6pm;
🚇 Unter den Linden)
Berlin Infostore Hauptbahnhof (Map p77,
B3; near Europaplatz north exit; ⏰ 8am-
10pm; 🚇 Hauptbahnhof)
Berlin Infostore Neues Kranzler Eck (Map
p133, E2; Kurfürstendamm 21; ⏰ 10am-8pm
Mon-Sat, to 6pm Sun; 🚇 Kurfürstendamm)

TRAVELLERS WITH DISABILITIES

Overall, Berlin caters quite well
for the needs of the disabled,
especially the wheelchair-bound.
You'll find ramps and/or lifts in
many public buildings, including train stations, museums,
concert halls and cinemas. Newer
hotels have lifts and rooms with
extrawide doors and spacious
bathrooms. Most buses and trams
are wheelchair-accessible and
many U- and S-Bahn stations
are equipped with ramps or lifts.
Stations are also getting grooved
platforms to assist vision-
impaired passengers.

For trip-planning assistance,
contact the **BVG** (☎ 194 19; www
.bvg.de). If your wheelchair breaks
down, call ☎ 0180 111 4747 for
24-hour assistance. Free wheelchair hire is available by calling
☎ 341 1797.

>INDEX

See also separate subindexes for Drink (p196), Eat (p197), Play (p197), See (p198) and Shop (p199)..

A

accessories, *see* Shop *subindex*
accommodation 150-1
Achtung Berlin 27
air travel 181-2
Alexanderplatz area 56-61, **57**
Alte Nationalgalerie 44
ambulance 184
aquariums 134
architecture 177-8
    German Democratic
    Republic 124
area codes, *see inside front cover*
Art Forum Berlin 29
arts 29, 30, 156-7, *see also* galleries, museums, See & Shop *subindexes*
ATMs 187

B

B&Bs 150
Barenboim, Daniel 27, 55
bars, *see* Drink *subindex*
bathrooms 91
beach bars, *see* Drink *subindex*
beer gardens, *see* Drink *subindex*
Berlin Airlift 114
Berlin Biennale 30
Berlin Marathon 29
Berlin Wall 15, 90, 115, 124, 160-1, 173

000 map pages

Berlin Zoo 134
Berlinale 26
Berliner Bierfestival 28
Berliner Dom 45
bicycle travel 24, 183, 187
Bismarck, Otto von 20
boat travel 188
Bonaparte, Napoleon 173
books 29, 157, 170, 179, *see also* Shop *subindex*
Bowie, David 16, 144, 168, 188
Brandenburg Gate 21, 46
Brecht, Bertolt 44, 54
buildings, notable, *see* See *subindex*
bunker tours 188
bus travel 181, 182, 183, 187
business hours 184, *see also inside front cover*

C

cabaret 23, *see also* Play *subindex*
cafes, *see* Drink & Eat *subindexes*
casinos 61
cathedrals, *see* See *subindex*
cell phones 188
cemeteries, *see* See *subindex*
Charlotte, Sophie 136
Charlottenburg 132-43, **133**
Charlottenburg Palace 12, 136-7
Checkpoint Charlie 114, 115

children, travel with 166
Chipperfield, David 49, 51
Christmas markets 30
Christopher Street Day 28
churches, *see* See *subindex*
cinema, *see* film
cinemas, *see* Play *subindex*
Classic Open Air Gendarmenmarkt 28
classical music 28, 86, *see also* Play *subindex*
climate change 181, 182
clothing 165, *see also* Shop *subindex*
clubs 13, 163, *see also* Play *subindex*
    Friedrichshain 130-1
    government quarter 79
    Kreuzberg, eastern 110-11
    Kreuzkölln 110-11
    Mitte – Alexanderplatz area 60-1
    Mitte – Scheunenviertel 74, 75
    Mitte – Unter den Linden 55
    Prenzlauer Berg 99
Cold War 15, 114, 115, 139, 173, 187
cosmetics 91
costs 186-7, *see also inside front cover*
courtyards, *see* See *subindex*

credit cards 187
cruises 188
cultural centres 99
culture 174-5
cycling 24, 183, 187

D

department stores 146
design, Bauhaus 82
Dietrich, Marlene 13, 23, 74, 84, 144
dinosaurs 65
disabilities, travellers with 189
discount cards 44, 83, 184
drinking 164, *see also* Drink & Shop *subindexes*
    Charlottenburg 141-2
    festivals 28
    Friedrichshain 127-9
    Kreuzberg, eastern 106-9
    Kreuzberg, western 118-19
    Kreuzkölln 106-9
    Mitte – Scheunenviertel 71-2
    Mitte – Unter den Linden 53-4
    Prenzlauer Berg 96-8
    Schöneberg 147
    Tiergarten 86-7
    tours 164, 187

E

East Berlin, *see* German Democratic Republic
East Germany, *see* German Democratic Republic
East Side Gallery 15, 124
Easter in Berlin 155
economy 175
electricity 184

emergencies 184, 186
environmental issues 181, 182
erotic clubs, *see* Play *subindex*
erotica 139-40
etiquette 176
events 25-30, 86, 155, 159
exchange rates, *see inside front cover*
expressionism 85, 114

F

fashion 14, 30, 165, *see also* Shop *subindex*
Festival of Lights 29-30
festivals 25-30, 155, 159
Festtage 27
Fête de la Musique 28
fetish clubs 61, 119, 120, 169
film 180
    festivals 26, 27, 30
    museums 83-4
fire services 184
flea markets, *see* Shop *subindex*
Folsom Europe 155
food 60, 152-3, *see also* Eat & Shop *subindexes*
    Charlottenburg 140-1
    festivals 26
    Friedrichshain 126-7
    government quarter 79
    Kreuzberg, eastern 103-6
    Kreuzberg, western 118
    Kreuzkölln 103-6
    Mitte - Alexanderplatz area 60
    Mitte – Scheunenviertel 69-71
    Mitte – Unter den Linden 52-3

organic 152-3
Potsdamer Platz 85-6
Prenzlauer Berg 95-6
Schöneberg 146-7
shopping 170
tours 188
traditional 153
football 35, 134
Foster, Lord Norman 16
Frederick the Great 12, 45, 85, 136, 172, 177
Friedrich, Caspar David 44
Friedrich I 12, 45, 136, 172
Friedrich II, *see* Frederick the Great
Friedrichshain 122-31, **123**
Fuckparade 28

G

galleries 156-7, *see also* See & Shop *subindexes*
    Charlottenburg 136
    Friedrichshain 15, 124
    Kreuzberg, western 114, 116
    Mitte – Museumsinsel 44, 46
    Mitte – Scheunenviertel 66, 67
    Mitte – Unter den Linden 44, 46
    Potsdamer Platz 18, 82-3, 84, 85
Garbo, Greta 48, *see See subindex*
gardens, *see* See *subindex*
gay travellers 28, 154-5, *see also* Play & Drink *subindexes*
GDR, *see* German Democratic Republic
Gehry, Frank 50, 178
Gemäldegalerie 18, 82-3

German Democratic Republic 162
  architecture 124
  culture 67, 98, 126
  museums 58, 126
  prisons 126
  tours 188
government 176
government quarter 76-9, **77**
Great Elector, see Wilhelm, Friedrich
Gropius, Walter 82

H
historic sites, see See subindex
history 172-4
  Berlin Airlift 114
  Berlin Wall 15, 90, 115, 124, 160-1, 173
  Cold War 15, 114, 115, 139, 173, 187
  German Democratic Republic 162
  Jewish Berlin 158-9
Hitler, Adolf 16, 47, 82, 134, 173, 180
holidays 185
Holocaust Denkmal 48
hostels 150
hotels 150

I
Industrial Revolution 173
interior design 140
Internationale Funkausstellung 28
Internationale Grüne Woche 26
Internationale Tourismus Börse 27

000 map pages

BERLIN >**194**

Internationales Literaturfestival 29
internet access 185
internet resources 185
  accommodation 151
  fashion 165
  gay & lesbian travellers 154
  public transport 182
Isherwood, Christopher 13, 144, 179
itineraries 33-7

J
jazz 30, see also Play subindex
Jazzfest Berlin 30
Jewish Berlin 158-9
  cemeteries 64, 90
  festivals 159
  Jewish Museum 17, 115
  memorials 48, 66
  synagogues 65-6, 90-1
  tours 159

K
karaoke 131
Karl-Marx-Allee 124
Karneval der Kulturen 27
Kennedy, John F 48, 144
Knut, the polar bear 134
Kollwitz, Käthe 48, 90, 135
Kreuzberg, eastern 100-11, **101**
Kreuzberg, western 112-21, **113**
Kreuzkölln 100-11, **101**
Kurfürstendamm 20, 156

L
Landwehrkanal 112
Lange Nacht der Museen 26, 167

Langhans, Carl Gotthard 21, 46
language 185-6
Le Carré, John 179
lesbian travellers 28, 154-5, see also Play & Drink subindexes
Lesbisch-Schwules Strassenfest 155
Libeskind, Daniel 17
Liebermann, Max 44, 90
lifestyle 174-6
  tours 188
lingerie 67-8
literature 29, 179, see also books
live music, see Play subindex

M
MaerzMusik 27
magazines 186
malls, see Shop subindex
Marienkirche 58
markets 30, 170, see also Eat & Shop subindexes
Mauerpark 90
May Day 27
memorials, see See subindex
Mendelssohn, Moses 17, 64, 158
Meyerbeer, Giacomo 90
Mies van der Rohe, Ludwig 85
Mitte – Alexanderplatz area 56-61, **57**
Mitte – Museumsinsel 42-55, **43**
Mitte – Scheunenviertel 14, 62-75, **63**
Mitte – Unter den Linden 42-55, **43**

mobile phones 188
money 186-7
    discount cards 44, 83, 184
monuments, *see* See *subindex*
multiculturalism 27, 175
museums 167, *see also* See *subindex*
    Charlottenburg 135, 136, 139
    government quarter 78
    Kreuzberg, western 17, 114, 115, 116
    Mitte – Alexanderplatz area 58
    Mitte – Museumsinsel 44, 46, 47, 48, 50
    Mitte – Scheunenviertel 66
    Mitte – Unter den Linden 44, 46, 47, 48, 50
    Potsdamer Platz 82, 83, 84, 85
Museumsinsel 42-55, **43**
Museumsinsel Festival 28
music 168, *see also* Play & Shop *subindexes*
    events 86
    festivals 27, 28, 30
    tours 188
Musikfest Berlin 28

N
Nazis 44-5, 48, 66, 116, 134, 154-5, 159
Neue Nationalgalerie 85
New Year's Eve 30
nightclubs, *see* Play *subindex*
nightlife, *see* Play *subindex*
Nikolaiviertel 58

O
Olympic Stadium 134
opera 27, *see also* Play *subindex*
organic food 153
Ostalgiana 125-6

P
palaces 12, 136-7
Palast der Republik 44, 50, 70
parks, *see* See *subindex*
performance spaces, *see* Play *subindex*
Pergamonmuseum 10-11, 50
phonecards 188
photography 135
planning 35
    discount cards 44, 83, 184
police 184
politics 176
Pop, Iggy 144, 168, 188
population 175
Porn Film Festival 30
Potsdamer Platz 80-7, **81**
Prenzlauer Berg 22, 88-99, **89**
Prussia 172-3
public transport 182-3
pubs, *see* Drink *subindex*

R
Ramones, the 66
Reichstag 16, 76-9, **77**
responsible travel 181
restaurants 152-3, *see also* Eat *subindex*
reunification 173-4

S
Sandsation 28
saunas 110, 119-20
S-Bahn 182, 183

Scheunenviertel 14, 62-75, **63**
Schinkel, Karl Friedrich 44, 47, 48, 55, 136, 177
Schloss Charlottenburg 12, 136-7
Schlossgarten 136
Schöneberg 144-7, **145**
sex clubs 61, 119, 120, 169
shopping 14, 170, *see also* Shop *subindex*
    Friedrichshain 125
    Kreuzberg, eastern 102-3
    Kreuzberg, western 116-18
    Kreuzkölln 102-3
    Kurfürstendamm 20, 156
    Mitte – Alexanderplatz area 59-60
    Mitte – Scheunenviertel 14, 67-8
    Mitte – Unter den Linden 50-1
    Potsdamer Platz 85
    Prenzlauer Berg 91-2
    Schöneberg 146
smoking 177
soccer 35, 134
souvenirs, *see* Shop *subindex*
Spree River 59, 76, 109-10, 128
squares, *see* See *subindex*
Stasi 162, 179, 180
    museum 126
    prison 126
statistics 175
swimming pools, *see* Play *subindex*
synagogues, *see* See *subindex*

T

taxis 183-4
telephone services
188, see also inside front
cover
Theatertreffen Berlin 27
theatre 27, see also Play
subindex
theme parks, see See subindex
Thirty Years War 172
Tiergarten 19, 80-7, **81**
tipping 188
toilets 91
tourist information 188-9
tours
art 157
Berlin Wall 161
boat 188
bunker 188
bus 187
cycling 187
drinking 164, 187
food 188
gay lifestyle 155
German Democratic
Republic 188
Jewish Berlin 159
lifestyle 188
music 188
Trabant 188
walking 187
Trabant tours 188
train travel 182, 183
trams 182, 183
Transmediale 26
transport, public 182-3
travel passes 183
TV Tower 59

000 map pages

BERLIN >196

U

U-Bahn 182, 183
Unesco World Heritage
sites 46
Unter den Linden 42-55, **43**

V

vacations 185
vegetarian food, see Eat
subindex
vintage goods, see Shop
subindex

W

walks 187
Wall, the 15, 90, 115, 124,
160-1, 173
wi-fi access 185
Wilhelm, Friedrich 12, 158,
172
Wilhelm I, Friedrich 172
Wilhelm III, Friedrich 136
Wilhelm IV, Friedrich 12, 136
Wowereit, Klaus 155, 174,
176
WWI 173
WWII 173

Y

You Berlin 30

Z

zoos 134

DRINK

Bars
Bar 3 71
Bebel Bar 53
CSA 127, 129
Eastern Comfort Hostel
Boat 130
Eschschloraque 72
Galerie Bremer 141
Green Door 147
Greenwich 72
Habermeyer 129
Haifischbar 119
Klub der Republik 98
Luzia 107
Madame Claude 108
Monarch Bar 108
Orient Lounge 108
Puro Skylounge 141
Raumfahrer 108
Rosa Bar 108-9
Rote Lotte 98
Silverfuture 109
Solar 119
Tausend 54
Windhorst 54
Würgeengel 109

Beach Bars
Deck 5 97
Kiki Blofeld 107
Strandgut Berlin 129

Beer Gardens
Café am Neuen See 86-7
Golgatha 118
Prater 98
Schleusenkrug 142

Cafe-Bars
Bar Gagarin 96
Freischwimmer 107
Kaufbar 129
Marietta 98
Mutter 147
San Remo Upflamör 109
Wohnzimmer 98

Cafes
Anna Blume 96
Bonanza Coffee Heroes
97

INDEX

Café Bravo 71
Café Richter 141
Tadschikische Teestube
   54

Gay & Lesbian Bars
Heile Welt 147
Möbel Olfe 108
Roses 109
Zum Schmutzigen Hobby
   98

Pubs
Ä 106
Ankerklause 107
Bellmann 107
Hops & Barley 129
Kptn A Müller 129
Möbel Olfe 108

🍴 EAT
American
Barcomi's Deli 69
Burgermeister 103
Tartane 70

Asian
Ishin 52-3
Kuchi 70
Monsieur Vuong 70
Sasaya 95
Susuru 70

Austrian
Sarah Wiener im Hamburger
   Bahnhof 79

Belgian
Brel 140

Cafes
Café Wintergarten im
   Literaturhaus 140

French
Bandol sur Mer 69
Café Nord-Sud 69
Major Grubert 104-5

Fusion
Spindler & Klatt 105
W-Imbiss 96

German
Curry 36 118
Fellas 93, 95
Henne 104
Joseph-Roth-Diele 86
Konnopke's Imbiss 95
Oderquelle 95
Renger-Patzsch 147
Schneeweiss 127
Schusterjunge 96
Schwarzer Hahn 127
Schwarzwaldstuben 70
Zur Letzten Instanz 60

International
Bond 140
Café Jacques 103
Foodorama 118
Grill Royal 52
Horváth 104
More 146
Tomasa 118
Weinbar Rutz 71
Zagreus Projekt 71

Italian
I Due Forni 95
Il Casolare 104
Miseria & Nobiltà 126-7
Sagrantino 53
Trattoria á Muntagnola 147
Vapiano 86
Zwölf Apostel 53

Japanese
Musashi 105
Uma 53

Markets
Türkenmarkt 105

Mediterranean
Hartmanns 103-4

Mexican
Dolores 60

Middle Eastern
Dada Falafel 69
Habibi 146
Meyman 126
Rissani 105
Schlemmerbuffet 96

Moroccan
Kasbah 69

Spanish
Atame 60

Thai
Facil 86
Moon Thai 141
Papaya 127

Turkish
Defne 103
Hasir 104

Vegan
Hans Wurst 95

Vegetarian
Cookies Cream 52
Yellow Sunshine
   105-6

Vietnamese
Mr Hai & Friends 141
Si An 96

INDEX

⭐ PLAY

Cabaret
Admiralspalast 54
Bar jeder Vernunft 143
Chamäleon Varieté 74
Friedrichstadtpalast 74-5

Casinos
Casino Berlin 61

Cinemas
Arsenal 87
Babylon Mitte 72
Cinestar Original & IMAX 3D 87
Kino International 61

Classical Music
Berliner Philharmonie 87
Konzerthaus Berlin 55
Yellow Lounge 86

Clubs
2BE 79
Bassy 99
Berghain/Panoramabar 130
Bohannon 60-1
Cassiopeia 130
Clärchens Ballhaus 74
Club der Visionäre 110
Cookies 55
Delicious Doughnuts 74
Felix Clubrestaurant 55
Icon 99
Kaffee Burger 75
KitKatClub @ Sage 61, 169
Maria am Ostbahnhof 130
Rosi's 131
SO36 110
Tape 79

000 map pages

BERLIN >198

Tresor 61
Watergate 111
Weekend 61

Cultural Centres
Kulturbrauerei 99

Erotic Clubs
Insomnia 119, 120, 169
KitKatClub @ Sage 61, 169

Gay & Lesbian Clubs
Ackerkeller 72
Connection 147
Kino International 61
Schwuz 121

Jazz Clubs
A-Trane 142-3
B-Flat 72, 74
Yorckschlösschen 121

Karaoke
Monster Ronson's Ichiban Karaoke 131

Live Music
A-Trane 142-3
B-Flat 72, 74
Dot Club 110
Lido 110
Magnet 99
SO36 110
Wild At Heart 111
Yorckschlösschen 121

Opera
Deutsche Oper Berlin 143
Staatsoper Unter den Linden 55

Performance Spaces
Haus der Kulturen der Welt 79
Radialsystem V 131

Swimming Pools
Badeschiff 109-10
Liquidrom 119, 121

Theatre
Admiralspalast 54
Berliner Ensemble 54
Deutsches Theater 74
English Theatre Berlin 119
Friedrichstadtpalast 74-5
Volksbühne am Rosa-Luxemburg-Platz 75

👁 SEE

Aquariums
Aquarium 134

Cemeteries
Alter Jüdischer Friedhof 64
Jüdischer Friedhof 90

Churches & Cathedrals
Berliner Dom 45
Friedrichswerdersche Kirche 47
Kaiser-Wilhelm-Gedächtniskirche 135
Marienkirche 58

Galleries
Alte Nationalgalerie 44
Berlinische Galerie 114
Daimler Contemporary 82
Deutsche Guggenheim Berlin 46
East Side Gallery 15, 124
Gemäldegalerie 18, 82-3
Halle am Wasser 78
Kunsthaus Tacheles 64
Kunst-Werke Berlin 64
Martin-Gropius-Bau 116
Neue Nationalgalerie 85
Sammlung Boros 66

Sammlung Scharf-
Gerstenberg 136
Temporäre Kunsthalle 50

Historic Sites
Berlin Wall 15, 90, 115, 124,
160-1, 173
Bernauer Strasse 90
Brandenburg Gate 21, 46
Checkpoint Charlie 114, 115
East Side Gallery 15, 124
Hitler's Bunker 47
Mauerpark 90
Palast der Republik 44, 50, 70
Stasi Prison 126
Topographie des Terrors 116
Wasserturm 91

Monuments & Memorials
Gedenkstätte Deutscher
Widerstand 82
Holocaust Denkmal 48
Neue Wache 48
Siegessäule 85
Stolpersteine 66

Museums
Bauhaus Archiv/Museum für
Gestaltung 82
Berliner Medizinhistorisches
Museum 78
Bodemuseum 46
Bröhan Museum 136
DDR Museum 58
Deutsches Historisches
Museum 46-7
Deutsches Technikmuseum 114
Emil Nolde Museum 47
Hamburger Bahnhof –
Museum für Gegenwart 78
Haus am Checkpoint Charlie
115
Jewish Museum 17, 115
Käthe-Kollwitz-Museum 135

Kennedy Museum 48
Kunstgewerbemuseum 83
Kupferstichkabinett 83
Mauermuseum 115
Museum Berggruen 136
Museum für Film und
Fernsehen 83-4
Museum für Fotografie 135
Museum für Naturkunde 65
Musikinstrumenten-Museum
84-5
Neues Museum 49
Pergamonmuseum 10-11, 50
Ramones Museum 66
Schwules Museum 116
Stasi Museum 126
Story of Berlin 139

Notable Buildings
Bundeskanzleramt 78
Hotel Adlon Kempinski 48
Karl-Marx-Allee 124
Reichstag 78-9
Rotes Rathaus 58-9
TV Tower 59

Notable Districts & Streets
Nikolaiviertel 58

Palaces
Schloss Charlottenburg 12,
136-7

Parks & Gardens
Schlossgarten 136
Tiergarten 19, 80, **81**
Volkspark Friedrichshain 125

Squares & Courtyards
Bebelplatz 44-5
Gendarmenmarkt 47
Hackesche Höfe 64
Kollwitzplatz 90
Pariser Platz 49-50

Stadiums
Olympic Stadium 134

Synagogues
Neue Synagoge & Centrum
Judaicum 65-6
Synagoge Rykestrasse 90-1

Theme Parks
Legoland Discovery Centre
83
Sea Life Berlin 59

Zoos
Berlin Zoo 134

🏠 SHOP
Accessories
Berlinomat 125
IC! Berlin 68
Ta(u)sche 93

Books
Berlin Story 50
Dussmann – Das
Kulturkaufhaus 51-2

Cosmetics
Biodrogerie Rosavelle 91

Department Stores
KaDeWe 146

Erotica
Hautnah 139-40

Fashion
14oz 67
Berlinerklamotten 67
Berlinomat 125
Faster, Pussycat! 116
Killerbeast 102
Lala Berlin 68
Overkill 102
Sameheads 117

UKO Fashion 102-3
UVR Connected 103
Vamp Star Salon 93

Food & Drink
1. Absinth Depot Berlin 67
Bonbonmacherei 68
Fassbender & Rausch 52
Goldhahn & Sampson 92

Galleries
Contemporary Fine Arts 51
Galerie Michael Schultz 138, 139

Gifts
Ausberlin 59
Die Imaginäre Manufaktur 102
Herrlich 116-17
Luxus International 93

Interior Design
Stilwerk 140

Lingerie
Blush Dessous 67-8

Markets & Flea Markets
Antikmarkt am Ostbahnhof 125
Christmas markets 30
Flohmarkt am Arkonaplatz 91-2
Flohmarkt am Boxhagener Platz 125
Flohmarkt am Mauerpark 92
Flohmarkt Strasse des 17 Juni 139

Music
Dussmann – Das Kulturkaufhaus 51-2
Space Hall 117-18

Ostalgiana
Mondos Arts 125-6

Shopping Malls
Alexa 59
Edd's 85
Friedrichstadtpassagen 52
Potsdamer Platz Arkaden 85

Souvenirs
Ampelmann Galerie 67
Ausberlin 59
Luxus International 93

Vintage
Jumbo Second Hand 102
VEB Orange 93
Zwischenzeit 93

000 map pages